Claudio Scardovi

Digital Transformation in Financial Services

Springer

Claudio Scardovi
AlixPartners
London
UK

ISBN 978-3-319-66944-1   ISBN 978-3-319-66945-8   (eBook)
DOI 10.1007/978-3-319-66945-8

Library of Congress Control Number: 2017951149

© Springer International Publishing AG 2017
This work is subject to copyright. All rights are reserved by the Publisher, whether the whole or part of the material is concerned, specifically the rights of translation, reprinting, reuse of illustrations, recitation, broadcasting, reproduction on microfilms or in any other physical way, and transmission or information storage and retrieval, electronic adaptation, computer software, or by similar or dissimilar methodology now known or hereafter developed.
The use of general descriptive names, registered names, trademarks, service marks, etc. in this publication does not imply, even in the absence of a specific statement, that such names are exempt from the relevant protective laws and regulations and therefore free for general use.
The publisher, the authors and the editors are safe to assume that the advice and information in this book are believed to be true and accurate at the date of publication. Neither the publisher nor the authors or the editors give a warranty, express or implied, with respect to the material contained herein or for any errors or omissions that may have been made. The publisher remains neutral with regard to jurisdictional claims in published maps and institutional affiliations.

Printed on acid-free paper

This Springer imprint is published by Springer Nature
The registered company is Springer International Publishing AG
The registered company address is: Gewerbestrasse 11, 6330 Cham, Switzerland

Foreword

Everywhere we look, digital transformation is at the top of the agenda. Publications, think tanks, consulting firms (including the one I lead) all have views on how digital transformation will rewrite the future of industries—and especially the future of the financial services industry.

Most agree, generally, on what digital transformation is: the profound impact of digital technologies on business activities, processes, and models. But they often disagree on how best to address it. How can organizations meet the challenges and seize the opportunities that digital transformation presents? How can companies develop the methods and tools they need to evolve their businesses in the right ways to truly become "digital"?

These are the questions that Claudio seeks to answer in this book. To do so, he offers an approach that he argues could help banking and financial services institutions to digitally transform while also becoming more stable and more profitable. Specifically, he says these companies should:

- take advantage of the dramatically increased availability of data and real-time information;
- use machine learning/AI to build more organizational intelligence;
- evolve a more inclusive, interconnecting intermediation model;
- develop solutions that add value to the overall economic ecosystem rather than playing a zero-sum game; and finally
- earn and trade on the trust that is central to the stability of the overall global financial system but that is often much more readily given to purely digital players.

Companies that take this approach could evolve into a new, digital breed of financial services institution: what he calls the "synapses bank". The "synapses bank" connects its various activities and partners in mutually beneficial ways, in much the same way that synapses connect neurons in a human brain. And in doing so, the "synapses bank", like the human brain, forms a whole that is greater than the sum of its parts. In Claudio's vision, financial services institutions that use digital technology to find new ways to add value rather than just extract it would become both more stable and more profitable.

Claudio does not predict that this "synapses bank" is the future of the financial services industry. But he does argue that it is an ambition worth considering. And he offers it as a lens through which to understand the financial services industry's successful and failed attempts at innovation and transformation—from payments to lending to risk management and insurance. And in doing so, he invites us to have a glimpse of what might be possible along the digital transformation journey.

Simon Freakley
CEO AlixPartners

Acknowledgements

With special thanks to Daniele Del Maschio and Andrea Rossi for their continued support and help in the development of this book.

Contents

1	**Unbearable Lightness of Banking**	1
	1.1 Unbearable Lightness, and Leverage	1
	1.2 Time (and Space) Lapses	4
	1.3 Capital Velocity (and Density)	6
	1.4 Intangible like Money	9
	1.5 Unsafe as a House	10
	1.6 Imbalanced, Disrupted and Dislocated	14
2	**Synapses in the Global Financial System**	19
	2.1 Synapses and Syndesis	19
	2.2 Five Senses: One	21
	2.3 Five Senses: Two	22
	2.4 Five Senses: Three	24
	2.5 Five Senses: Four	25
	2.6 Five Senses: Five	26
	2.7 Data, Going Open	27
3	**In Transformation We Trust**	31
	3.1 The Risk of the Frog	31
	3.2 Death by a Hundred Technologies	34
	3.3 BBVA: Rebooting Digital	36
	3.4 Conquistadores, Bit by Bit	38
	3.5 Goldman Sachs: The Remaining 99	42
	3.6 Digital Goldman	43
4	**Cyber Capital at Risk**	47
	4.1 Credibility to Gain, Trust to Lose	47
	4.2 War on Cash	49
	4.3 Cybergeddon: Watch Your Bytes	51
	4.4 Quantum Security	54
	4.5 Cyber Trust as Scarce Resource	55
	4.6 CISO in Cyberspace	57
	4.7 Banking on the Basics: One	59
	4.8 Banking on the Basics: Two	62

5 Digital Transformation in Payments 65
- 5.1 Payments in Paper-Less Societies 65
- 5.2 Breaking up the Payments Value Chain 68
- 5.3 Closed Loop 71
- 5.4 The Opportunities for a Synapses Bank 74
- 5.5 Distributed, Therefore Exists 75
- 5.6 If the Bank Wears Prada 79
- 5.7 Loyalty for the Public Good 81

6 Transformation in Funding 85
- 6.1 People's Cyber Capitalism 85
- 6.2 Artificial Investing and Real Life 88
- 6.3 Dealing Digital for Digital Dealing 90
- 6.4 Everybody Is a Dealer Now 92
- 6.5 Artificial Retail, Banking on Intelligence 94
- 6.6 Understanding Customers' Customers 97
- 6.7 Shifting Channels 100

7 Transformation in Investment Management 105
- 7.1 Money Management, Power to People 105
- 7.2 Better Mouse Trap 107
- 7.3 Investment Synapses 111
- 7.4 Wine and Dine 2.0 113
- 7.5 Ex-Ex: Extended Externalisers 114
- 7.6 Trading Machines: Faster, Smarter, Richer? 117
- 7.7 Capitally Connected Markets 119
- 7.8 Market Utilities: Clubbing Together 122

8 Transformation in Lending 127
- 8.1 Lending: A Social Business 127
- 8.2 Creditworthy: A "Witticism" 128
- 8.3 Alternative Lending Models 131
- 8.4 From Retail Banking to Retailers Banking 134
- 8.5 Alternative Models of Deposit Taking 137
- 8.6 Buying and Selling Money—Like a Brain 138
- 8.7 The Future of Buying and Selling Money 140

9 Transformation in Risk Management 143
- 9.1 At the Core: Holistic, Proactive, Integrated 143
- 9.2 Credit Scoring: Mind the Present 145
- 9.3 Granting Education 148
- 9.4 Credit Work Out: Getting Digital 151
- 9.5 Digital Risk Management: Optimizing the Trade off 154

	9.6	Shifting the Isoquant.	156
	9.7	Bricks After the Storm	157
	9.8	Real Estate, in Real Time	160
10	**Transformation in Insurance**		**163**
	10.1	Next "In-Line" or Next "On-Line"?	163
	10.2	Beyond the "On-Line"	166
	10.3	Digital-Insuring, at Your Peril.	169
	10.4	Mutually Insured, Completely Electronic	174
	10.5	Healthy as an Insurer	177
	10.6	Claim What?.	181
	10.7	Synapses in Insurance.	183
11	**Digital for the Greater Good**		**187**
	11.1	Innovation, Here to Stay.	187
	11.2	Digital for Good.	189
	11.3	A New Way of Digital Living	192
	11.4	A "Digitally" Inverted Pyramid	194
	11.5	Data Divide (et Impera)	196
	11.6	Data Addicted.	199
	11.7	Synapse Yourself and Break Free	201
	11.8	(Block) Chain Reaction.	202
12	**The Synapses Challenge Ahead**		**207**
	12.1	The Sky Is the Limit.	207
	12.2	Bank, Alexa Bank Is My Name	208
	12.3	The "Next" Amazon in Financial Services	211
	12.4	From Wall Street to Chinese Walls.	215
	12.5	Building Tunnels	216
	12.6	Digital "In a Box"	218
	12.7	Digital Minds	222
	12.8	Digital Maturity	224
	12.9	I, Robot. You, Bank.	226
	12.10	Out-of-the-Box: Getting IT and Business Together.	229
	12.11	Synapsezation.	231
Bibliography			**235**

Unbearable Lightness of Banking

Abstract

The traditional business model of banking, and of most of the financial services incumbent companies now operating in the global financial system, were designed and developed on the basis of a number of "leverages"—both tangible and intangible. These "leverages" have contributed to the success and dominance of current set of incumbents, but also to the cyclical crisis that over time brought this industry to his knees. These "leverages" have now become even more unbearable and a new kind of lightness is in need, in order to reinvent the financial services industry to face the challenge of the many digital disruptions to come—as technological innovation is now changing the system once and for all.

Keywords

Global financial system · Banking crisis · Leverage · Duration mismatch · Securitization

1.1 Unbearable Lightness, and Leverage

Banks were born light, and leveraged, almost by design. As the first dollar of equity capital was put at work to allow a bank to start operating, a number of other dollars were then gathered on the basis of this, and from multiple sources (from individuals, small business and corporates) to fully fund the bank's balance sheet, with a mix of short term (e.g. deposits and current accounts, short term notes) and mid-to long term debt products (e.g. mid-long term and subordinated debts).

A leverage of 40–60 (40–60 dollars of other liabilities funding the bank, on top of the one dollar equity capital) was not uncommon prior to the Lehman Brothers debacle, providing a very compelling proposition to the risk/return trade off of the shareholders of the bank (multiplied returns, if the bank was going to perform, and limited losses, largely shouldered by the mostly non-professional debtholders—or by the taxpayers, in case of a rescue with public money—if the bank was not). It all followed the simple rule "private gains, public losses".

Whilst now running at leverages of 20–25, if not less, given the heavy re-regulation and extra capital buffers that have been put in place after the Lehman bankruptcy in 2008 and the unfolding to our days of the global crisis, this "unbearable lightness" of the bank's business model still holds true. Just consider the full balance sheet of a typical retail/commercial bank: with a 60–70% of its assets lent to retail and corporate counterparts and an extra 10–20% of other financial assets—either held for sales or held to maturity: a minimal volatility in the net (e.g. considering its mix of funding liabilities) value of its lending portfolio would immediately wipe out most of its equity capital; and even a similar, limited volatility in the net value of its financial assets would most likely put the bank in a position of extreme weakness—should the regulatory capital (in our basic hypothesis equal to the equity capital) fall below the minimum required by the regulators.

The bank would then be forced to raise capital, or sell assets and reduce risks in difficult times and in a rush ("deleveraging" and "de-risking"), most likely experiencing significant losses, given the limited liquidity of such assets and the fire sale requirement. Should any of these fail, the alternative solution for the bank would be to consider its partial liquidation, or outright resolution with the systemic impacts we all well know. This first, "unbearable lightness" of the bank's business model that brought it to dominance and success (but also to so many crisis) driven by the leverage of assets over equity is not, however, the end of the story.

If we think of the bank as the sum of two pyramids, the first one sitting on its larger base, this one representing the overall liabilities insisting on its "one dollar" equity capital (the peak of the pyramid); and the second one, inverted, with the large base of the overall assets spreading upwards from the same "one dollar" equity capital, to then match the liabilities, we would immediately perceive the intrinsic instability of the two.

And we could even consider fatter tails adding to the basis of these two inverted pyramids. On the "gathering" side, banks (or, more correctly, financial services conglomerates) are managing other big chunks of money, coming from their asset and wealth management and insurance businesses. True enough, this money does not directly fund the balance sheet of the bank—thus, these fat tails should be shown as dotted. But it provides further leverage to the same basis of capital, as the "one dollar" equity is also providing the basic mean to run these businesses, and to cover less obvious but still relevant operational, business and reputational risks that are related to these businesses—as depicted in the following Fig. 1.1—The inverted pyramids.

1.1 Unbearable Lightness, and Leverage

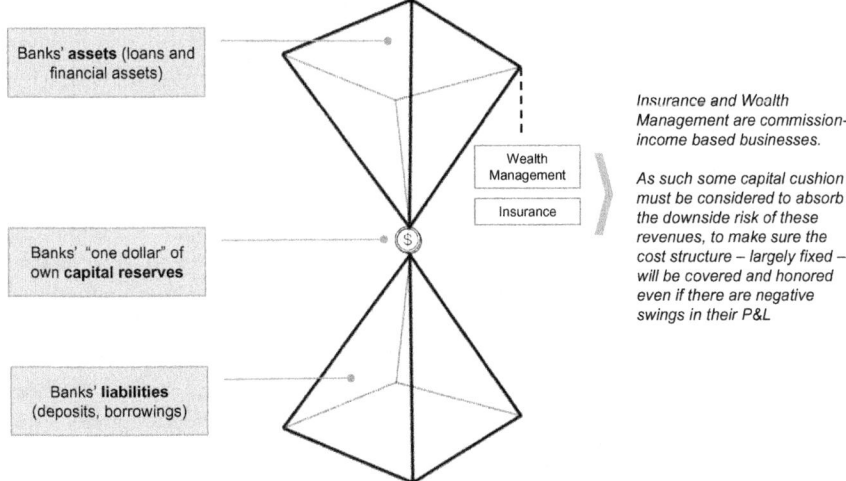

Fig. 1.1 The inverted pyramids: lending and other assets managed over equity leverage

More specifically, on one side, these are all commission-income based businesses, and as such some capital cushion must be considered to absorb the downside risk of these revenues, to make sure the cost structure—largely fixed—will be covered and honored even if there are negative swings in their P&L. On the other side, a number of operational risks (including, for example, the risk of fraud and misconduct, or of cyber-attacks that could originate losses to the bank's clients that the bank will likely have to cover anyway, not to mention other minimum regulatory requirements and the impacts on its reputation) need also to be "covered" (either in a funded or unfunded way) by equity capital, or alternatively by other liabilities, thus adding further leverage.

The "meta-leverage" that includes also the asset and wealth and insurance businesses (not to mention many other commission generating businesses, such as the payments/settlements one) has been scarcely understood and considered up to now, but could represent a further, significant threat to the stability of the banking system, as banks keep developing into financial conglomerates to build huge commission businesses, with assets under management often mirroring or even surpassing the total amount of the banks' lending assets.

Both the assets that fund directly or indirectly the bank's balance sheet are then invested by the bank, thus fully exposing the complexity of the business that is often dubbed, in academic contexts, as the "risk transformation" one, operated—it is often argued—to the benefit of the overall economy and society. The bank gathers money from many, dispersed counterparts, all seeking a moderate risk/return profile, and then extends loans to more risky and concentrated counterparts, pursuing more aggressive risk/return profiles, allowing the matching of the funds and uses of economically rationale counterparts with different financial expectations via the cushion provided by its own capital buffer—the usual one dollar equity one.

This risk transformation is in fact more perception than reality if the capital cushion is thin, as there are high chances that some of the losses will be borne by the debt holders (among which are the individuals that are deposit holders), or by the tax payers—should the State step-in last minute to save the bank and bail it out, to avoid the systemic effects of the bank's failure (the domino effects generated on other banks, at domestic and international level, and the dry up of the interbank and monetary markets that could then develop into a more structural lending freeze and even lead to the blockage of some part of the global payments system). On this perception-deception, most of the contemporary global financial system has been built, with its unbearable lightness that starts with the two inverted pyramids—that are not, however, the end of it.

1.2 Time (and Space) Lapses

The unbearable lightness of being a bank is generated by the equity multiplier (either in its purest form, or in its "meta-leverage" extension that we just discussed). It is however just a first dimension of this lightness (the gravity force visually represented by the two pyramids, one placed bottom up and the other top down and insisting on the very same one dollar of equity). A second, also well-known, further dimension is in fact driven by the time laps (or maturity gap, in more technical parlance) existing between the overall set of liabilities and related assets that the bank is managing to cover its costs and produce a decent return for its shareholders.

A common "weighted average time to maturity" (duration) of all the liabilities of a typical retail/commercial bank could in fact point to a typical 2–3 years range, with the same measure pointing to an typical 8–10 years on the asset side, with an implicit "refinancing risk" or "time lapse multiplier" of 4–5 times (the bank's assets need to be refinanced 4–5 times, with corresponding liabilities, before they reach their maturity).

This duration mismatch, if not by design, turns to be a pretty structural outcome of the banking business and of the "time transformation" it has operated since the origins of finance. On one side, riskier projects need more time to develop and work-out, and the longer the time horizon, the higher the chances that some initial negative swings in the venture will be absorbed and fully resolved. On the other side, the savings provided by families and individuals, small businesses and corporates, need theoretically to be more easily available in the short term (even if the "behavioral duration" of sight deposits could usually be calculated in the range of

6–9 years, their "technical" duration is zero, as they could be withdrawn at a moment's notice).

It is also worth to remember that the basic business of banking could be referred as a "buy the money—sell the money" one, with the bank gathering as many liabilities as possible, given its one dollar equity, and with the cheapest average cost of funding, and then extending as many loans (or investing in as many financial assets) as possible, with the highest expected yield, so to net a very high spread (the difference between the interest matured on the bank's assets and the cost of their funding, expressed as a percentage) and interest margin (the dollars generated by applying this percentage spread to the overall value intermediated).

This interest margin still drives most of the intermediation margin (or total revenues—interest margin plus commission income plus other P&L from principal trading activities) generated by a bank, and—in a typical situation of upward sloping yield curves—this margin will increase if the liabilities have shorter durations that the assets (as the spread gets higher). It all therefore contributes to the acceleration in the return generated on the one dollar equity, which is shouldering now not just the force of gravity of the inverted pyramids, but also the one generated by this time lapse, or duration mismatch—as the banks wants to invest long whilst borrowing short, in theory ensuring the safety of this time transformation with their buffer capital.

As in the case of leverage, this unstable time equilibrium (the second unbearable lightness) tends to precipitate when things go nasty—and false perceptions show again their dangerous nature of false deception. Should the bank start losing money, and should the general state of the financial markets worsen significantly, the demand for short term liabilities would increase, as well as the one from clients for longer term assets—further increasing the duration mismatch and the bank's exposure to the interest rate structural risk.

It won't help that the duration of most of the collaterals of the lending assets of a bank are even longer or indefinite (as it is the case with real estate assets), and with lengthy time to recovery/to sale estimated for reaching the full monetization of these assets and of their related collaterals when needed. And it also won't help that this time mismatch is also paralleled, in many cases, particularly for the banks operating at international level, by a space mismatch, where the intermediation game is played by raising funds from stable, mature, typically more developed countries, to then lend them to higher growth emerging countries—characterized by a higher risk/return profile, as there is no free lunch in competitive markets, and higher growth rates are usually associated with higher volatility (e.g. downside risk), as a number of "emerging markets" financial crises and debt crashes has been showing in the last few decades (as shown in Fig. 1.2).

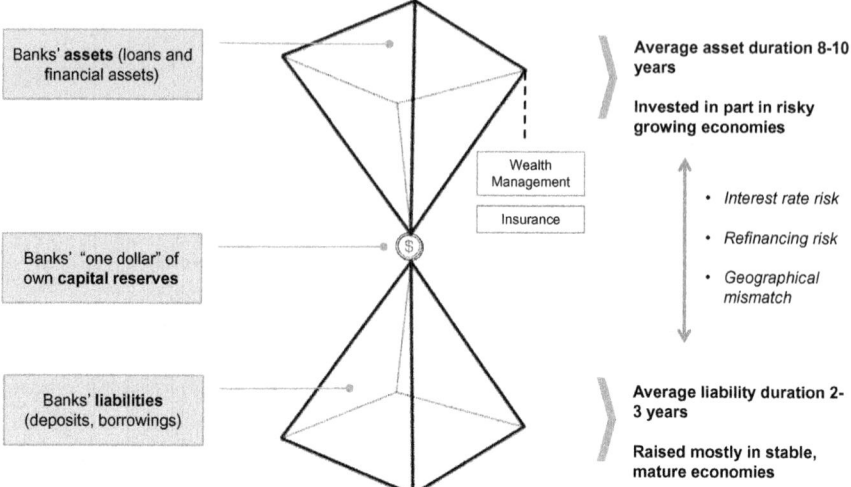

Fig. 1.2 The inverted pyramids: duration and geographical leverage

1.3 Capital Velocity (and Density)

Should the "quantity" (the two pyramids' force of gravity insisting on the one dollar equity) and the "acceleration" (the time and space lapse, or mismatch, between the liability and corresponding assets that contributes to the growth of the bank's profitability through time and space) effects not be enough, a third one—here referred as "capital velocity"—is adding to the definitely "unbearable lightness" of being a bank, as described in the Fig. 1.3—capital velocity and the securitization game.

Inventory velocity and turnover is a very obvious driver in manufacturing optimization: the more times you make your full inventory turn around over a year, the more efficient is the operating model of the business you operate, and the more efficiently and effectively your invested capital can be put at work to produce a decent return. A similar concept could then be surely copied and considered for implementation to put the one dollar equity of a bank at an even better use, if just there was a similar mean? That mean exist, and is usually referred as "securitization" (and often dubbed as financial innovation—improperly, as the mechanisms of securitization are nothing new, even if its aggressive development in terms of volumes structured and transacted greatly accelerated in the last decade before the Lehman debacle).

In its most basic application, a securitization allows a bank to segregate a specific portfolio of assets, that is then going be sold to an SPV (a "special purpose vehicle" owned by the bank or otherwise "orphan") which is funding their acquisition by issuing bonds then subscribed by third party investors (sometimes, as it

1.3 Capital Velocity (and Density)

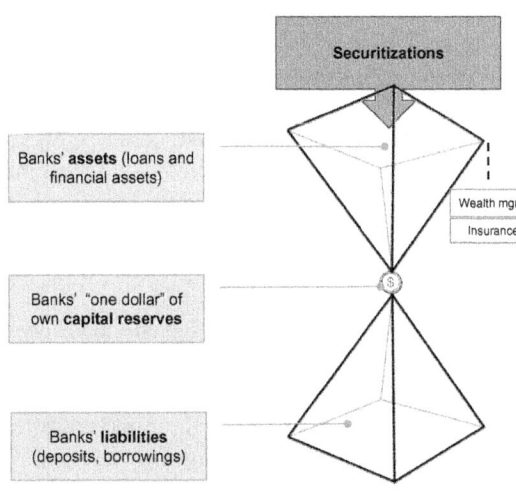

Fig. 1.3 Capital velocity and the securitization game

was common in the recent past, with the same bank among them, chipping-in with some part of its equity capital to buy the equity and mezzanine more risky tranches), thus reducing its overall leverage but at limited or almost non-existing de-risking (and with the senior tranches going to long-only institutional investors).

The securitization can also easily allow a repackaging of different assets, to create a given diversification effect and new, hybrid risk/return profiles. Also, given the approach to the trancing of the bonds issued by the SPV to fund itself, very different categories' of investors (from pension funds, insurance companies to private equity and hedge funds) can be targeted—given the "cascading rule" used to allocate the proceeds coming from the reference portfolio being securitized (they satisfy first the credit rights of the most highly rated senior tranches, then of the less senior ones and then down to the mezzanine and to the junior equity).

In principle, it follows, the securitization mechanism works beauties and for multiple counterparts. It allows to the bank to build highly diversified portfolios, by combining bits and pieces at the whims of the investment banks advising on the transaction, thus allowing the transfer of risk/return profiles in a "synthetic" way (the loans could actually be kept in the bank's balance sheet and served by it—with just their risk ownership being shifted to the final buyers) and theoretically reaching out the best holder of any of such profiles.

It also allows to the bank to create a liquid market for assets that would be untraded by definition, should they be held to maturity by the originating entity, thus supporting an efficient price discovery process as well—a process that could (theoretically) contribute to the transparency and liquidity of the overall financial system.

It allows finally the multiple usage of the bank's capital during the fiscal year time frame—the long duration lending portfolios are not held to maturity, but can be sold during the year at will, and the bank, with the proceeds obtained, can extend further loans, making its capital "rotate" multiple times during the year. The multiple usage (or "capital velocity": the number of times the one dollar equity of the bank is re-used and re-leveraged to get funding and extend credit, and meet the regulatory capital minimum as required) is thus contributing further to the growth in the profitability of the bank, and is also de-risking its balance sheet, if the securitizations are finalized as "true sales", e.g. without the bank retaining any of the riskier tranches.

Unfortunately, the lessons learned from the global financial crisis have been quite different. In a number of cases, they have provided an easy way for banks to re-leverage themselves and to further extend their time lapse or duration mismatch (when they started to consider the long dated portfolios and the opportunity to securitize and sell them in a much quicker time frame, repackaged as a salami of uncertain composition and healthiness)—thus further increasing their inherent instability along these two dimensions.

In many other cases, they have resulted—given the number of conflict of interests at play—in a "hot potato" game (the banks selling their worst quality assets to third, ignorant counterparts, at the price of jewels, and with a very high credit rating assigned to them by external agencies that were in turn conflicted as consultants of the banks). With huge risks being transferred undetected and being not fully understood across the global financial system, to counterparts still related to the banking system and thus prone to the same domino effect.

A similar reasoning could be used to argue how this third "unbearable lightness" has also been driven by the "density" of equity capital usage, for principal investing and risk underwriting purposes, via the use of complex, structured derivatives (or even plain, insurance-like, financial guarantees), sold for a premium as unfunded, thus allowing the further "densification" of the bank's equity capital to drive its risk/return profile even higher, to an almost un-investable level (for their perspective shareholders—should have they known).

In conclusion, after the quantity and acceleration, this capital velocity/density effect has allowed to further compound and multiply the almost unbearable lightness (or instability) of the traditional banking model, that ultimately resulted in the burst of the global financial crisis affecting a banking system that, re-regulation after re-regulation, has not yet regained the apparent stability of times long past and is actually posing even more fundamental questions—regarding its fundamental "raison d'etre" and its chances of having a sustainable, profitable, if at all, future—now that other digital challenges lie at the horizon.

1.4 Intangible like Money

Just consider how flimsy a piece of paper money is: be it the "one dollar" bank note we have used as our reference bank's equity capital, or even a "10" or a "100 dollars" bill one. How perishable it is, and with no immediate, material use (apart from its transactional value that is set by "fiat" e.g. based on and potentially enforceable by the rule of Law and printed at whim by the Central Bank of the relevant Country—also called, for this very reason, the "bank of banks"). And still, a bank note is more tangible that a string of 0–1 digits that is now making up the vast majority of the (electronic) money that is freely flowing in the global economy.

Actually, the cash, paper money has in fact a unique characteristic, as it allows (as exception, should we forget about the marginal forms of barter that still do occur in some part of the economy) the conclusion of some commercial exchange between individuals or companies without the intermediation, in some way or form, of financial intermediaries—like banks, payment providers, regulated capital markets or central banks.

The vast majority of our savings, investment and consumption acts is, in fact, materializing via some kind of interaction with the largely regulated global financial system and with its main institutional players: retail/commercial and wholesale/investment banks, asset management and insurance companies, payments/settlement providers and central banks and many others. It all rests on the most immaterial of things, e.g. the money, that has been used successfully through centuries to regulate and foster the international commerce (avoiding, that is, the bartering and keeping wars and expropriation by force to a minimum), and to tax individuals and allow the development of democratic nations that are based on social participation and individual rights. It has also allowed the transfer of goods effectively and efficiently through time and space, to optimally allocate the most scarce and productive resources across the economy, often allowing the shared participation of a multitude of people or Countries to indivisible, high scale projects... and so on.

It all rests on the most intangible of things. As cash money could be lost, stolen or burned. And also digital money, even more ethereal in nature, could be lost, stolen or destroyed, as some recent and rather scary cyber-security attacks have shown. Not to mention that money could be de-based—as it happened in the night of times when the County leader (usually the King, or the tyrant) started putting bronze or something else of little value into the (otherwise thought of as pure) gold coins.

This debasement still happens today, when the "fiat" originating principle is abused, and Central Banks start printing money (either paper money or, more likely, electronic) with no restraint, to finance budget deficits of the local Government or else, just throwing "helicopter money" at people to keep them at bay, creating an excess of money that in the long run (via the "Fisher equation", that also contemplates the velocity with which such money is used) should turn into higher, long term inflation; and it still happens when, in regimes of managed

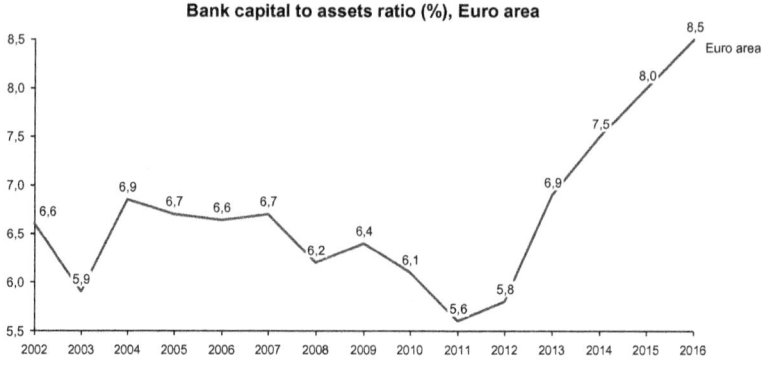

An even minimal volatility in the net value of a bank's lending portfolio (i.e. considering its mix of funding liabilities) would immediately wipe out most of its equity capital

Source: International Monetary Fund, Global Financial Stability Report

Fig. 1.4 Capital core T1 increased in last years to rebuild banks' credibility and trust

exchange rates, a specific currency is forcefully depreciated to "beggar thy neighbor", increasing the international competitiveness of its reference Country and export unemployment on the basis of an unfair currency exchange ratio.

Given such intangibility, and the risks inherently involved in it, it is crucial to understand how money is built on a promise that is worth the credibility of the one that commits to deliver on that promise. Money, and the global financial system, we could argue, are in fact ultimately built on faith and delivered on trust.

The ever increasing efforts aimed at providing a common set of internationally recognized and enforceable set of regulations to ensure capital adequacy, adequate risk management and the compliance to a number of other procedures, and the focus on the political side to make sure that the financial system is perceived as stable and safe (even in case of a forced resolution) are contributing on the direction to retain and rebuild that trust. Certainly, as showed in the following Figure, a much higher capital buffers have been rebuilt in recent years in the banking system, to at least partially address, with "hard money" the weaknesses built on the trust side (Fig. 1.4).

1.5 Unsafe as a House

Another quite relevant contribution to the perceived greater "tangibility" of the "castle of cards" of money has been historically played, with a greater and greater role since the end of World War II, by the real estate sector. The banking system has in fact played a crucial role in the real estate and infrastructure re-building effort after the war. And it has supported an ever increasing rate of home ownership for most of the families in the developed Countries—thus contributing to their social stability and further economic development.

The real estate sector, as a consequence, has become extremely interconnected with the financial system, providing the "tangibility" perspective with its very concrete collaterals, either used as guarantees to retail mortgages or to corporate loans, as trophy assets owned by the banks for their headquarters and branches or as "long term" invested asset pertaining to their insurance and asset/wealth management managed portfolios.

Banking and real estate has been a very peculiar marriage indeed, of the most intangible with the most concrete of sectors: their intertwined relationship has apparently worked well—till the global financial crisis hit. Till then it had been spurring the growth of the real economy, the accumulation of savings for families and individuals (the retail mortgage being maybe the simplest and most effective way to allow and force a human being to save and accumulate a transferrable wealth) and making the banking and financial services sector look more solid and stable, and with a more limited volatility in its value (a house will never lose value in the short and in the long run: as long as there is no reliable "mark to market" of the value of the real estate assets, that is... as there is no liquid, fully comparable market; and as long as you forget about the cost of inflation).

It is then important to understand why this synergic relationship, apparently overcoming most of the dimensions of the bank's "unbearable lightness", has now become unsustainable as well, actually driving further systemic risks and fueling potentially vicious circles of booms and busts. And why a new model of banking needs to be thought of as starting from a very different premise than the "safe as a house" one.

For the sake of this discussion, we could safely argue that banks and real estate are not just strongly intertwined sector, mingling together in a number of different and sometimes novel (albeit less understood, as in the asset backed securities—ABS—case) ways: banks are in fact by far the largest and most active players in the real estate sector which they end up, if not controlling, influencing in a very strong way.

Let's take into consideration a typical balance sheet of a retail/commercial bank, as shown in Fig. 1.5—Bank and real estate: a shaky relationship. The bank, working now at a 15/20 leverage ratio (the ratio of the total assets on its equity capital), will own directly some real estate assets, for its own use as head-quarters (typically trophy assets to convey the sense of prestige and credibility to its corporate and retail customers) and branches—becoming redundant by the day, as most of the businesses and operations of banks turn digital.

The bank as "real estate principal and trader" will also directly own a bunch of other real estate assets, as it develops its leasing proposition—bearing directly the risk of the swings in the value of these assets, including the operational risks related to their potential malfunctioning and the liabilities coming from the resulting damages to people and to other goods. The bank will also, finally, own directly other real estate assets as a result of its repossession activities carried out on its

		Starting situation		RE market contraction: -10%		
		Initial Assets (Base: 100)	RE value (Base: 100)	RE value (Base: 100)	Hypothesis of correlation ratio	Final Assets (Base: 100)
Tangible assets	Mortgage	8.5	19	17	1:5	8.1
	Loans to RE developer	5.8	12	11	1:2	5.2
	Prop assets/ Leasing	2.1	4	3	1:2	2.0
	Non Performing Loan	1.9	4	3	1:3	1.7
	Other tangible assets	80.5	-	-	-	80.5
Intangible assets		1.2	-	-	-	1.2
Total assets		100.0	38	34		98.7
Liabilities		96.0	-	-	-	96.0
Tangible equity		4.0	-	-	-	2.7
Liabilities and equity		100.0	-	-	-	98.7
Tangible equity		4.0		2.7		
Tangible assets		98.8	4.1% ratio	97.5	2.8% ratio	

(Tangible assets total: 18.3 initial → 17.0 final; change -1.3)

Note: Decreases to 1.5% and 0.1% in case of RE contraction of -20% and -30%

Fig. 1.5 Banks and real estate: a shaky relationship

non-performing loans (NPLs) portfolio—usually after a bidding process aimed at disposing those assets via an open market auction and "true" sale.

More importantly, the bank will own "indirectly" multiple stacks of real estate assets, as it lends to retail clients (with real estate assets tied to mortgages as collateral), small businesses, medium and large corporates and public finance institutions (again, leveraging the tangibility of real estate as guarantee against the default of the counterparts); and it will own "indirectly" the brown and green field new developments carried out by the real estate developers it is financing, that are literally using the money lent to them by the intangible banking system to build other concrete houses: burning the money to make further bricks, so to speak.

Some of these loans will in turn become near, sub, or non-performing, making the "indirect" ownership more stringent and with clearer implications on the profit and loss and balance sheet of the bank. Finally, the bank will also indirectly own real estate assets as part of its investment portfolio dedicated to the asset management products it sells to its customers or that it manages as technical reserves for its insurance business (if it has one, as it's often the case for banks that developed into financial conglomerates). More specifically, these reserves are meant to meet and serve the policyholders requirements (including minimum return guarantees that the bank may have promised to clients) and therefore the value of the assets they comprise are really meant as a protection layer over and above the bank's equity capital.

In summary, in its ever running challenge of creating stability out of thin air, and of turning the intangible money into something hard and concrete, the bank becomes an almost fully fledged real estate company, with a long position on its economic cycle, and with multiple functions and roles played along its value chain.

1.5 Unsafe as a House

As the lending supply has a strong influence on the demand and supply of real estate assets, the bank is also contributing to the success of the sector itself—and in turn of its own—in a kind of "self-fulfilling prophecy": you lend a wall of money to the real estate sector because you are positive on it, and this in turn keeps growing in size (the number of new buildings keeps growing) and price (the price of traded homes is also growing, spurred by an inflated demand, driven by an easy, abundant and cheap access to mortgages). It obviously follows that this "self-fulfilling prophecy" leads in turn to the formation of asset bubbles that undermine the very basic hypothesis of this "real estatization" of the banking sector (e.g. that houses are safe and the banks too because of them, and you just need to wait, for accumulating a great value out of them).

The "real-estatization" of banking and of the finance sector—and the parallel, excessive "financialization" of the real estate sector has led, among few other things, to the prickle of the asset bubble in 2008 and to the global financial crisis that had dominated international markets and economies since then. Houses are in fact unsafe, as many other assets used as repository of value—and for sure they are much less liquid.

The demand of houses is determined by the available income of people and companies, and by the mortgage supply (obviously enough, the more money is available to buy bricks, the higher the chances their demand will pick up). It is also determined by the level of rents on such assets (rents being the best proxy of a yield on real estate: the higher it gets, the more attractive it becomes as investment opportunity, or as "own" versus "rent" option for individuals and firms that can afford it), but many other factors are also influencing this market, including, just as a matter of example: the structure of the society and the average size of a family (given multiple, smaller families coming from splits and divorces and from lower demographic trends), the higher the ask of small, multiple houses; the mobility of people (given higher mobility, for business and pleasure, the higher potentially the ask for second and third houses); the social engineering (the greater the industrialization and polarization of wealth, the strongest the "gentrification" trend, with big cities becoming even bigger and with the richest people willing to get and live in their downtown, at all costs, the higher the swings in real estate values, with city centers reaching stellar valuations and the periphery loosing value big times etc.).

It is now easier to understand why this "real-estatization" of banks (and the corresponding "bankization" of real estate companies) has really been a double sword process for their and the systemic stability of the overall economy. As they have become more tangible, because of the direct and indirect ownerships they have been building over time via their interlinkages with the real estate sector, banks have become more exposed to the real estate risk—a largely ignored and little understood risk. And as this last one turns out to be largely influenced by the GDP cycle, by the level of interest rates and money supply, it has often behaved in unexpected ways.

Also, its "value at risk" (the maximum potential loss that is expected, given certain hypothesis on the distribution of frequency of events and a set confidence level) is still perceived as largely unknown, mostly because of the unavailability of reliable "mark to market" prices for the valuation of the real estate assets underpinning the banks' loan portfolios. As it has grown big, the real estate risk has then kept being little understood and measured and vastly under managed—with just few reactionary policies designed for when the bubble burst and with limited proactive planning, control and work out—from banks and regulators alike.

In the last few years, since the Lehman Brothers debacle in 2008, the size of this real estate exposure has brought many banks to their knees, and an almost "minimal" downward volatility of 10% in the value of those assets could still cause a major decline in the equity and regulatory capital of many global and domestic banks, forcing them in turn to deleverage, de-risk and raise capital—thus likely further undermining the real estate sector, as the lending supply dries up and the normal interplay of demand and supply of houses becomes clogged in the midst of a financial markets that works through imbalances, disruptions and dislocations.

As the banking real estate connubial relationship falls apart, an obvious question arises, with regard to what kind of other assets could help the stabilization of the financial system, and create new, durable goodwill for banks, potentially helping them to address and solve the three unbearable drivers of lightness—rebalancing the asset/equity leverage, the time mismatch and defining a velocity of capital usage that is still relevant and profitable but sustainable as well, with limited risks of making some part of the system spin around and crash.

1.6 Imbalanced, Disrupted and Dislocated

Global and domestic banks, as much as the remaining pack of institutional players active in the international financial systems, are now facing—as a consequence of all this—a number of unprecedented challenges: something requiring a real transformation, or radical, almost genetic evolution—way above what was needed in past financial crisis. This is because the 2008 crisis, as we have argued so far, has not been a typical, temporary crisis (just) led by speculation, market gyrations or simple fraud, but it has been grounded in more structural issues that have created and still make up most of the "unbearable lightnesses" described.

This need of real transformation has now become common parlance and almost a "buzzword" in the industry and, in truth, some sense of urgency has started surfacing in the otherwise fairly static world of finance. Banks, still recovering from the global financial crisis, are now trying to find ways to re-balance their inverted pyramid structure, putting limits to their leverage, time lapse mismatch and increased (unchecked) velocity in their inventory of structured financial products: and they are doing this whilst the external world is rapidly changing around them, further increasing their risk of becoming obsolete and irrelevant by the day.

Most of them are still burdened by past financial excesses, not yet fully recognized into their P&L and regulatory capital structure. Some of them—retail/commercial banks—are still struggling with regard to the bulk of NPLs accumulated since 2008—mostly in continental Europe, but not only. Others, including global wholesale/investment banks and international, universal banks are still potentially impaired by their heavy weight of Alt-3 legacy assets—the derivatives and highly structured credit products that are deemed as almost impossible to value, because of their sky rocket complexity, opacity and limited or non-existent liquidity.

Other, non-financial legacies from the past are also making life even more difficult for senior bankers, and the change of their organization looks almost impossible to design and drive to full execution. On one side, the last few years have been marked by ever increasing regulatory costs (where the re-regulation has become a very heavy duty process, apparently never ending and developing in often confused and heterogeneous ways—different across diverse geographical jurisdictions and sub-sectors) and compliance ones (where the compliance and red-taping is taking very stringent and multiple forms, fueled by the social angst caused by the taxpayers costs that were observed and contested as consequence of the banking crisis).

It almost comes as a logical consequence that the new regulatory and compliance requirements are also paired by the very high costs coming from litigations and regulatory fines, consequence—in some cases, as for the anti-money laundering (AML) regulation, of a principled approach that puts to the banks the burden of the proof of having behaved correctly—with the tolerance on any potential misconduct in the financial system brought almost to zero, as banks bashing as become one of the preferred sports of media and politicians alike.

Past legacies, acting as a constraint on the bank's willingness and ability to change, are not however the end of the story. Apart from these, to paraphrase Marcel Proust, many other worries about the future are almost making the day to day life of banks executives impossible to bear. It then follows that the attention and focus required from them and from the organization to execute the transformation right is not just there.

Looking at the very near future, a number of geopolitical imbalances, between developed, emerging economies and under developed economies, are still threatening the stability of the system, with currency wars, sequential "tit for tat" devaluations and "beggar thy neighbor" economic policies on the remaking (or "unmaking") of the main international trade agreements. Even the re-emergence of the military assertiveness of some of the major economic blocks of the present and of the recent past—from China to Russia, not to mention the Arabic states and other major economic Asian heavyweights such as India and Japan, and the continuous threats of international terrorism are further adding volatility to the overall ecosystem.

Other secular movements in the overall structure of the global economy are also producing new sources of uncertainty and risk: from the serial dislocations of the oil market and the development of alternative energy sources, to the emergence of digital and of artificial intelligence as disrupters of all kind of traditional industries, to the early successes of the shared economy and of the internet of things that are impacting the way money is spent, save and invested, to the revolution of 3D printing and the likely impact it will have on global and local manufacturing... All these new factors, and many others, are bringing further instability into a system that was always been perceived as too introverted and with limited capacity of reaction—particularly so when, as in these days, it looks fully dedicated to solving its own solvency and profitability issues.

The list of grievances for banks would be indeed much longer, and we could just mention the negative impacts on their reputation and credibility coming from high profile misconduct cases (like the miss-selling of insurance protection in the UK, or of unwanted retails products in the USA). Or the macro environment now dominated by extremely challenging monetary policies—with very low interest rates turning even negative in some regions, mining the very basic principle of the banking intermediation—buy money and sell money—and its ability to generate an healthy interest rate spread. Or the rising cyber security threats posed to banks and other financial intermediaries by terrorists, anarchists and traditional burglars—as they have become a primary target, as they represent the "financial plumbing" of the global economy and the driving force of the capitalistic system. Or, finally, the still obvious over-capacity (mostly in the developed Countries, with huge numbers of unbanked people still in the emerging and underdeveloped ones) and excising fragmentation of an industry where in many Countries, a mix of private, public and private-public operators keep confusingly competing with each other's and not always using market prices as reference for trades.

A last threat to banks and incumbent financial intermediaries is eventually worth mentioning—this one already evident in the market place and for sure catching most of the attention paid by private equity and venture capital funds, even if its full realization points out to a much longer time horizon.

We are referring to the rise and early successes of new, so called "FinTech", digital challengers—often working in the shadow of the official regulatory definition of "financial industry" and thus able to avoid most of the rules that are instead applying to banks—potentially introducing great gains for the customers but also very relevant pains for the incumbent players unable to react and change, fast and effectively. The FinTech—digital challengers topic will indeed be further discussed later on, with greater detail and with a more articulated vision of what is happening and could happen to any of the most fundamental functions played by the global financial system, given the new entrants' disruptive strategies and the incumbents', largely defensive and unable to drive real transformation, reactions. For the time being, it is worth taking a pause on this last point of the "destruens part" of our discussion, to start asking ourselves few open questions.

What, if anything, could rebuild a sustainable proposition for banks and other financial intermediaries, overcoming this state of imbalance, disruption and dislocation? Transformation can in fact be more or less well design and executed, but still needs, and is informed and driven by a final end state—a business and operating model—that are qualifying this new target, incorporating the set of competitive invariances that will define the winners and definitely set the destiny of the losers.

What is then the Nirvana of this new target business and operating model? And what would be the ambition and vision that can allow banks to break from the constraints of the past, overcoming the worries of the future to fully live the present, to then change at the right time, in the right way and for the right reason? What is, therefore, the bank of the future—that is, if the bank has a future at all? And what fundamental pillars could be considered to address and resolve, once and for all, its unbearable lightness?

Synapses in the Global Financial System

Abstract

As traditional business models appear increasingly unable to cope with the new digital ecosystem and the challenges brought by innovation across multiple dimensions, so traditional frameworks of competitive analysis looks in need of reshaping, if not of a more radical change. The synapses framework of analysis is built on five key pillars: advance data/information management, applied analytics and machine learning/AI, a new way of doing business in a richer, more value adding, multi-stakeholders way (dubbed "interconnecting by junctions"), new solutions and use cases that create truly incremental value for the overall economic system and, finally, trust—e.g. the importance of being credible and with a good reputation in an upcoming age of digital uncertainties, cyber risks and warfare, loss of privacy and of individual conscience and many others. This is particularly true for the financial services, an industry built on the pinnacle of the intangible—as money (already digital) gets unregulated, with new services offered by unknown digital dotcom.

Keywords

Synapses · Data management · Applied analytics · Machine learning · Artificial intelligence

2.1 Synapses and Syndesis

Complex economic systems have often been compared to living organisms, in the way they behave and develop—through cycles of innovation, maturity and decadence, and for the way they tend to react to exogenous factors, as they potentially mine their chances of survival through the unavoidable periods of booms and busts (from a financial or evolutionary perspectives, respectively). As a critical component of this economic system-living organism, we could then think of the global financial sector as a fairly complex nervous system, working as a structure that allows the diverse components of the larger economic organism—the muscles, the bones, the blood pulsing in the veins and the skin covering the outside—to work effectively and in full coordination with each other—allowing almost everything to become possible... from the simplest movement (like the waving of a hand to say hello) to the most complex ones (like performing a critical somersault).

More specifically, we could think of the financial system as ultimately pursuing a process of continuous evolution. With steps forward preventing the terminal events that could come from inside or from external shocks, and driving the continuous recombination of its genetic components then driving the evolution into stronger off springs and species. A critical component, in this interpretation of the world of finance and banking, would be played by synapses—in general terms and with specific reference to a nervous system.

Synapses (also called "syndesis") refers, more broadly to the pairing of two homologous chromosomes that occurs during meiosis. This pairing ("fastening together", the original mean of the Greek word) allows the matching up of homologous pairs, prior to their segregation, and the possible chromosomal crossover between them. This crossing over, known also as genetic recombination, provides the important function of increasing the genetic variability within the offspring. Think about the variability of business and operating models—and the multiple constraints posed by regulations and technology, not to mention culture and behavior—politics, bureaucracy and syndication, now prevailing in banking and limiting its chances of changing successfully.

Against this back drop of internal and external constraints, and given the continuously changing and increasingly threatening ecosystem, a set of repeatedly recombinant synapses would have the general effect of allowing genes to move independently of each other through successive generations, allowing for the independent concentration of beneficial genes and the purging of the detrimental ones—an essential step for the successful meiosis, and for the evolution and survival of the species. Setting free the recombinant synapses, from illogical rules and IT legacies, doctrinal culture and prevailing behavior and bureaucracy, would rise the chances of evolution of the system, and of its main players' (banks and other financial intermediaries) survival.

Synapses—arguing one step further in this biological digression—has an even more interesting specific definition when referred to the nervous system, as it works as a structure that transmits an electrical or chemical signal to another neuron—even if via non neurological contacts, or junctions. Synapses are essential to neural functions because via neurons they pass signals to individual target cells, driving them to perform their correct function in a logical, coordinated way—making the body wave or shake hands or perform a fairly critical somersault. Regulating the neurological transmission allows then to make the system work, performing its fundamental function and in a "smart" way—reducing to a minimum the neurons required to perform and making sure their (business and operating) model works in the most effective and efficient way. What would then be the approach to rethink the global financial system as an interconnected synapses process? And what would be the critical elements to characterize the new role of the bank as the synapses main driver?

We will assume, as our funding hypothesis, that five critical components, or pillars, are now supporting and will be increasingly driving in the future the successful synapses that needs to happen in the global financial system to support the development of the overall living organism—the economic system as a whole, as it unfolds and perform at international and local level. We will then discuss how a number of new major regulatory events—among them the open data movement and related "requirements"—are further acting as a catalyst of the fast paced evolution process. And, finally, how a couple of well-known, leading global—regional banks —Goldman Sachs and BBVA, incumbent leaders on the investment banking/wholesale and retail/commercial sectors respectively—have initially reacted to the challenging forces now at play in the financial services industry, leveraging digital innovation to change their business strategies, apparently in a very successful way.

2.2 Five Senses: One

We can define these five critical components, or building blocks, as "senses" that help banks in predicting, understanding, navigating, contrasting and reacting to the new external ecosystem in which they are now increasingly competing—as it is progressively dominated by digital and other technological innovation. In our working hypothesis, these "five senses" include (as shown in Fig. 2.1): data and information advance management; intelligence by applied analytics, machine learning and artificial intelligence (AI) management; interconnectivity and junction management; new business solution design and management; trust and credibility management.

Data and information (as defined as some more structured combination of data, characterized by a particular arrangement or sequence of things), stand out as the first critical block, that needs to be designed, built and protected, with particular reference to the personal digital identity of clients, by the "synapses bank". Data and information have always been at the center stage of banking, but new technological developments are suggesting now some kind of discontinuity in their role and importance.

New data capture and storage technologies are now making technically possible and economically feasible the accumulation of unprecedented quantities of data— derived from multiple sources (quantitative—structured—and qualitative and with an increasing role played by the social sites of the world wide web—unstructured) and managed in multiple ways—allowing more flexibility in the rules for data retrieval, combination and sequencing. The "internet of things", e.g. the real time connectivity allowed by the digital devices that can now be easily installed on

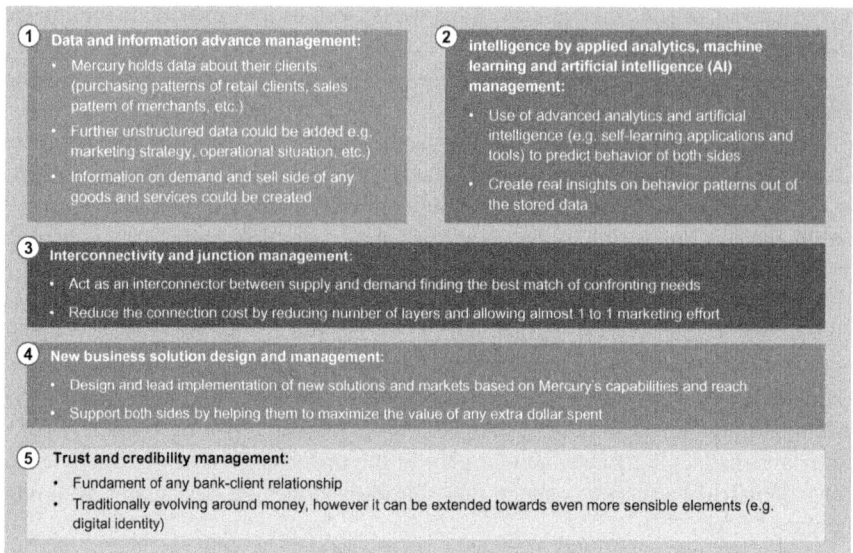

Fig. 2.1 Five senses to read and navigate the new banking digital ecosystem

almost everything—from a T-shirt to a car—is just going to compound the trillions of data further becoming available and produced on a continuous basis and in real time.

Not only that. As new regulations (the PSD2 on payments, and the MIFID on derivatives and other investment management products) come into play, banks and other financial intermediaries are forced to open up their own data to let the customer know how they operate, how much they are charging them, and for what service. Hence, new sources of meaningful data once jealously preserved by banks are now becoming available for customer and—given their approval—to other aggregator/price comparison players. In turn, this extended freedom of data access and the related shift in the bargaining power to favor the end customers, opens up to new competitive dynamics, and favors the entrance of new "shadow banking" (mostly digital) players.

2.3 Five Senses: Two

Quantity and quality of data may however turn out relatively unfruitful, if it is not matched by a parallel development of models, techniques and approaches to derive intelligence out of them—that is the ability to define multiple, logical and serviceable "cause—effect" relationships among those data and the information. The ultimate aim is therefore to use applied analytics, machine learning/AI and anything else that that can produce recommendations that are useful enough for the business strategy and scope of the "synapses bank". It is intelligence with a clear aim in mind that allows the build-up of goodwill out of data and information.

More specifically, the recent sophistication and industrialization of machine learning and artificial intelligence (AI) tools is now making possible the "robotization" of the easiest bits of the reasoning process that produces intelligence out of raw data and sequenced information. As AI is threatening to revolutionize or displace large segments of the financial services job market, it is also offering a number of new functionalities and applications that can really turn the needle of the productivity attained out of the enormous amount of data and information now being captured, organized and stored. In a way, applied analytics and the use of AI systems are raising the yield on the new intangible capital of the financial system, e.g. the data/information capital—helping to overcome its relative scarcity and excessive abundance (in many instances, scarcity—of very relevant, immediately intelligible data/information, and abundance—of all kind of other "white noises"—coexist and only machine learning/AI can help make sense of the latter, whilst leveraging the former).

As of today, most of the data gathered by financial intermediaries have been stored without following basic golden rules (such as the full verification of completeness, existence, accuracy, valuation, ownership etc.) and in multiple legacy systems that make the consistency and easiness of any comprehensive extraction and elaboration very difficult to master, with high investments required for any new use case, with long time frames required to extract and elaborate data and with high chances of errors and mistakes along the way—with potential fines and liabilities deriving from the wrong use of data—given stricter confidentiality rules.

The use of middleware solutions, able to retrieve data from multiple legacy systems, doing elaborations based on flexible rules hosted in the middleware and then ensuring the reconciliation in 1–2 days on batch elaboration, has partially addressed these serious issue, but not ensured a full competitiveness of the incumbents, vis a vis the unstructured, multi-sources but unified flexible, agile data bases mastered by the new digital players—where queries drive the structure and elaboration ex post—a la Google, without requiring any pre-determined and rigid articulation "once and for all" of data and information.

It is also worth noting that frantic "data accumulation" excesses by global and local banks have lead in many cases to huge over-investments and high running operating costs not justified by any final use-case yield. And that the effort of digitizing historical data written on paper has proved long and costly, exposing the now-fully-digitalized data sets to the increasing cyber-risk, where data directly owned by the bank or on behalf of its customers could be destroyed or stolen—potentially threatening the confidentiality of the digital identity of clients and the very existence (risk of destruction) and ownership (risk of theft) of their money.

2.4 Five Senses: Three

Banking, at times, has been described as one of the easiest and most boring jobs in the world—assuming you had the money and power required to start with. As we discussed in our "pars destruens", the well-known saying that banking is a "3-6-3" job—meaning, you buy money at 3%, sell it at 6%, and by 3 p.m. are at the golf course—is obviously long gone. But the overall tendency to rely on intermediation as "core business" of banking is still there, even if most of its competitive strength —related to the sometimes described "segmented oligopoly"—is mostly lost, and ready to be further disrupted by the digitization of markets and societies alike— breaking any further boundary of the potentially segmented addressable markets. In truth, calls to get back to the pure intermediation businesses have been high—after the more aggressive forays in the principal investment space brought hell to the sector. But, as it was implicit in our discussion in Chap. 1, intermediation lies at the heart of the traditional lending business and is actually generating—and is in turn supported by—the three "unbearable lightnesses" of the current business model of banking.

Firstly, intermediation happens when the bank gathers data from multiple retail sources seeking low risks/low returns opportunities, and extend loans to few, more risk taker corporates (the magic transformation is in theory ensured by the diversification and by the bank's capital buffer—but we have argued that the magic tends not to hold in time of crisis). Secondly, intermediation happens when lower duration funds are employed to finance longer durations uses (again, with a magic transformation happening by virtue of the ALM—asset liability management capabilities of the bank—and of the usual bank equity buffer—but we have argued that ALM time lapses tend to become impossible to refinance when the market is illiquid and risk appetite collapses).

Finally, intermediation happens in a multiplied way when the bank does not hold loans to maturity, but sell them (either as true sale, or just as mere deleverage that is not truly de-risking its balance sheet) via securitizations—effectively extending its intermediation from retail clients to corporates (traditional business), to wholesale investors (the buyers of the securitization notes) to retail again (if these investors are then putting part of this notes in the portfolios of mutual funds, pension funds or insurance companies).

In our vision of the "synapses bank", mere intermediation should evolve and extend, becoming the ability to interconnect, via junctions, as in the neural function example, a larger number of stakeholders, and in smarter, more value adding ways —to allow the economic system to work, performing its fundamental functions in smarter ways, e.g. reducing the transaction frictions and the neurons required to do the job in the most effective and efficient way: in a way not just finding the minimal two counterparts required for any deal, but finding the multiple best ones—so as to maximize the total value created by the transaction, minimizing as well all associated costs and risks. This should in turn help the system become more stable and profitable, as the three unbearable lightnesses are reinforced by the new mix of stakeholders put at play—with the synapses bank acting as intelligent match maker of different quantities of money available, time horizons and risk profiles, so as to produce an higher economic output (no matter how it is then shared).

2.5 Five Senses: Four

Building on the logical extension of this "junction management" ability, the "synapses bank" could then compete on the solution seeking, designing and delivery—e.g. not just limiting itself in interconnecting the best possible counterparts to a trade and in the smartest, most efficient/effective way, but also finding innovative use cases (or business solutions) that enable the development of new, valuable, economic possibilities. These in turn should allow and support the development of new, successful business models. In this way, the bank could capitalize on data and information to create intelligence that drive interconnection by selective junctions and support as well the development of innovative economic solutions or use cases. A simple example could help in clarifying the different dimensions of the four senses so far discussed.

As a start, a typical bank will own "structured" data on the purchasing history of its retail clients, and on the sales patterns of its merchants and of their suppliers. The bank could then start considering to add to them other unstructured data, such as the personal behavior and preferences of its retail clients, and the marketing strategy and operational situation of its merchants. It could create a powerful set of data and information on the demand and sell side of any specific kind of good and service (sense 1). On this basis, with the use of applied analytics and machine learning/AI, it could also start to predict the potential behavior of both sides of a trade to create real, insightful intelligence out of the data and information gathered and stored (sense 2).

Acting as a meta-intermediary (or via junctions, to use a better terminology) the synapses bank could then selectively interconnect the best counterparties to a deal: the trendy teen ager looking for a new cerulean pull-over and the merchant that is high on the stock of this, and the manufacturer that is just planning the colors to produce for the next, upcoming season (as in the "Devil wears Prada" Hollywood movie—and in the notorious discussion, between Merrill Streep and Anne Hathaway—on the power of fashion and designers). The junction will work better if it can use the minimum required number of neurons (e.g. allowing an almost 1 to 1 marketing effort, moving away from the typical bombardment of broad band marketing material and communication and without the multi layered middle-men sales structure), and seeking the best match, in real time, of confronting needs—to buy or sell and produce that cerulean pull-over (sense 3).

More importantly, the synapses bank could seek, design and lead the implementation of new "solutions" or "use cases" that could be developed on these basis: e.g. supporting its customers in optimizing the value they get from any extra dollar of spend (not just ensuring better deals as "value for money", but also by having the bank playing the buyer's advocate role, advising and helping the client in designing and fulfilling a targeted and aspirational life-style). Following this "solution seeking role", the bank could, for example, help merchants in organizing their marketing campaigns—both pre, and post sales—to achieve a better penetration of new clients, their fidelization and optimal satisfaction (we will discuss later how banks could help merchants in setting up and managing MFO and CLO—merchant funded offers/card linked offers—loyalty systems based on points earned and cash rebates driven by their purchases).

The banks could then end up supporting the manufacturers in planning and producing the goods demanded by its target customers and with the acceptable level of associated quality/price tag and creating a fully integrated supply chain. In both examples, the bank would end up not just doing better its old intermediation work (by creating and sustaining new ways of interconnections among multiple counterparts), but would also create new businesses (the MFO/CLO) and better ways to allocate and use the scarce resources in the economy, to the overall benefit of the system.

2.6 Five Senses: Five

It is easy to understand how far from all this the traditional banking model is, and how it is still mostly focused on reaping the benefits of the "low hanging fruits" coming from the mere intermediation (of money and of other financial products) in the retail/commercial side and from the broker—dealer business model on the wholesale/investment banking side. The "synapses" banks would go much further than that, trying to act as the enlightened match maker of multiple stakeholders active in markets and societies alike; and as the skillful designer of new, value adding solutions that would create incremental value in the system (and not just redistribute the existing one), potentially defining and supporting new lifestyles and behavioral core values.

Such a powerful and almost omniscient "synapses" would not act in a vacuum and would need to be built on the credibility and faith entrusted to it by millions of customers, ready to leave the inefficient and ineffective "safe known" for the unknown risks potentially introduced by the new offerings and players. Such credibility and trust in the banking sector appears however in bad shape, after the recent, multiple sectorial scandals that have been observed, reported and sometimes magnified by media and politicians alike.

It follows that a fifth final sense, or building block, is required to complete the overall picture and sustain the potential feasibility of the synapses bank—and of any emerging FinTech winner alike. Such a bank (or emerging FinTech) will in fact need to develop working on all four preceding pillars, but on the basis of the "trust capital"—the fundamental required foundation of any sustainable innovation and development to come.

Trust has been, we have already commented, the very basis on which the superbly intangible global financial system has been born and built through time. A bank's value is based on the word's value of the bankers, and on their reliability in keeping faith to it. Trust should then be recovered and amended from past mistakes, and then further developed and capitalized for the even more immaterial potential role played by a synapses based business model (whether played by transformed banks of by FinTech). Such a business model would in fact end up not just managing the already sensible "money" of people and companies, but also other even more sensible stuff like the "digital/personal identity" of customers, the intelligence that can be derived out of their social and economic subsystems and consumer and investor behaviors. The synapses bank could end up creating more and better value for the overall system, allowing for a more transparent, competitive and socially acceptable sharing of the richness and well-being that should become available out of it. But it can ask for such a vast and holistic mandate if it is widely trusted by markets and societies alike.

Let's then stop for the moment in the discussion of our suggested theoretical framework (the "pentagon) to assess the digital transformation that will disrupt banking and the global financial system, and let's briefly consider a further potential tipping point towards the creation of "synapses" based winning business models: the "open data" movement and the implications it opens up in terms of competitive strategies.

2.7 Data, Going Open

Banking, at times, has been described as one of the easiest (and most boring) job in the world—assuming you have the full control and ownership of the data that can allow you to perform an all too easy intermediation game. Banks know, or should knew, most of the financial health, issues, worries and ambitions of their customers, and can act accordingly, linking the counterparties that are long on funds but short on ideas with the ones that are long on dreams and energy, but short on cash, and for a spread or a fee (or both).

The control and ownership of customers data has allowed banks to build through their history a significant negotiating power and to build a quasi-segmented oligopoly structure of their market, fending off the competitive attacks of new players and capitalizing on the information they already got to cross and up-sell their customers, or influence their consumption and investment patterns across other value chains.

Their control of customer data has also allowed them to increase the stickiness of their customers, because of the mess and the time lost that you need to go through once you decide to change bank, and to reduce the overall transparency of their pricing: money, as a commodity, should be fairly ease to compare, but the complexity of the products and services offered, along with the limited availability of customers data on their usage of financial services, has helped in preserving the fogginess around the bank's competitive proposition. A major regulatory breakthrough, an almost quasi-philosophical movement, is now potentially mining the basis of this fundamental competitive advantage[1] providing more badly needed transparency to this industry.

According to this breakthrough, regulators are demanding that banks provide customers with detailed transaction data in the belief that better-informed consumers will make better decisions and drive greater competition. To facilitate the availability of such detailed data and information, the European Union's new Payment Services Directive 2 (PSD2) will soon require banks to share transaction-level data with third parties. The PSD2 and the standardization of banking API (Application Programming Interfaces) that helps to make use of open data will help in boosting customers' engagement by improving access and accelerating the development of third party apps that can analyze data and recommend best products and services.

In advance to the EU, regulators in the United Kingdom have started applying considerable scrutiny to the market for personal accounts—reflecting concerns that banking may lack competition and real break-through innovation, thus delivering, as a result, poor value to customers. By order of the Competition and Market Authority (CMA), these API may soon become the market standard, even in advance of the PSD2 implementation, and help anticipating some of the discontinuities expected across international markets.

Ideally, on the positive side, a combination of app developers, price comparison web sites and banks' new use cases (where banks can also try to play the customer's advocate role, or pre-empt the independent price comparison web sites by launching their own comparison methodology, to be "selectively" communicated to current and target clients) can afford banks to take their selective bets on this new breakthrough. Eventually, the open data disruption will allow consumers to use historical account data files to compare accounts and the cost of any other financial products and services—and answer few fundamental questions about the competitiveness of what they get from the incumbent traditional banks. Financial technological innovation around tailored accounts could then help banks in boosting engagement by providing insightful analysis that promotes improved outcomes, potentially driving further cross and up selling and more tailored solutions. But FinTech challengers could as well prove that their value proposition is simply much better, for the peace of mind of old, dying incumbents. In fact, on the negative side, this "open data" regulatory change and the associated "open data" apps and digital players that should be mushrooming on the world wide web, is promising to be disruptive for the financial services industry—with money becoming more of the fully comparable commodity it really is and banks loosing most of their negotiating power born out of the control and ownership of data, and of the related limited transparency and comparability available in the sector.

---

[1] Current account comparison, David Branch, AlixPartners, July 2016.

A major challenge still lies ahead for a successful deployment of the open data initiative, as such account data have to be rich enough to enable a valid comparison —whether received in a downloadable file or transmitted via API. And they must allow for an easy comparison—by no means assured, when data inputs are affected by a range of choices that must be made to reconstruct accounts under different terms and conditions. Unless the banking industry can agree on common standards in relation to those choices, customers will likely keep getting significantly different answers from different sources, thereby undermining their confidence in price comparison web sites and causing confusion as opposed to creating clarity and transparency.

Even if via a process of trials and errors, the industry will ultimately get it, driving a further acceleration towards the unbundling of the incumbent banks: they will be deconstructed in terms of what they are precisely offering and at what price, and they will be competitively challenged along their integrated value chains, at any single point where a better offering by a digital challenger could be more likely to hit and win customers. The open data will then facilitate the development of the "synapses" model—whether played by traditional banks digitally transformed or by new FinTech players—as this model actually starts from the full availability and optimal management of data and information, to derive intelligence, new ways of interconnecting customers and solutions and use cases that could be designed and implemented to deliver better value to the end customers—something that should be very high in the agenda of any players in the financial space. But even traditional banks could address these "value delivered to clients" concept and profit from it.

In fact, the "value delivered" to clients is clearly a complementary opposite (the ying of the yang) of the "customer's value created for the bank" that needs to be measured and communicated to re-address their competitive relationships with clients: banks are not just there to financially gain from customers but also to deliver to them relevant and measurable financial value. In the aftermath of the global financial crisis and of the following banks' bashing, this message has a number of positive communication and marketing fall outs. On one side, it would send a message to customers that there is value in banking for them after all, and that their bank is at the forefront of it: open, transparent and confident of its own proposition to build long term trust with its customers.

On the other side, it would also send a message to consumer associations and to the many local banking regulators/anti-trust authorities that the bank can become best practice in transparency and client management—setting a fair trade with customers. It would also send a message to incumbent and new digital/shadow players, that the bank is at the forefront of this and is proactively addressing the price comparison engines now available on the web, and setting a standard methodology, at its preferred terms.

Finally, the communication of the "value delivered"—by traditional banks to end customers—could also open up a powerful new way of engaging with their client base—therefore potentially leading to new ways of maximizing the traditional "customer value's created for a bank"—reconciling the apparently unsolvable trade-off found in a client-bank relationship ("I gain, you lose"). In a more radical application, the bank could be even willing to provide a fully comprehensive and transparent price comparison application, and to help then its customer in sourcing the best products and services as if he/she were acting in an open architecture setting, as it already happens in most of the asset management industry.

Even this "client's advocate" role, that helps him/her in navigating in an open architecture world looks quite consistent with the "synapses" bank approach, where the bank drives the meiosis and the synapses, interconnecting different parts of the system, but without actually assuming any direct, captive driven, principal position —neither as the manufacturer of the products and services being sold, nor as the underwriter and holder of the risk being underwritten.

As data owned by banks open up, by virtue of by rule of Law, a number of third party applications will naturally surge—with their imagination and ingenuity limited only by the devices that can host apps and by the data available to feed their creations, ready to analyze almost everything: from the amounts, types, locations, and times of client's spending; to the cost of banking products (e.g., current accounts, mutual funds, payments etc.) across the wider market; to the user-entered data regarding budget keeping and spending limits.

Banks customers will then have an unconstrained view of their real-time financial positions across their various bank accounts, credit cards, and mortgages or consumer finance products. And they will be able to use innovative functionality to understand, visualize, and therefore adjust their spending or saving patterns in ways never previously available: from the increased availability of price comparison, where the transparency of different prices and condition could change the traditional inertia of customers in switching across accounts and products; to the reduction of overdrafts, where most of these are generated by poor information and planning across the multiple current accounts and saving pots used by clients; to the increased usage of robo-advice, able to suggest real time, at the tap of an app, how to best manage your our own assets and liabilities—the universe of potential applications looks infinite, with wide reaching consequences.

Some of the work banks have so far done has involved their reconstruction of account histories under different terms and conditions to also see, for example, what would have happened to the customers' accounts had they been held by another bank (or by a new FinTech). Some are also venturing in building their price comparison models, but for their internal use, or for their "selective" commercial use (calling on the clients only when their pricing offer is better than the ones of the competitors). But the potential applications of this "open data" discontinuity are really going to extend much beyond that on a potentially transformative setting.

In fact, as data will get open, and fully comparable, so the financial services industry will need to be.

In Transformation We Trust

Abstract

Incumbent banks are facing a crucial challenge as they need to embrace digitalization and aim for a significant transformation of their business and operating models, overcoming all kind of constraints driven, for example, from creeping legacy IT systems, silo-ed business divisions and central support functions and the cultural resistance well engrained in an industry that has been heavily regulated for decades and, maybe, too protected by the attacks of non-traditional competitors. One key element of this challenge is represented by trust and credibility—and by how banks will be able to successfully recover them in full. As trust is becoming and even more important factor in an increasingly digitized global financial system, cyber security and cyber trust are becoming one of the most serious risks banks will need to face and overcome.

Keywords

Digital · Banking transformation · Cyber security · Trust · Reputational risk

3.1 The Risk of the Frog

Risk has always been a peculiar factor to manage, particularly so in the financial service sector. By no mean "scarce", it has been seen for years as something to just avoid "tout court", then as something to measure and minimize, then as something to plan and control—for regulatory purposes and to reassure shareholders, debtholders and policymakers alike (as banks tend to have a systemic effect when they go down, and big banks tend to be saved, at tax payers expense, because of the potential negative externalities they would bring to the overall economy). In any case, it has had a consistently negative connotation, and following a taxonomy definition that has been extended through the years, starting (for the banking sector) from the credit and interest rate risks, to the (other) market risks, to the more recent operational and conduct risks.

In truth, risk is one of the key—if not the most critical—"production factor" of almost any business—even more so in banking and in the financial services industry. In fact, there is no return without some corresponding risk and best strategic and managerial decision making is mostly about setting this trade off right, maximizing the corresponding value creation opportunities and the risk adjusted performances of any company.

For banks, and for companies alike, the real performance and value creation should be assessed on the basis of the "economic capital" absorbed by the risks they are underwriting—taking into consideration their risk driven cost of equity capital. In this setting, banks and other financial intermediaries have then a more specific role, as a main part of their core business, as we said, is all about offering risk management products and services for other counterparts, retail and corporate alike: via financial derivatives and guarantees, insurance policies and other alternative structured solutions offering pooling, sharing or the outright transfer of risks.

We have spoken at length, in the beginning of this book, of the many "traditional risks" that have brought the traditional banking model to its knees: from the risks driven by its excessive leverage and potential illiquidity, to the credit risks linked to the "core" lending business, to the market risks associated to proprietary trading (equity, foreign exchange, interest rate, commodity), to the structural interest rate risk driven by the different durations of the assets and liabilities intermediated, to the earnings at risk driven by commission fee based business and to the real estate overarching risk.

In more recent years, operational risks, associated to the internal failure of people, processes, IT plus other negative external events has also risen in importance, as multiple failures (also associated to the "conduct risk" linked to the behavior of the employees of the bank and on how they could miss-sell products, act on the basis of conflict of interests etc.) have caused significant direct and indirect losses—with multi-billion fines coming from regulators and serious damage to reputation.

All these risks are now progressively well understood, at least from a methodological and theoretical perspective, and certainly the focus of a continuously strengthened and sometimes unbearably cumbersome regulation—you can find a detailed representation of the so called "traditional risks" on most of the Global SIFI financial statements, with ever increasing investment budgets and renewed management attention. As most of these risks are now addressed, a new set of risks are emerging and often growing whilst still little recognized, poorly understood and usually not fully addressed (if not, sometimes, at all) in the scope of the CRO (Chief Risk Officer) mandate.

These "new risks" are potentially introducing new instability into the system, and impacting on the traditional risks as well. Most of them, we could state, are driven today by the rapid and disruptive innovation happening across sectors— something that has been dubbed the "fourth industrial revolution" and going even wider and deeper than the current digitalization transformation addressed in our discussion. It is, therefore, for the incumbent banks, a risk of being leapfrogged on the innovation frontier, and made irrelevant and redundant by the new players—the FinTech and the likes, better able to jump on new opportunities.

Let's take for example the 3D printing revolution: as it is going to impact all kind of manufacturing sectors, redesigning entire value chains and changing the competitive proposition of companies, clusters and even Countries, it will impact on their respective credit worthiness, and on the way banks are now allocating capital at risk, across all kind of credit risk factors—with most of the credit rating models in need to be revised if not redesigned accordingly. They entail therefore radical changes, and the risk that somebody, starting from scratch, will be better able to design—for example—better credit rating tools and allocation policies for addressing these discontinuities.

Or take the example of robotization and artificial intelligence, with its potentially profound social implications in terms of the millions of jobs potentially lost and of the likely creation of further disparity in the income distribution across people. Or just consider the different impact coming from advances in quantum computing on the productivity of companies, sectors and Countries alike—it all should lead to different client segmentation approaches and to the analysis of new credit risks factor that today are not even considered in the overall taxonomy of the CRO mandate. Again, new player could be better placed in designing and implementing new underwriting approaches and tools to address these opportunities.

The innovation happening across sectors would then not be just about credit risk, as the implications coming from the development in nanotechnology, biotechnology or in genetic engineering will change dramatically how long we live, what we eat, how we dress and travel and with which kind of lifestyle. Our world of physical and intangible capabilities could just be extended and augmented to unprecedented levels, not to mention other ethical implications worth to consider—all these should also lead to all kind of further impacts and changes on the more traditional risks: from health to mortality and other "pure" risks.

These radical innovations and the economic and social scenarios they are opening up are by no way science fiction: most of them are already happening and changing in sometimes brutal ways the competitive structure of entire sectors and even the long time cemented comparative advantages of Nations. For such risks there is no VaR (Value at Risk) reporting in the financial statement of banks, nor are the regulator well equipped enough to understand in full what could happen to the "traditional" risk factors should some of these scenarios come to be realized in full. It all changes and no CRO looks now set to spot in advance the next train (or trains) coming at the end of the tunnel.

Whilst this discussion is worth of a much more deep analysis, the main point is that there is now an emerging, hyper critical, potential terminal risk that the financial players and banks specifically are now facing, e.g. the risk of being digitally leap frogged by new digital "FinTech" challengers, just stepping ahead of them in one go, putting at risk the stability of the entire global financial system—

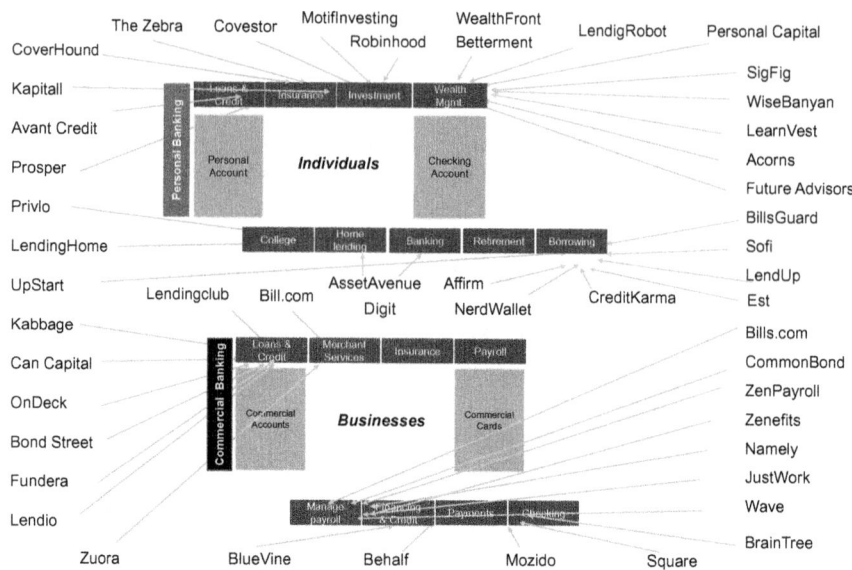

Fig. 3.1 Banking value chain is breaking up following attack by FinTech start-ups

but also introducing new opportunities for the value creation of the system (see Fig. 3.1—Banking value chain is breaking up).

3.2 Death by a Hundred Technologies

Digital and more broadly technological innovation for banks is becoming not only an opportunity to get to incremental returns—driven mostly by better productivity and by a much more enlarged convenience offered to clients—but also a risk to become obsolete and irrelevant, with then a rapidly deteriorating revenues capacity. The margin compression and loss of market shares and of entire pots of revenues and of millions of clients is in itself, in our view, stands today as a much larger risk than the parallel impacts on the traditional risks and something that no CRO or regulator is now ready to identify, assess, evaluate and let alone to predict. It is the job of the board of directors and of the CEO of main financial players to address this digital/technological innovation risk, and to make sure that the digital capital and related goodwill of their companies can be developed competitively and in the most effective way—to make sure banks remain relevant.

The taxonomy of the technological innovations taking shape is extending by the day. New, agile technology allows software development where requirements and solutions evolve dynamically through the collaborative effort of self-organizing cross functional team—something FinTech players can master better than banks, and therefore getting more productive and developing software faster, better and

3.2 Death by a Hundred Technologies

cheaper. Cloud computing allows then an internet-based shared computer processing, and shared data coming from multiple sources and can be traced back from multiple devices on demand. But again, banks are not well placed to leverage this new opportunity, because of the many internal (e.g. old legacy systems) and external (e.g. regulatory) constraints.

And similar examples could be made in relation to robo-advice, or virtual and augmented reality, advanced robotics, quantum computing, cognitive computing, block chains, machine learning, artificial intelligence and many others discontinuities now emerging and taking shapes: new start up players, born as digital, are simply more likely and better equipped to successfully embark on these new technological innovation, with traditional incumbents trying to catch up, but almost inevitably sand-bagged by a number of constraints.

On one side, outdated IT systems can be the biggest Achilles' heel for established banks seeking to compete against digital start-up companies. Their IT infrastructure is in fact holding them back, seriously limiting their ability to exploit the new digital tools and the multi-faced technological innovation already happening across sectors, and taking shapes in markets and societies alike. Legacy systems coming as a patchwork from multiple past M&A are also limiting the opportunity of using the big data already owned by the bank for practical use cases, as their systems will often not be able to have a single view of the same customer, or to share the relevant information across legal entities and businesses and all kind of other organizational silos to derive the intelligence that could vice versa be easily attainable—if the data were on the same data base.

On the other side, the patchy legacy systems and the constraints coming from the bank's infrastructure are often just used as an excuse not to do what real innovation would require, e.g. changing radically the operating and business models, the organization and the processes to fully take advantage of the value they can potentially unlock. The natural resistance to change is larger for older organizations, and the more structure is an organization the more difficult is to change it. Even the cultural approach of banks is far from ideal, as it nurtures preservation over change, conservation versus evolution and the avoidance of risks at all costs instead of the undertaking of measured risks that entails a potentially significant entrepreneurial pay off. Whilst some entrepreneurs are still working for banks, its best ones tend to fly away; and a bank full of bureaucrats and technocrats is not the ideal "incubator" of new ideas and "accelerators" of change plans.

As with many other cases related to the risk of being leapfrogged, the best risk management strategy rests however with a proactive approach to change, to drive the transformation and evolution of the company. There is hope after all, until the bank can retain and nurture talents and act as a catalyst of change, either by virtue or necessity, of the overall service offerings it is bringing to market and potentially to the benefit of the overall global financial system. This digital transformation—the embracing of all kind of new technological innovations that can be relevant for doing a better business—will however need to become the imperative of the financial services companies that want to preserve their fair chance of survival. This digital transformation will then benefit the global financial system as well, and will potentially ensure its relative stability—something that is required to support the growth rate in the economy and the optimal allocation of scarce resources at global level. The trust and commitment to this transformation is then the first step to consider: something that is a "need to have" for the incumbent players to survive into a new geological era.

As of today, the list of unsuccessful attempts at this would be so long to become almost pointless. Change management has never been—we said—the core competency of banks and of other financial services companies that were protected overtime by regulations. There are however some initial success stories, and we will now review how a couple of leading retail/commercial and wholesale/investment global banks have started to react to the digital challenge, reviewing radically their business and operating models and industrial and commercial strategies as a consequence of their "thinking digital, playing digital and feeling digital".

3.3 BBVA: Rebooting Digital

BBVA, a leading multinational Spanish banking group, with presence that extends to Latin America and the US, born out of a merger of Banco Bilbao Vizcaya and Argentaria in 1999, and emerging almost untarnished from the global financial crisis and with a decent return on equity, asset quality and market capitalization, could be defined as the ideal prototype of a "boringly safe and dull, mostly retail, international banking group", well versed in deposit taking and in mortgage making, with some corporate banking extension to fill the gap. Far from sitting complacently on these almost inertial competitive advantages, BBVA has been almost paranoid on its requirements to keep changing and embracing as much as technological innovation as possible.

Run for the last few decades by a Chairman, Francisco Gonzales, that has been once an IT-coding programmer and by a relatively young CEO, Carlos Torres, that was formerly its head of digital, the bank has now crystallized a vision of a radical transformation journey to became a global digital bank—leader at global level, and ideally one of the 4–5 few that will be allowed to be a truly global leader—regardless of the home Country geographical starting point—by the economics of this frontier-less business. More precisely, in the words of Gonzales, "BBVA will be a software company in the future". And "our goal is to turn BBVA into a totally digital company, including all our products and services, and with our more than 100,000 employees working digitally[1]". Towards that end, the Chairman has been driving a digital transformation journey for almost a decade and through the global crisis, with a skillful combination of vision, governance, development of internal know how and talent pools (from which it emerged the running CEO) and some targeted acquisition as well.

---

[1]BBVA's investor presentation, October 2015 VA's investor presentation, October 2015.

3.3 BBVA: Rebooting Digital

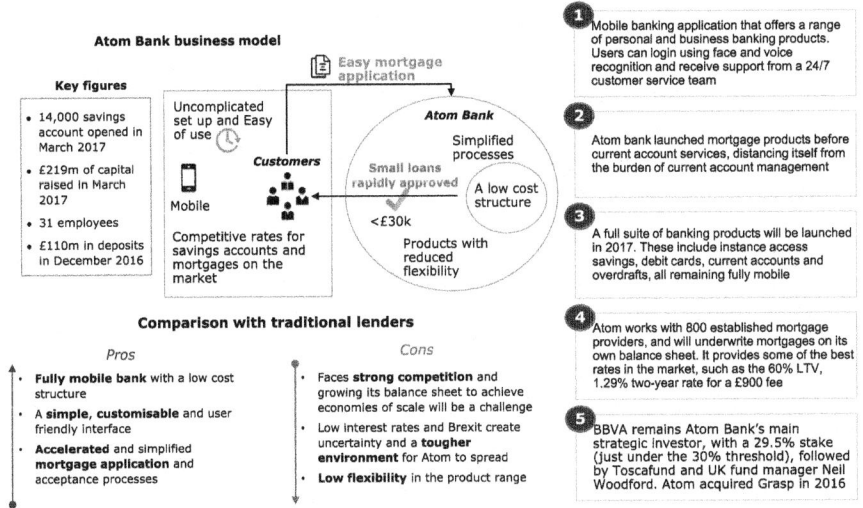

Fig. 3.2 Atom bank: a fully mobile bank with AI into its mortgages

At the end of 2015, BBVA could already claim 30% of his customer base[2] of 51 million as digital customers—online and mobile, seen as much more engaging with the bank—performing 11 times more transactions annually than traditional, non-digital customers. The bank has then much more ambitious targets to come.

The vision of "building the best digital bank of the 21st century", began with a taunting task, building out and re-platforming its core technology for digital banking—e.g. moving from a spaghetti like wrangle of past and mostly outdated legacy systems to a newly built, fully integrated and digital one. That has allowed a safe scaling of the customers transactions and the design and development of a number of innovative use cases aimed at transforming the way the bank does business with its mostly retail and small business/SME clients. The digital banking area, previously lead by Carlos Torres, has therefore been tasked with the responsibility of developing existing distribution channels, adapting internal processes and designing a new range of digital products and services, to deliver the best possible end customer experience.

Apart from this internal effort, BBVA has also reached out and has been increasingly engaged with the digital start up community, ending up acquiring FinTech companies such as Simple and Madiva, and more recently a significant stake in Atom Bank as well—the first mobile-only UK bank, to accelerate the adoption and innovation of its digital services, as shown in the Figs. 3.2 and 3.3—focusing on AI and unstructured data management. In February 2016, the bank has then spin off its portfolio of FinTech ventures and has created a FinTech focused venture capital firm called Propel Venture Partners. The early lessons from the

---
[2]Capgemini, BBVA, "rebooting banking for a digital technology", 2016.

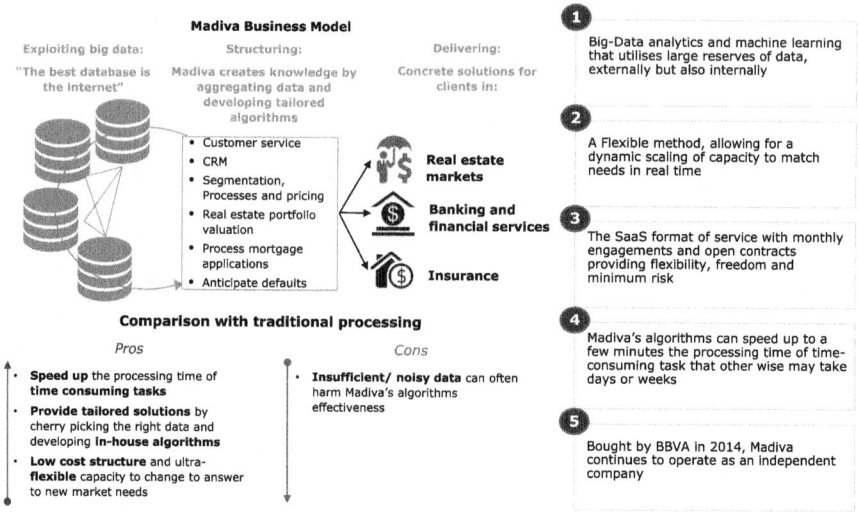

Fig. 3.3 Madiva leverages on big data analytics to extrapolate meaningful information from unstructured data

BBVA inward and outward looking digital transformation experience so far could be five-fold.

3.4 Conquistadores, Bit by Bit

As a first, the bank's digital transformation should start from the basics, e.g. with a new IT system that re-platforms most of the past legacy ones, including both front and back office system wrangles, progressively de-commissioning most of its obsolete software. This can allow in turn the developments of new, digital and use-case driven applications in an agile, flexible, inexpensive and quick way. It's really hard to build a new house if its foundations are creaky, and any credible strategy of disruptions needs to be designed and crafted in doable, pragmatic way, ideally starting anew on a clean, solid ground that is receptive to fast digital innovation.

More specifically, the stated aim of BBVA has been of developing a real-time, client-centric, modular and scalable platform, that would support future clients' transaction volumes and data, fostering open data innovation and ensuring fortress-like cybersecurity walls. This task, for a traditional bank, is well described by the words of Gonzales when he notes that "to build the banking IT platform from scratch is like changing the pieces of an engine of a lorry as it zooms down the highway"—and it needs to keep working along the way.

Secondly, the digital area defined internally should not be considered as a stand-alone division, or business unit, but reach out to all kind of front-to-back business applications of the bank, to drive a change that considers the overall capabilities portfolio of the bank, and not just part of it. "Seamless integration" could be a too much of a statement in real life, but still some kind of consistency in the way clients interact via different channels (the omni-channel strategy, to use a consulting buzzword) should be ensured and delivered.

More importantly, the area should not be led by some brilliant IT geek with limited understanding of banking and perceived as an exogenous virus to the ecosystem, but by a highly talented individual that could actually make it to the top, as was the case of Carlos Torres, then promoted to Group CEO. BBVA has in fact focused a lot of its efforts in building an effective governance model for digital transformation (moving from the digital banking division to the digital banking area —to encompass marketing, omni-channel distribution, technology innovation, strategy and talent management among others)—driving the change from analog to digital, at all levels of the businesses (all client segments, products, geographical areas and channels are now covered).

Thirdly, whatever the realm and level of sophistication of digital innovation, it must start from a robust and valuable end customer use case, e.g. it must have a client ready to pay for it, as it perceives a solution to some of his/her complex or nonetheless relevant and urgent needs. A seamless banking experience is useless if it is built around the solution of a badly defined or irrelevant client need. Many digital start-ups have not, in fact, become "unicorn" (worth more than 100 Bln USD) because of their prowess in digital innovation and brutal technological dominance, but just because they were able to identify some ignored, pent up demand, addressing a simple need or opportunity (e.g. to share thoughts with a forum of friends and followers—Twitter, or to make some money out of existing, underutilized assets and some free time—Uber, or AirBnB).

AI (artificial intelligence systems) and deep/self-learning techniques will also come to the fore, to help in supporting and drive this hyper-customer-centricity of one, e.g. potentially being able to spot, via the big data and building intelligence via applied analytics, a relevant need or opportunity—sometimes ignored by the same customer—and to offer a solution that is both scalable (and therefore efficient) and effective. Who would not fancy a banking assistant ready to help in managing basic, repetitive and time-consuming financial transactions, or to advice on our savings management, or insurance coverage—even if we are not worth a "private client" definition? BBVA virtual, intelligent banking assistant Lola works like Apple's Siri (with a nicer name) and simplifies the clients' digital interactions, potentially offering in the future valuable advice as well.

Fourthly, no matter how hard you try, the banking environment, dominated by regulations and compliance, heavy syndication on decision making, organization made by a matrix of vertical and horizontal silos, and the stratification of values, behaviors and praxis that usually lead to the emerge of power brokers keen "to change everything so as not to change anything at all"... is not exactly the best one to envision and deliver innovation. That's way the bank should consider alliances and acquisitions with FinTech ventures that can ensure some truly "out of the box" thinking and some first stage innovation phases that take weeks, instead of the almost unavoidable banking years.

And the bank can offer them the capital and the scale (e.g. immediate access to integrated legacy systems and to millions of clients, under the umbrella of a well-known brand) that they will need at later stages. To this end, BBVA has set up a network of innovation centers in key hubs around the world, including New York, but also Madrid, Bogota and Mexico City—they work closely with FinTech and all kind of digital disrupters to go beyond its own internal innovation efforts, to anticipate IT developments and trends as—in the words of Gonzales, "We see disruption as an immense opportunity that can find new ways to generate growth by offering transparent, ultra-convenient and data rich solutions for customers".

Finally, as a fifth element comes the recognition that an optimal, risk-return investment process in new ventures can only happen if you skip the internally regulated, heavily syndicated processes, the army of bureaucrats that never made a penny in real business and you assign—in a free-market-like way—responsibilities and roles/levers and promote a proper incentive system for venture capital investment talents that could end up working for the bank's sponsored, independently managed fund as they could do in a similar thing in Silicon Valley. If you want the best talents in the markets you have to be ready to offer them the best incentive package of the market—the leveraged returns you will get on the capital they are going to invest will more than compensate the extra costs you will have to face in the short run.

BBVA role as limited partner (only) in Propel Venture Fund has also helped so far the new FinTech focused investment company in focusing on few key areas that are not necessarily the business priority of the former parent company, letting it drive initiatives that could be seen as potentially competing with it. Including working on Open API related initiatives that are aiming at disintermediating existing banks, playing an aggregator and price-comparison role that could help the clients to shop around, and find the best deal out of financial products (including BBVA's ones) that are, as we argued in the beginning, the greatest commodity of all (money is money after all).

BBVA is taking upfront the open data challenge, and in a very courageous way. It recently announced[3] its intention of opening up access to customer data, with bank's customer permission, so that other companies can use the information to offer bespoke financial services—a first in promoting "open banking" by an incumbent. The bank, ahead of the regulation that comes into force in 2018, is expected to radically change the face of banking, by allowing merchants, technology companies and other groups to provide financial services, potentially through collaboration with established banks behind the scene—hence the proactive, anticipatory move by the Spanish lender. Whilst the move opens up opportunities for competitors, it also open the opportunity to gain more customers and

---

[3]Financial Times, May 24th 2017, "BBVA to share customer data with other businesses", Emma Dunkley.

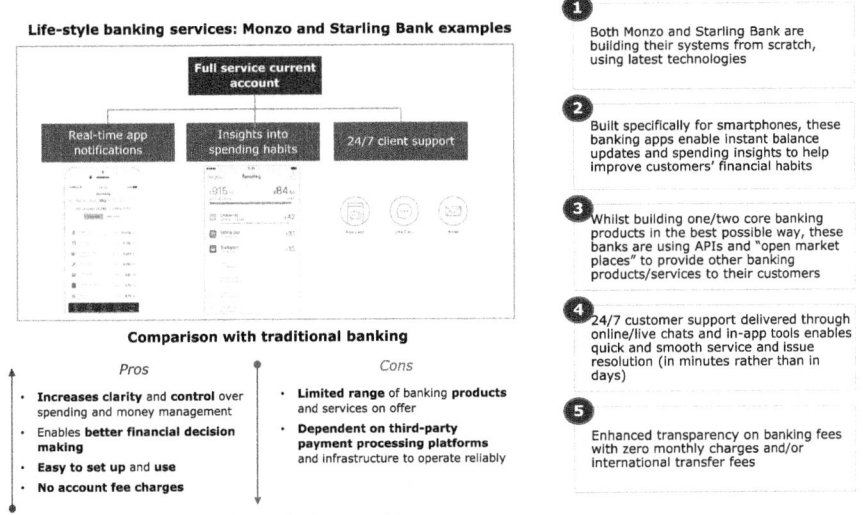

Fig. 3.4 Monzo and Starling: from products to lifestyle offerings

originating more loans—for example, a retailer could inform a customer when they are able to gain a preapproved loan from BBVA, accessible at the point of sale.

It's not, however, just about selling more stuff. Companies, on the basis of the greater data, information and intelligence available, will also become able to offer lifestyle services—for example, a number of start-up banks in the UK, such as Monzo and Starling, have already developed money management services that categorize spending based on transactions (see Fig. 3.4, on the progressive evolution of offerings, from products to lifestyle management). This "categorization" could then be used by advanced banks such as BBVA to offer deals such as discounts at a customer's favorite coffee shop, in line with their spending habits. And other services could include enabling customers to make a purchase though a merchant's site, with immediate access to preapproved consumer finance, or being able to view all their accounts in one place.

Raul Lucas, head of BBVA's initiative, has pointedly stated how BBVA's belief is that data belongs to customers, and the bank just want to make it easier for them to share their information with those companies that offer them value and are able to deliver the best services for them. Opening up the market, after the data. And now, differently from the past, in a completely global setting, even for regional banks like BBVA.

As Coca Cola was pompously aiming, few years ago, to build a dominant market share not just in the fizzy drinks segments worldwide but in all kind of drinks except tap water, BBVA is now aiming to be the leader in digital banking at global level, as geographical frontiers become almost worthless. As far-fetched this vision looks like, it is something to watch out, and maybe argue for, from a customer's advocate point of view. With BBVA well positioned on this, unless a new Twitter, or Uber or AbnB, comes along, before the Spaniards do.

3.5 Goldman Sachs: The Remaining 99

Goldman Sachs has been, in recent times, not only derided (the "great vampire squid" of the Rolling Stone magazine) and criticized, for being greedy and arrogant, and for being the very essence of the "rotating doors" approach to network and business building (with top public figures being hired by Goldman and moving easily from public to private, or from private to public, and then back to public/private again, jobs—from Paulson to Monti, to Draghi and Barroso, just to many a few),[4] but also it has being envied as the "smartest investment bank in town", and the very blue blood pin-striped essence of the once godly and mighty investment bankers.

Goldman Sachs still commands a great brand name in business and its financial performance has been pretty good, through the last troubled economic cycle, and able to be profitable even in the worst years of the past global financial crisis. However, very much like the rest of its industry, it has neither fully recovered the competitive positioning that was ensuring to its shareholders an easy double digit return on equity. Also, as any other of its traditional global competitors, it has not reached yet a new fully industrialized business model that could allow the bank to easily get to the lower but more stable and still interesting high digit return of an financial services sector increasingly pushed to become a utility one. As things gets tougher, we could expect Goldman to play an even heavier and heavier hand in its play in the investment banking sector, doubling up it un-relentless focus of the past on being number one or two in any specific product line, or in getting out fast.

It is, in fact, playing a very different (and digital) game. As it developed and grew, before the last crisis and even before the Dot Com bubble of the late nineties, its own mostly custom-based IT system, the bank has increasingly focused on IT and software as key competitive advantages, nurturing talents in these fields as it would do with top deal makers and traders. The story of Goldman being Goldman because it is a super well connected team of deal makers and traders sitting on top of a software company is a well-known one in the industry, as the bank has built ad hoc, top performing software solutions ahead of the market, refusing to offshore to low quality Countries and to out-source to just partially controlled third parties.

Goldman Sachs has however become lately more than a software company, and with the ambition to lead as the most digital of the pack, and not just on Wall Street but on Main Street as well. It is a story, as it unfolds, where the adoption of the new digital technology is paralleled by a very different competitive positioning that is moving the bank away from its traditional turf and is driving its market and client extensions.

---

[4]The Economist, October 29th 2016, "Too squid to fail" and "Rebooting".

Whether it is the business strategy that is driving the digital re-platforming of the IT systems of the bank or vice versa is a "chicken and egg" question not really worth a definitive answer. The most important assumption, underpinning both strategies, is in fact that money is digital after all, a pure theoretical concept that gets concreteness primarily through an electronic construct. It follows that banks should be, at their "qualifying" core, technology companies whose business is to make sure the overall electronic plumbing of the global financial system stands still and keeps working safely and efficiently. Whilst their "winning" core, we have already argued and we will further develop later, is to put some logic into this, e.g. making sense of the many end means of money and of the economic and social positive solutions that it can bring about.

In a world of finance increasingly dominated by digits and by unprecedented amount of electronic data and information made available, logic will help the "mosquito in getting out of the bottle"—following the Wittgenstein argument—finding the relevant intelligence and the value adding solutions that give a much more important and ultimately more legitimate and nobler sense to money and banking. From a commercial strategy point of view, it also looks like Goldman is now focusing on the remaining 99% of the mosquitos flying into the bottle and with almost no hope of getting out of it, and not just the top VIP 1% that was usually referred as being the target and the main beneficiary of the bank's offerings and related fortunes.

3.6 Digital Goldman

A new Goldman is then (again) ahead of the pack in finding this logic and making its digital transformation a mean to an end qualified by many relevant use cases for large corporates and financial institutions and retail/SME clients as well. A number of new initiatives seek to take technology into entirely new lines of businesses.

In a first example, the bank is now automating and streamlining its traditional wholesale businesses, identifying 146 steps across 45 systems that can be simplified and almost fully digitized in an initial public shares offering (IPO); but also, it is launching a new internet banking business, named Marcus, to lend to consumer clients leveraging the digital innovation already experienced by other FinTech players—to address the retail business.

Where once—not that long ago—600 people worked on a vast floor trading shares, with traders yelling and slamming phones, with 66 distinct actions amenable to mechanization, now Goldman has 2 people that trade equities and another 200 software engineers who work on its digital systems that do the job on their own. Where once—still to our very days—branch tellers were waiting for (or more lately, chasing) people to apply for a consumer loan and going through a paper heavy, bureaucracy driven, lengthy and nasty underwriting process, now native digital clients connect on line, are mapped by psychometric analysis as they flip between web pages and move the "loan to value" cursor, and get money (or a negative answer) in a matter of minutes.

It follows that the communication with clients changes as well. As the bank was once interacting with them via "wine and dine" and business meetings, or phone calls, electronic orders and e-mails, it is now managing communication via a client portal called "Marquee" that gives access to tools such as Goldman's risk analytics for trading shares or structuring hedges, even allowing to corporate clients to create their own, self-tailored strategies for executing large share buy-backs—with a service called "Athena".

Quite similarly to BBVA, it also incubating a number of FinTech start-ups. One, Symphony (described in Fig. 3.5), offers a messaging platform to rival more established players like Bloomberg—it offers seamless incorporation of data and communication that makes the terminal the most important conduit in finance (even the physicality of Wall Street has long become a mere metaphor). Another, Kensho (Fig. 3.6), offers a kind of real-time encyclopedia—screening vast amount of structured and unstructured data and information readily available on the web -to find correlations between world events and price-sensitive assets (never heard of Brexit and Trump?). Where traditional statistically based pools failed miserably, much better predictions come apparently from "black box" applied analytics mining written, qualitative information coming from social web sites. In the following Figure, a description of Goldman's new initiative on the consumer finance for mass market clients is also described (Fig. 3.7), as the global investment bank starts addressing the "remaining 99%".

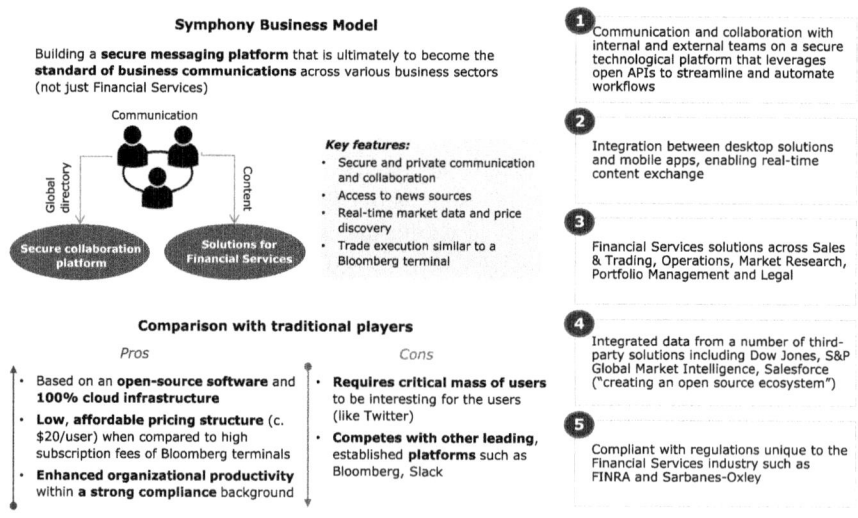

Fig. 3.5 Symphony's secure communication platform enables effective collaboration among key FS and other industry players

3.6 Digital Goldman

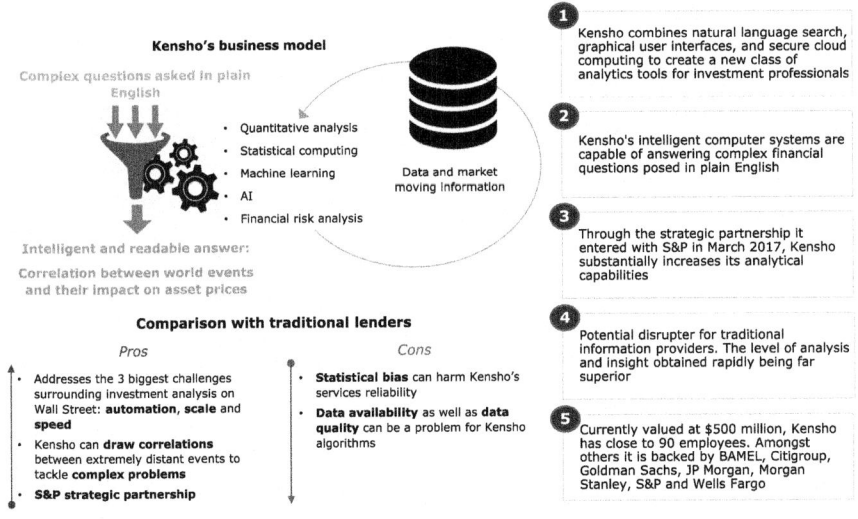

Fig. 3.6 Kensho is an information provider leveraging on big data and AI to address complex issues

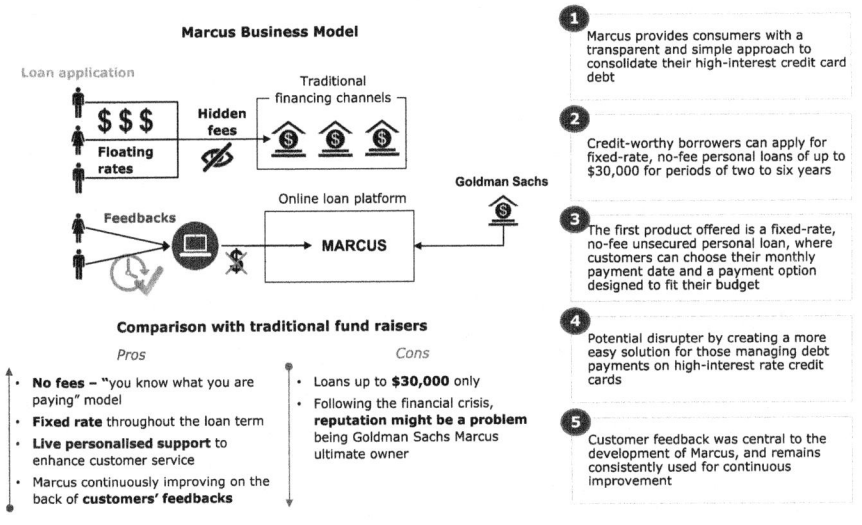

Fig. 3.7 Marcus is addressing mass market's credit needs

As Goldman, as most of the banks operating at global and local level, is now looking at reducing its risk underwriting and principal investing businesses, also spurred by regulators and credit agencies alike, it is now looking to become more and more of an intermediary. It is then looking at ways to augment these basic functions, introducing new value added services and finding new ways that realize noticeable new use cases (our "interconnectivity" functions, leading to new, meaningful solutions for the ecosystem). And it is doing so pursuing alliances with other old incumbents and new FinTech players as well, on a range of topics: from P2P lending to crowdfunding, from block-chain technology and even thinking of patenting a new digital crypto currency—doing all these for more people (the remainder 99%) and with a lower take of capital at risk.

A final challenge lays ahead for Goldman, as it tries to move away from the traditional cultural model of investment banking (with banks being perceived as parasitic, greedy and reactionary, and FinTech as much more cool, healthy and innovative places). The bank (or software company?) will in fact have to change the core values and the "prototype" person (or "Goldmanite") it is looking for—it has now a good 25% of its employees with a background in technology, from a 5% of just a few years ago (still the reference number for many other banks)—not even including the IT people working in outside ventures like Symphony and Kensho.

Will the godly and mighty, pin striped investment bankers—the deal rainmakers and the fat finger traders—also be destined to extinction, supplanted by an emerging crowd of geeks, rocket scientist in both finance and technology? With the proverbial, old time hero, Gordon Gekko becoming part of the 99% forgotten ones? The challenge of changing its people, whilst working with best people all the time, looks daunting.

Cyber Capital at Risk

Abstract

In a world of finance that is progressively de-materializing (as everything gets digitized, not just money, but everything from the branch network, to the back-office processes and paper work, to the people supporting sales and advice) the fifth element of trust and credibility gest even more critical, albeit in a different a different shape. As cyber risk becomes dominant in the digital-based global financial system, so it becomes digital trust and its nemesis cyber capital at risk. On this basis, and with a very strategic perspective, banks and other intermediaries will be called to allocated scarce digital trust and cyber capital at risk across products and segments, innovation opportunities and applications, and to invest in cyber-security as to maximize the return they get on their cyber-capital at risk—given its impact on business and clients.

Keywords

Cyber-security · Capital at risk · Cyber-attacks · Cyber trust · Business impacts

4.1 Credibility to Gain, Trust to Lose

Just consider a simple paper based note of "cash money" (as opposed to the dematerialized money being created by Central Banks as a digital string of "0–1" digits). A 20 Euro bill, for example, with its geographical map of Europe (including UK and other Countries not joining the single currency), a bridge in the background, six stars and the signature of Mario Draghi, the Governor of the ECB (European Central Bank).

Formal and sophisticated as it may appear (it has to be accepted as a mean of exchange by the rule of Law, and the paper on which it's printed has a number of features that makes the printing of fake—e.g. unofficial—notes very difficult, albeit never impossible), the 20 Euro bill note has (along with any other kind of coins and notes) a remarkable characteristic, as it stands as the only way to conduct business, consume goods or services or invest in all kind of assets without the (further) involvement of the global financial system—of their financial intermediaries, regulated capital markets, payments systems and Central Banks. All the remaining transactions are in fact inevitably intermediated by these, as money used for business, consumption, investment etc. gets exchanged and funneled through the highly structured plumbing of the financial system.

Paper notes (or metallic coins) are, in a way, the only way we can do without banks and the likes (leaving aside the use of bartering or the of alternative repositories of wealth, such as gold, diamonds, Rolex watches or precious wines to set an independent reference for the value being exchanged). And even for paper notes or metallic coins, their current use and broad acceptance works well until it is built on credibility—as the enforcement of the rule of Law is never applied, save in some critical cases where the credibility of specific currencies has been completely eroded by hyperinflation.

This "credibility" of physical (as opposed to digital) money is then built on the fulfillment of many promises. One of this is the promise of not being misused by the Tyrant of the day, that could print at his/her own will to buy all kind of stuff, or to finance the Public Debt that the running Government could wish to issue, to reduce to zero the taxation and spur all kind of social investments, in the aftermath of the election cycle, just to be re-elected (as this exercise would not be a "free lunch", the ensuing inflation would then significantly eat away part of the purchasing power of citizens).

Another obvious promise is coming from the enforcement required in order to not allow the immoderate growth of faked notes in the economy (a number of fake money is always at play, but usually on a minimal scale). And another one is related to certainty that they are accepted by other international counterparts, with a relatively stable currency exchange ratio, as devaluation policies will not be used by the current Government to "beg thy neighbor" and export unemployment (making the domestic citizens much more internationally poor as their purchasing power on transactions denominated in other currencies is decreasing).

And finally, a further promise could relate to the assurance that the purchasing power of the notes holders is not taxed—not just by hyperinflation or currency devaluation, but also by negative interest rates as charged by banks, should we decide not to park our paper money under the proverbial mattress. As it stands, it takes a lot of energy to fulfil these and many other similar promises, and quite a long time to build a consistent track record of delivering them, thus building credibility into the system and on the part of its main players and components.

It just then takes a moment to loose trust. This loss of trust has actually become one of the main issues of the global financial system after the great crisis of 2008, and the subsequent reverberations in the public and private sectors: banks, and most other financial intermediaries have now an issue of trust that needs to be rebuilt, because of their misconduct and the obvious fragility (the "unbearable lightness") that, even if not new, was put in the limelight after the debacle of Lehman Brothers.

More importantly, the loss of trust is now underpinning the overall monetary system, with Central Banks now pursuing all kind of non-traditional policies (including QE—the printing of huge quantity of base money, or Quantitative Easing) to spur the economy; currency devaluations—to foster domestic competitiveness in the short run and allow an easier repayment of the public debt owned by foreigners; and negative interest rates—an almost unprecedented measure now being tested and used to fight a deflation that could lead to the further stop of consumption and investment.

Not only that. The loss of trust comes in new digital ways—because of the radical technological innovation taking shape, as the very "basic" component of the global financial system is now at risk of being "substituted" in the best case, or disintermediated, in the worst one. Notes are just a very small part of the problem in a system were everything gets digital and even traditional money (either physical or digital) run the risk of being leapfrogged by some new crypto currency. What about then the trust of a paper money (and of its digital, immaterial version, that has however, in any case and by rule of Law, the right of being converted into paper and coins) that is considered for substitutions by its very creators and guardians the Central Banks?

4.2 War on Cash

Just consider a simple paper based note of "cash money" (as opposed to the dematerialized money being Riksbank, the Central Bank of Sweden, is already working on that, on a project to create a digital only eKrona, potentially aiming at the complete elimination of any cash left in the economy). Still unclear whether it would be designed as a rechargeable card, an app or in another way, it poses questions regarding its impact on the monetary policy and financial stability of that Country and abroad. And what about BitCoins and the other crypto currencies now potentially competing to set different market references for trading and exchange?

The technology needed for the creation of digital currencies is now up for grabs to many people and constituencies, and a lot of attention has been focused on Blockchain, a complex set of algorithms that are "minted" by a very high number of servers working according to a decentralized and almost anarchic structure, in order to create the so-called cryptocurrencies, the BitCoin being the most obvious example (Fig. 4.1).

Blockchain technology allows digital currencies to be created and traded and verified over a network of computers without any "central ledger" (i.e. as opposed to the "distributed ledgers" way of working) acting as the final "certifier" of the trade. If no central certifier of last resort is needed, then even the absolute necessity of the global financial system and of its main players and components, central banks

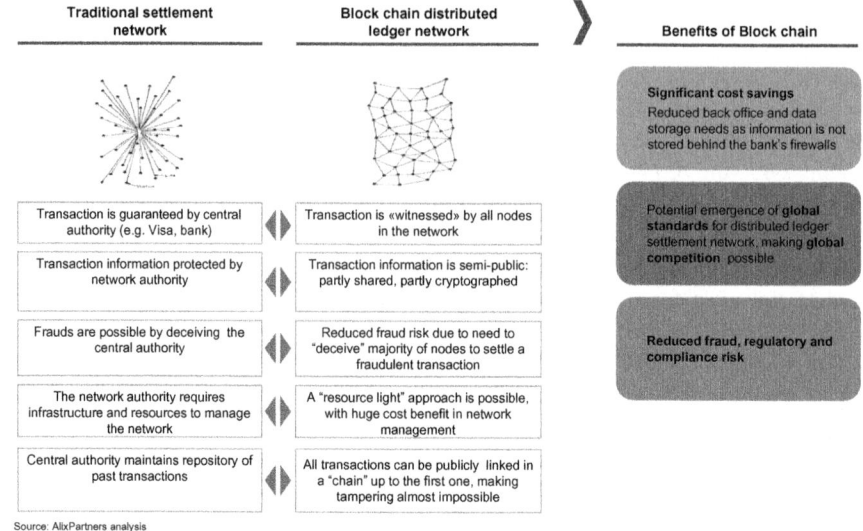

Fig. 4.1 War on cash: disruptive technology can radically change banking

included, can be argued and contrasted. Distributed ledgers are then potentially opening up the markets to an even more worrying scenario, where paper money is not just substituted by its demiurge the Central Bank, but disintermediated, along with the very same Riksbank, ECB and FED of this world, by third party players that... could actually not even exist (how would you define the counterpart—still unknown—behind the creation of BitCoins? Who would you reference as its ruler? How would you classify its ethereal governance system?).

Blockchain, often described as "distributed ledger"—a secure protocol where a network of computers collectively verify a transaction before it can be recorded and approved, it is now creating trust by enabling people that do not know each other to collaborate without having to go through an independent central super-authority e.g. a custodian bank, a central bank, a payments provider or whoever is in charge of any kind of institutional, public or private, "central ledger".

And this shared, programmable, cryptographically secure and trusted distributed ledger that no one controls and is still transparent to everybody, could extend its applications way beyond the financial system—from birth, marriage and death certificates, educational degrees, insurance claims and medical records, land titles and even to on-line real time voting systems.

Blockchain offers therefore the opportunity not just to rebuild trust, in a different way, in the financial system, but to also extend it into other sectors, and supporting the development of the shared economy (or "on-demand" economy), where goods and services are consumed in novel ways—again by leveraging platforms that help to match supply and demand of diverse and unknown counterparts, gluing everything together with a new, different form of digital trust. A digital trust, certified by social web sites and building the premises of a shared economy, that allows a better exploitation of under-utilized assets and poses eventually more radical questions on what it is really worth to own directly and what is less or not worth at all, in a "synaptic" world.

As Uber is the largest taxi company, owning no taxis at all, and Facebook the most popular media owner, without creating any content, and Alibaba the most valuable retailer, with no inventory at all, and AirBnB the world largest accommodation provider, with no real estate… it is not impossible to imagine, in a not too distant future the largest financial institution by market value as not owning any financial balance sheet at all—leveraging a model where the synapses it manages are more and more frictionless, real time, at almost zero marginal costs and value adding in the customers' use cases it can offer—with no direct reliance on either any centralized general ledger or system wide structural plumbing governed by regulators and incumbents. Banks could just do so if they could just recover and master the trust that is so critical in financial services.

As trust is challenged in novel and digital ways, banks' transformation into "synapses banks" needs to find new, specific solutions. Banks trust issue is in fact much more profound than the re-definition of values and culture (away from the "lazy and greedy" Gordon Gekko style set of values) and well above the re-basement of commercial conduct (away from aggressive cross selling of unwanted, mispriced products and services).

We have seen as both BBVA and Goldman Sachs, best in class in their own traditional turfs and emerging as leading global "digital players" (even if not yet fully digital in their business and operational nature), are considering trust, and trust rebuilding, as a key component of their transformation strategy. It is then worth to further develop the notion of credibility and trust in a digital world, discussing how it could recover in the aftermath of the global financial crisis and how it could evolve in the increasingly open battlefield, and in the new financial cyber-space where traditional incumbents, and emerging "synapses" banks and new start up FinTech challengers (and other well established players like Apple, Google or Facebook) will end up competing.

We will therefore discuss how cyber-risk can have a significant impact on this trust and how it should be managed, as one of the most critical dimensions. Remembering how it takes a world of effort and a lot of time to build credibility, delivering consistently on the expectations set, and just a few seconds to lose this trust.

4.3 Cybergeddon: Watch Your Bytes

Just imagine yourself one day, waking up and logging on as a customer to your online banking account to find out that your lifetime savings have been completely depleted, over-night. With a number of digital strings (representing your well-earned retirement money) being pocketed and spent by someone, at any possible time and in any possible place—you are really at a loss, as it will probably be your bank, with the only possible boundary to focus the search of your stolen money being the universe of the many servers where the world wide web runs, uncontrolled, unrestrained, almost anarchic and certainly ethereal in nature.[1]

Imagine then one day that the bank you run as a top manager stands still—literally freezed and unable to wake up from its digital, deadly torpor. With online applications being devoured by some terrifying worm of a digital nature, and your operating systems being unable to process any of the simplest to the most complex of its core processes—the cash-in of a few dollars by a branch based bank teller, or the clearing and settlement of a structured derivative on the wholesale global markets. It's not just the money you stand to lose by the day—the unclosed trades, the unrecoverable money and the likes, till some kind of recovery plan will act and solve the problem; more importantly, you could end up harming your reputation with customers and regulators alike, with loss of business for the long term, fines, costly remediation plans and further capital requirements.

Imagine, finally, that your job is, as regulator, to supervise the global financial system, and that its structural plumbing, its main financial intermediaries, capital markets and payments systems—just to mention a few—are experiencing similar disruptions, with personal and systemic data being stolen or deleted, and money robbed, or created a new, at the whims of cyber barons operating from some far away island. Panic of retail and corporate customers alike, severe dislocations in domestic and international markets and the blockage of the main fundamental functions of the global financial system would rapidly ensue, followed by further breaches, defaults… and potentially bringing the overall economy to a hard stop, leading to uncontrolled mess, social unrest and maybe protracted violence leading to the topping of democratically elected governments.

It could have been even worst. In the "Internet of Things" (IoT) scenario that is rapidly developing and taking place, we could have lost control of our home appliance, or self-driving car, or medical-check out not to mention the occasional chemical reactor and intercontinental warfare system digitally controlled by "super-safe" passwords expressed in ever-changing combination of bits and bytes—now being cracked by a lunatic geek sitting in an Internet café and playing with real nuclear arsenals as it were a videogame.

A number of cyber barbarians are in fact just waiting at the portal of the global financial system, obviously attracted by it because "that's where the money is" (in the words of a famous banks' robber) and ready to strike on its weakest link (including the many FinTech now operating within the global financial system), bringing about a collateral damage that is hard to predict, and potentially too high to even contemplate.

This "Cybergeddon" scenario just described is much more real that generally thought, and becoming more likely by the day, as the quantity of data and information accumulated and stored into the system grows exponentially, as the number of new applications and gateways of access increases, as open data and cooperative software development solutions grows, and given the ubiquity of the world wide

---

[1]Watch your bytes, AlixPartners position paper, Claudio Scardovi, Lorenzo Grillo, March 2017.

web that just keeps expanding. We all follow the un-relented pace of technological innovation—as digital becomes more and more embedded in our everyday life we simply cannot do without it and we are then exposed to the unknown.

Cyber terrorists and hacktivists, cyber robbers and spies are motivated by different motives—the former looking to mount viral sabotage attacks on vital economic and social systems, the latter simply aiming to steal money and critical data to make an easy buck—from financial intelligence, to personal, confidential data, to trade secrets. But their means look increasingly similar, as do the targets they tend to concentrate on—with the global financial system and its financial intermediaries and markets becoming one of the most obvious.

Let's consider banks, for example. As we have previously discussed, they are still sitting on an almost unbearable ("un-investable", in the words of Tidjane Thiam, CEO of Credit Suisse[2]) business model, that allowed them to have an easy living till few years ago. They multiplied the money supply by leveraging their equity capital—getting funds from multiple, low risk sources and giving it away to fewer, more risky lenders (risk transformation), to build an interest rate spread for themselves, on the assumption that banks were never going to fail or would have saved at all costs in such extraordinary events.

They then multiplied this fungibility of money across time and space—building time and geographical lapses, or mismatches, in their balance sheet (time and space transformation), to further enhance that spread, based on the normally upward sloping term structure of yield curves (and taking advantage of the interest rate spread between developed economies and emerging economies). They finally multiplied their ability of undertaking risky lending and underwriting—increasing the velocity and the density in their equity capital usage, via asset sale securitization (thus increasing the velocity of usage of a dollar of equity in a given time frame) and the use of structured derivatives (the density of equity up-risking), just to further augment their risk trading proposition.

They are now all trying to move away from this unbearable lightnesses and transform themselves and become digital, e.g. playing digital, thinking digital and being digital in nature, on the basis of increasingly digital business and operating models. We have then been arguing that their new transformation challenge, moving away from the three leverage-risk/time-space and density-velocity transformations described) should be around reinventing themselves as a "synapses-like" organization on the basis of few building blocks.

The first, leveraging data and information advanced accumulation, preservation, extraction and management. The second, leveraging the use of applied analytics and self-learning machines/AI to derive intelligence from the data and information. The third, focusing on the development of new ways of interacting with customers via Omni-channels distribution strategies that allow them to still crucially sit in the middle of the buy/sell trade, but offering a richer proposition of interconnections among multiple stakeholders. The fourth, focusing on the identification of new system solutions and customer new use cases that provide incremental value to the

---

[2]Bloomberg, Financial services conference, London, November 2017.

overall ecosystem. And finally, the fifth, leveraging trust and credibility, as the starting point and founding "horizontal" block of the "synapses" model and of the overall transformation and rebirth of the industry. But what about this very same horizontal, underpinning block is under the threat of a multiple, critical attacks?

4.4 Quantum Security

Not all sources of technological innovation are however bringing new and more complex risks, further adding to the complexity of doing business in an increasingly digitally dominated economic system. We already mentioned the Blockchain technology, ideally promising not only to build code much harder to crack and dope, but also to be treating data in a much safer way as it keeps storage of them on multiple servers (because of its "distributed ledger" nature), thus reducing the risk of losing critical, unique information or of having them "cooked up" by some cyber gangster (as he/she would need to do this on any single server of the network).

Quantum mechanics—the theory of behavior at the atomic level developed in the early 20th century[3] and on of the most promising technological disruption to come—is also promising to contribute to the preservation of cyber security, thus supporting the re-building of the credibility and trust of the sector. Quantum mechanics, broadly speaking, substitutes the notion of a clockwork, deterministic universe with a reality that deals in probabilities rather than certainties—one where the very act of measuring affects what is measured.

Out of this quantum mechanics general principle was then born the (at least) theoretical possibility of building quantum computers—out of the abilities to trap, poke and prod single atoms and other particles of light called photons. Quantum computing is now becoming a factual reality, with computer chips getting faster and cheaper and smaller—with infinite potential applications to all kind of sectors and industries.

From a cyber security point of view, a global network of communication links whose access is protected and underwritten by unbreakable physical laws could represent a very appealing and almost definitive solution. In this network, signals could be encoded using either superposed or entangled particles that cannot be intercepted, duplicated or passed on—as this very acts would influence their status and behavior—according to the Heisenberg principle of indetermination—it could as well work for the global financial system, should this be able to entirely replace, sometime in the future, the existing worryingly uns Figure and unsafe plumbing with a new quantum one—also computing power would be multiplied by a very high order of magnitude.

Using algorithms that recast problems in quantum forms, new computers could perform calculations that today's best supercomputers would take millennia to crack, with obvious applications to the world (for example) of credit risk

---

[3]The Economist, Subatomic opportunities: quantum leaps, March 11th 2017.

underwriting, financial derivatives hedging, proprietary trading and investment management and so on.

Quantum computing would eventually render obsolete today's cryptographic techniques which are based on hard mathematical problems, the "enigma" that were already used during the second World War to protect secret military information. But also quantum hackers would develop stronger algorithms maybe able to break into new security systems—security is eventually all about a "catch me if you can" never ending story.

Whatever the final end game (or continuously moving target), in the new, upcoming but still under development business model of "synapses banking", a "bit" of credibility is—more than ever—everything.

As the saying goes, for digital banks it takes a lot to build credibility, and just a (lost) bit to loose trust. In their new digital strategy, the intangibility of their unbearably light, almost ethereal business model is even greater, and based on the quantity and quality of data and information being managed—increasing exponentially as we speak. If a cyber-attack could harm their very basic attributes (the "golden rules" of data/information management), the very basis of the banks' operating model would be compromised and put at risk.

Even more so if the intelligence being produced by the system could be sabotaged, lost or stolen, or if the blockage of some critical part of the system could freeze and impair the day to day functioning of the banks' intermediation/interconnection role and disrupt the normal functioning (or introduce a malicious, often undetected, malfunctioning) of the ecosystem solutions and customer use cases that are ultimately justifying the distinctive value adding role of banks and of the other financial intermediaries acting in the economy.

Everything in this new, digital world is therefore built on trust or, actually, cyber-trust—as this one truly emerges as the real "scarce resource" of the new digital business and operating model of the synapses bank. Cyber-trust, or cyber-capital, is therefore the ultimate stakeholders value to preserve and that needs to be allocated at best across multiple risk/return opportunities, managing accordingly other limited resources (such as the "franchise capital", coming from the business relationships with customers; or the "knowledge capital", coming from the pool of talents and headcounts the bank has; or the "financial capital", as the regulatory buffer it can deploy or accumulate at best, and as the cash at hand that could invest across multiple options).

4.5 Cyber Trust as Scarce Resource

This credibility, built over many years and out of the best management of trillions of bits and bytes, can be measured, as cyber-trust goodwill, or as cyber-capital at risk (the two being the two different faces of the same medal), to then drive the digital business and operating strategy of the bank. Cyber-security is definitely not a buzzword as it is now usually associated with a long list of "tick the box" checks and balances that the bank needs to put in place, and with an even longer list of software solutions aimed at addressing its failings, in an undifferentiated way and following a "bean counting" logic (one bean is a bean, full stop).

Getting the basics right and overcoming the simple blunders, starting from the physical safety of data and environments, and from the appropriate selection, controlling and monitoring of people (employees and customers/suppliers alike), is of course a good starting point and a "need to have". But the road towards a more scientific and still pragmatic approach to the optimal management of cyber risk must encompass some form of objective quantification—as seen not as an end in itself, but as a necessary mean to a different end.

Let's start by clarifying that by "cyber trust valuation" and by "cyber risk quantification" (its nemesis) we are referring to the process of evaluating the cyber risk that has been identified at the bank (or at any other financial intermediary) and then measured and analyzed, leveraging all available cyber data and past data and information by using the most sophisticated modelling techniques—from the traditional conjoint statistical analysis, to the other applied analytics "black box" techniques such as neural networks, fuzzy logic, genetic algorithms, gradient boosters and all kind of other AI (artificial intelligence) applications.

These analysis can work out how to accurately and dynamically (in the case of "self-learning" AI machines, as they will readjust as new data and information come available) represent the financial intermediary's cyber environment e.g. using a Monte Carlo simulation to run millions of times a cyber-attack outcome scenario to derive the organization's loss distribution—considering all kind of direct and indirect impacts on business.

The analysis should also cover all of the business critical applications, databases and IT systems and associated exposures in dollars. And the potential losses that could derive directly or indirectly, including for example: the costs of straight-through robberies, regardless of their full or partial cover from the bank's side; the costs from potential disputes arising from customers, and even from suppliers and employees, in case their personal, confidential data are stolen and used in fraudulent manners; the regulatory fines associated with failure in compliance and the regulatory capital requirements top up associated with a weaker cyber security system (via the operational risk capital charge requirement); the disruption in the day-to-day operations, with consequent lost business and reputational harm; the more long term persistent damage caused to the brand value of the bank that would impair its commercial goodwill and ability to attract the best digital talents; And many others.

On the basis of these potential losses, and of their relevant distribution of frequency, the expected severity (or cyber-capital at risk) should be calculated, in two different and complementary ways. On one side, as the maximum unexpected loss for a given level of confidence—e.g. a given number of standard deviations—that drives the capital buffer needed by the bank to target a certain credit rating level. On the other side, as the mean of the same distribution of frequency that should be considered and built into the pricing structure of any product and service, on the basis of their cyber-riskiness and given the target return on cyber-capital—to define

4.5 Cyber Trust as Scarce Resource

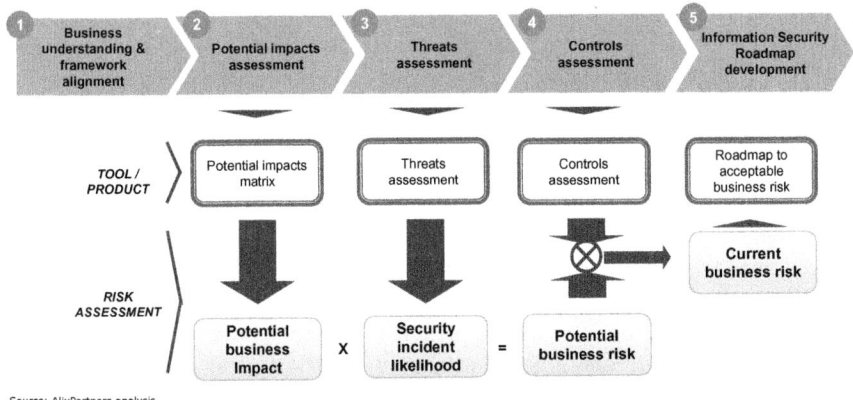

Fig. 4.2 An information security risk assessment approach

ideally a risk adjusted cyber return on cyber capital at risk (see in the following Fig. 4.2 a suggested approach to quantity business impacts as key component of the cyber capital at risk).

This "as is" analysis of the digital business and operating models riskiness should then be matched by the considerations on the bank's network topology, the defenses that have been put in place based on specific cyber frameworks such as NIST, ISO 27002 or CIS 6.1, the strength and maturity of each framework and so on.

That means, cyber-attacks success rates and collateral damages are not built in a vacuum, and the CISO (Chief Information Security Officer) job should not (just) aim at identifying, evaluating and controlling/monitoring existing or emerging cyber threats, but at proactively and reactively managing them at best as well.

On the basis of all this, the very strategic planning process of the bank should be driven on the basis of the consideration of how much incremental cyber capital at risk is generated by new opportunities, the innovation pursued, the applications developed by the products and client segments heads. On this basis, a return on the cyber capital al risk generated should be considered, including the potential reduction of such a risk via insurance coverage (and considering its costs into the equation), and how much it impacts on the overall business of the bank. Also, all kind of investments considered to prevent cyber risk should be analyzed on an ROI basis, to make sure the limited budget allocated to this gets employed on the most critical tail risks.

4.6 CISO in Cyberspace

This credibility, built over many years and out of the best management of trillions of bits and bytes, can be

Cyber-attacks could then be prevented and their success rate could be reduced significantly, following an approach were the scarce resources are critically aligned and focused on the unacceptable risks—e.g. allocating the investable budgets on the no-regret projects that allows to maximize the return on cyber-capital, covering the fat tails and unacceptable spikes of the risk distribution.

Cyber-attacks are however never fully avoidable, and the ex-post reactionary component of the CISO job is as important as his/her ex-ante proactive one—it drives the minimization of the loss given the event—addressing all direct and indirect damage—including business ones—associated with robbers, terrorist, spies and hackers.

As we have seen, there is a clear bonding between credibility and trust, and between cyber security and a better management of the cyber-trust and goodwill and related cyber-capital at risk—the real and increasingly crucial scarce resources that could maximize the value creation potential of the synapses bank—or of any other financial intermediary acting digitally in the global markets—for shareholders and stakeholders alike.

The CISO could therefore drive not only the design of the best risk management system (organization, processes, models and IT infrastructures and applications) aimed at addressing cyber security as the key risk among the many that the bank faces, in close coordination with the CRO (Chief Risk Manager) for the bank-wide risks aggregation activities and to ensure consistency in their management. But also the design of the best planning and control system (targeting, budgeting, reporting on risk adjusted performance) that can help the CFO in allocating at best the synapses bank's capital at risk, and the COO in correctly defining its optimal cost structures and capital budgeting plans, and the CIO/CTO in designing the best cyber-risk consistent IT system.

Out of the comprehensive analysis and objective quantification of the cyber-capital at risk, and on the basis of the best proactive/reactive courses of action that the CISO (working in partnership with the CRO, CFO, COO and CIO) aims to drive, the best strategies to hedge/cover part of this cyber-risk (e.g. via insurance guarantees provided by primary counterparts) should also be defined and put in place.

As a warden of the cyber-trust, and guardian of the cyber-capital at risk, the CISO should therefore frequently report to the CEO and to the Chairman with regards to the ever evolving cyber risk taxonomy that the bank is facing, and how it plans to address this—on the basis of the risk/return appetite of its share and stakeholders (regulators included) as expressed by its Board of Directors. Far from being a mere "thick the box" approach, or a formal, boringly technical discussion, this promises to be a very interesting and challenging one as it addresses a new worry, if not, ultimately, "the main worry", that keeps the CEO awake at night, with hallucinating dreams of a financial cyberspace where an unrestrained and con-strainable digital warfare could suddenly erupts—melting most of infrastructure supporting the global financial system.

4.6 CISO in Cyberspace

Cyberspace—a term coined by William Gibson, a science-fiction writer, has in fact come to represent, in the words of Gibson, the "consensual hallucination experienced daily by billions of legitimate operators". Just imagine if this should become the hallucination of the myriad of people, professionals and every-day customers alike, usually dealing with some of the fundamental functions of the global financial system. A financial cyber-space that crosses every dimension of time and space, projecting a virtual representation of all the data that could be extracted and maliciously manipulated (for sabotage, terrorism, espionage or simple robbery does not really matters) to express a different reality. A financial cyber-space that could create, at the tip of a mouse, new Lehman-like domino-effects, failures of payment systems that get us back to bartering, and the creation of few hyper rich, at the cost of billions of robbed people (with the already poor likely suffering the worst).

This cyber-threat of mass financial hallucination is even greater than the one, referred to by past US President Barrack Obama as "one of the gravest national security dangers" his Country is facing: because every cyber-financial-space hallucination is transnational in nature, and encompassing the very fabric of the global economic system and of civil societies. In this cyber-war, the bank needs to keep at bay the unacceptable risks, whilst accepting that a zero-risks policy is just unattainable—or not economically convenient.

A lot is in fact at play and a new, fundamentally different approach to cyber-security is needed, for traditional and for synapses banks and for any other relevant financial intermediary alike. And a greater role, both in proactive and in reactive risk management, is called for the CISO that, short of having a "license to kill" must have the right to call the shots—from an organizational and resource levels perspective. As every bit counts.

4.7 Banking on the Basics: One

Banks were born light and leveraged, almost by designed, we have argued at the beginning of this book. But they have also played an incredibly important role, probably as the leading actor, in sustaining the fundamental functions that, from the beginning, have represented the very "reason d'etre" of the global financial system—valuable functions of economic, social and political relevance, that have contributed to the continued creation and accumulation of wealth and to development of the civilization of the human race.[4]

Banks, as other financial services intermediaries, have been "banking" on these functions to then provide other, potentially more profitable services, but still making sure to keep performing the very basic functions (or "utilities") required to pursue an optimal allocation of resources at a global scale, to maximize the sustainable growth rate of economies and the wellbeing achieved by Countries and

---
[4]The future of financial services, World Economic Forum report, June 2015.

societies alike. There are multiple definitions of these basic functions, usually converging on a fundamental set of few (usually 6–8).

First, the global financial system was born to support the free exchange of products and services, and the development of domestic and international trade, by ensuring that a safe, efficient and effective finalization of deals is reached via the payments system, and the clearing and settlement associated with any financial and commercial transaction.

Payments have then allowed to liberalize markets and support the specialization of Countries and companies alike on the basis of their comparative advantage and, as we have seen, the modern payments systems has allowed to overcome economic systems based on bartering or war and expropriation. Paper and digital money and payment services and main infrastructures—often referred as the basic plumbing of the system, are now promising to be disrupted by the digital revolution, as a new world of challenges opens up many opportunities for incumbents, and for the synapses bank willing and able transform itself.

On one side, new crypto currencies will try to gain market share, and to become accepted as widespread means of payments, potentially disintermediating official currencies, and diminishing the role of the Central Banks and the efficacy of their monetary policies (how could they control the money supply of crypto currencies?). On the other side, the distributed ledgers/block chain technology introduces an even bigger risk, for them and for the other financial intermediaries, as transactions could happen outside the traditional "rails" and with no intermediation at all of any of the traditional financial intermediary.

Leaving aside all these, the pace of innovation in payments is just unprecedented, allowing more and more convenience, but also making payments, and the money exchanged, more and more ethereal, and therefore prone to cyber risk. And as new players, offering P2P payments services, become widespread, they can use this channel to monitor the spending behaviour of consumers and companies, and cross and up sell accordingly—tell how you spend, and I will tell you who you are (or you wish to appear or to become).

Second, the global financial system was devised to allow the conservation, capitalization and transfer of value across time, to optimize the life consumption pattern of individuals and allow the sharing of the accumulated wealth across different generations. This "savings and investment" function, and related support to consumption, has developed along with the financial literacy of people and has been driven by the financial innovation that was created in the last decades in the wealth and asset management sectors.

The level of active participation of individuals in this "savings/investment" process, and the availability of more sophisticated approaches to risk/return analysis and portfolio targeting is also being discontinued by the new digital innovations now taking shape. Investing can in fact become a social business if digital venues are created and accommodate investors communities made up of millions of small retail investors, willing to share their tips and specific know how (no insider trading, just common information that, aggregated, can tell a lot: if multiple people starts complaining about the service offered by the Hotel Chain ABC, it's time to sell the stock; if multiple people are now suggesting that the new smartphone by DEF is great, it's time to buy.

As the use of machine learning/AI and other technological advancements become widespread, a diverse synapses approach can also take shape, with new roles being potentially played in the meiosis process of the asset gathering and wealth management processes—why shouldn't a robot do a better job in advising me on my pension plan or in picking up stocks and building a superior asset allocation, making away with the judgment bias of traders and ensuring (in its coding) that no conflict of interest is leading to some foul play. Not to mention the current, still relevant proprietary trading business of banks and insurance companies, where a new quantum computing powered set of super intelligent machines are potentially going to displace human traders and even legendary investors a la Warren Buffet, ensuring again no conduct risk.

Third, a critical function performed by the financial system has also been its ability to pool limited resources from a very large number of different sources and to use them together, to finance quite large, sizeable and indivisible projects (e.g. the construction of a bridge linking Sicily to the Italian continent) that—apart from the sheer amount of money required—are also suggesting a disaggregation and distribution of their risks, in order not to destabilize the overall economic and financial system in case of failure. The overall process of getting new finance into the system has been continuously evolving through time, being mainly driven by the liberalization and deregulation of the financial markets and by its globalization. However, also for this function, digital technologies are now introducing new business and operating models to do just that.

Crowed funding initiatives are now mimicking seed/venture capital raising and even IPO (initial public offering) processes, without the involvement of investment banks, regulated capital markets and the likes—allowing a tailoring of the business plan each investor is willing to consider for underwriting, the segmentation of the potential shareholders and a very personalized match making. Crowding out traditional, wholesale middle men, these new business and operating models are also promising to redefine venerable segments of the investment/wholesale banking market, where the senior bankers' Rolodex with their high level relationships where key to get to the big mandates on anything from M&A to global finance.

This would, in a way, "democratize" this segment of finance and allow a greater accessibility to the international world of finance—with more opportunities for everybody—in a more synapses driven world where data, intelligence and digital interconnections are the real qualifiers to get a chance to play, developing innovative solutions that, based on the required trust, can hit the market and create new success stories.

4.8 Banking on the Basics: Two

Fourth, the global financial system is also providing the crucial structure to allow a safe and reliable transfer of funds across counterparts—some of them long on capital and short of entrepreneurial ideas and energy and vice versa, and across time and space. Since time immemorial, banks have played along a "fully integrated" business model, bundling together both the deposit taking and the lending making activities—but are now facing the competition of unbundled players, that acts as intermediaries (as the banks did and still largely do) but without providing a capital buffer in between: no more "promise" of safety (hugely overstated, as we have seen in the discussion of the inverted pyramids) provided to deposit holders, but instead greater transparency and socialization, of both profits and losses from the "buy the money, sell the money" traditional business.

Digital technologies are in fact now making possible the efficient interconnection of multiple counterparts and the competitive adjudication of financial resources via a real time matching that the development of API, of third party price comparison tools and the likes can only foster. This match making can also allow now a deep profiling of the risk/return chosen, as saver and investor, or as borrower and consumer (or entrepreneur).

Also, the availability of unprecedented amounts of data and the development of applied analytics techniques, leveraging deep/self-learning machines and artificial intelligence, is now potentially introducing a further revolution on the way credit scoring and rating tool models are developed, and therefore on how the creditworthiness and underwriting risk of a counterpart is assessed—potentially leading to a reallocation of resources that follows different, more real time and "social knowledge" criteria, with tectonic shifts in the way wealth stocks and funded opportunities could be migrated away from traditionally opaque power brokers.

Fifth, another fundamental function being performed by the global financial system involves then the analysis (and pricing), the pooling and sharing or outright transfer of financial risks, via the intermediation of wholesale/investment banks (usually acting as mere intermediaries, when they structure some risks sale to counterparts that could be their best holders, for a fee). Financial risk management products can then be traded on either OTC (Over The Counter) or regulated markets (via the use of financial derivatives like futures, forwards, options etc.). Alternative to the usual set of forward, futures, swaps, options, financial guarantees can also be designed and provided by insurance or by other institutional counterparts.

On this dimension, the potential evolutionary driver introduced by digital innovation are represented by new risk management models, able to master both structured and unstructured data and build better predictive models out of machine learning/AI applications, solving most of the "backward looking" and continuous maintenance and fine tuning issues that are typical of more traditional models based on statistical analysis.

4.8 Banking on the Basics: Two

Also, the world-wide web offers new places to design, aggregate and fine tune risk management "structured solutions" that are then pooling multiple stakeholders together, to sell, share or underwrite risks for a fee, without the involvement of an investment bank (and with no guarantee of any equity capital buffer in between). More broadly, in world of ever changing risk taxonomy, the digital innovation is promising to introduce many innovative and value adding solutions, but also new fundamental risks—including the major one we discuss of "being digitally leapfrogged".

Also, the global financial system was born to provide transparency on the comparative value of things, through its price discovery process that is best taking place in highly efficient and liquid markets. This "efficient market" role has included other significant provisions, such as the ability to manage effectively a number of information asymmetries driven issues, including moral hazard, adverse selection and the principal-agent ones. But also the availability of common infrastructures, or "market utilities" that can pursue the broader public good (e.g. providing a credit scoring database for the overall population, as in the case of the US FICO information system) or, more broadly, allowing to reap the economies of cost and scope that can be reached by the aggregation of greater volumes onto single platforms, or nodes, of the overall ecosystem.

Traditional price discovery mechanisms, via the interplay of supply and demand on regulated markets, and the solutions provided to some information and other public goods failures could also be up for disruption, with opportunities for synapses banks to replicate old markets into different and more agile forms, or for new digital challengers to perform them instead, in new ways that could be either complementary or alternative to the existing one. In a way, even the global financial system—as a system comprising financial products, financial markets and financial intermediaries working on common infrastructure could also end up being disintermediated, or changed in a significant way—to end up in very different forms and shapes.

One example of the transformation to come could be, for example, as later discussed, the creation of new utilities, born out of the carve out and pooling from multiple banking peers of existing IT and operations; or the creation of alternative, fully digital, or quantum powered, "rails"—new infrastructure interconnecting the multiple ends of a significantly different system, where products, markets and players change after their basic infrastructure.

Sixth, and finally, the global financial system is also allowing the pooling and transfer (or sharing, according to a principle of mutuality) of non-financial, so called "pure risks"—including mortality and life extension, morbidity and health and the ones related to the value of properties and to other general casualties. These can be insured (covered) either via insurance policies provided by insurance and reinsurance companies, or via financial contracts and capital market solutions (like the CAT—Catastrophes Alternative Transfers, usually in the form of bonds whose yield is indexed to some weather catastrophic events like tornados, hurricanes or heart quakes; or the ART—Alternative Risk Transfers, that take many different shapes and forms).

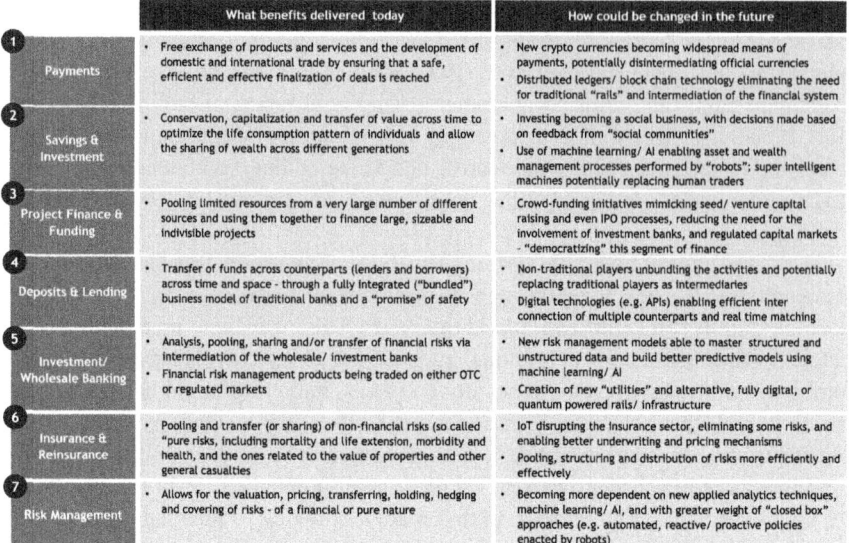

Fig. 4.3 The seven functions of a transforming global financial service industry

Digital innovation is going to impact even more greatly on this last function and in an more radical way, as the internet of things (IoT), made up by advanced sensors and wearable computers and by data accumulator and transmitters that can now be incorporated in everything we normally use, from houses to cars, from glasses to (even) our own body with just change the dimension, quality and timeliness of information on our everyday life. Not to mention other forms of technological information where, for example, the advances of self-driving machines are promising to eliminate up to 99.7% of the street casualties (also eliminating most of the traffic and its related pollution, the value of parking slots and need itself to own a car).

In many other examples, we could then find that, by using a synapses approach, insurance companies could not only aim at a better underwriting of risks, but also seek to contribute to the solution of the risk itself, as in the case of the self-driving cars, or in the case of specific illness that could find better therapies and quicker pharmaceutical tests via the use of real time, unstructured data that are analyzed with the help of the best (digital) intelligence. Also, the digital innovation is promising to introduce new ways of disaggregating and pooling, structuring and distributing pure risks in a more efficient and effective way.

This could well put at risk some part of the competitive positioning of life and P&C insurance companies, and of other venerable markets like the Lloyds of London. Ultimately, each of us could choose to take some risks (or "bet" some money associated to their Value at Risk) with regards to specific event, including business related ones, as the failing of a new major movie being released—they could get a ticket for free, and just pay double if the movie goes bad during the first week end (Fig. 4.3).

Digital Transformation in Payments

Abstract

All main fundamental functions played by the global financial system are potentially ripe for disruption. A disruption mostly introduced by digital innovation, but not only, as a full spectrum of technological changes are happening across multiple fields and converging into a new future steady state that is difficult to predict. The payment sector looks like the first and most obvious entry point for new FinTech challengers—encompassing a number of innovations that extend to the creation of crypto currencies and of new "rails" where transactions can be cleared and settled—potentially without any role left for traditional financial intermediaries (including Central banks) and in real time and at almost zero costs. In an increasingly frictionless, timeless and super transparent digital payments systems, new revenues opportunities are however manifesting, with new extended roles for the "controllers and miners" of data—banks but not only (or not necessarily), with an intermediation (interconnection) role extending to all kind of goods and services.

Keywords

Digital payments · Clearing · Settlement · PSD2 · GDPR · MIF interchange · SEPA · Crypto-currency

5.1 Payments in Paper-Less Societies

Cash is at the basis of common people's understanding of the nature and working of the main functions provided by the global financial system. It is an old notion, since (time immemorial) some King or Emperor started coining some form of money with the legal power to be accepted as a mean to clear transactions, limiting the bartering alternatives and progressively reducing the frictions and the costs associated with deals, as the coins (the "cash") where increasingly used across Counties and Countries, regardless of the "real" value of the material with which coins where forged (e.g. progressively debasing the gold value that was initially used to build their credibility as a mean of exchange and as a permanent store of value).

Cash was then progressively dematerialized, and it is now mostly occurring in a digital form, as we pay with a credit card, or settle with a wire transfer, or allow our debit card to be charged with no bank notes or coins changing hands—they are still there, at the basis of the collective imagination of the notion of money, but their quantity becomes increasingly marginal, as cash becomes bank note and coin-less, and fully digital.

In paper-less societies (using here "paper" as reference to both bank notes and coins), the payment function provided by the global financial system minds even more, at least initially. Everything is digital and digitally controlled by regulated financial intermediaries—by banks and credit card companies and other payment providers, by IT infrastructure systems and local and global authorities overseeing the overall system. And a key role is also played by Central banks, still at the core or this global financial function and, in a way, the "clearers of last resort", also setting the terms of trade among multiple foreign currencies.

However, as the money gets more digital, and therefore critically difficult to control, the risk of the global financial system of being attacked and progressively disintermediated by other FinTech players increases as well. A new wealth of opportunities opens up to new digital challenger and shadow banking players (the two dimensions are often interconnected and fused in the same company, as digital is used to find ways to avoid heavy regulations and compliance requirements), and even to new digital money, or crypto-currencies.

The "official" payment industry has indeed evolved significantly over time, particularly since the introduction of credit cards in 1950s, debit cards in the 1980s and the rise of e-commerce in the 1990s. Notwithstanding the growth in popularity of e-payments, and the bold approaches taken recently, for example by the Central Bank of Sweden (with its project to introduce a new digital currency and to dematerialize money even further from coins and paper) and by the Central Bank of India (that has taken out of the economy the paper money of greater value, to reduce the risk of corruption and to make the black economy came out in the open) the full displacement of cash and cheques is still some way off in other developed Countries —with other under developed economies (e.g. in Africa) that are instead jumping towards digital money, as the rapid development of M-Pesa is showing (Fig. 5.1)— a mobile phone-based money transfer, financing and microfinancing service launched by in 2007 by Vodafone for Safaricom and Vodacom, the largest mobile network operators in Kenya and Tanzania.

Notwithstanding the rapid adoption of digital money, several critical challenges still need to be overcome to make the world truly cashless and to offer eventually the opportunity for radical breakthrough in the function—at international and local level. On one side, electronic transactions done in the traditional way are still relying on a number of intermediaries, usually coordinated by large scale-based

5.1 Payments in Paper-Less Societies

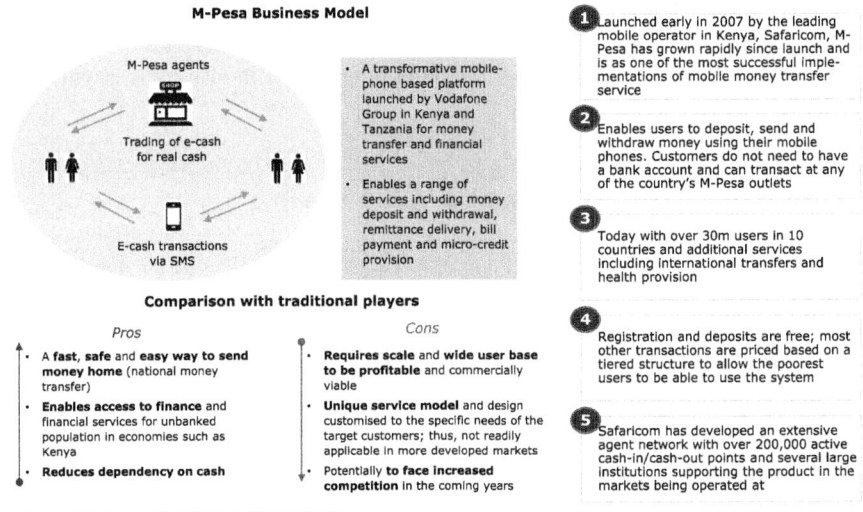

Fig. 5.1 M-pesa: a pioneer in mobile banking and beyond

payment networks: they ensure acceptance and security into the system and have been providing a number of benefits to customers and other stakeholders alike, such as their traditional convenience, efficiency, traceability and protection.

On the other side, the shift towards a truly cashless society will need to retain most of these benefits and overcome critical hurdles as well, such as the adoption from all kind of merchants and businesses (and private individuals as well) of ways that allow to settle transactions and transfer money just digitally. This adoption will require an appropriate level of trust that should be based on an adequate degree of accessibility, convenience and protection from cyber fraud. And a cultural shift in how people think of money.

A number of innovations have emerged recently that could act as powerful accelerator towards a truly cashless society, such as the creation and development of mobile wallets and mobile-based merchant payments solutions, or the provision of integrated billing services, for the use of both customers and merchants, and of other value added services that tend to modify the front-end payment and settlement processes to improve customers and merchants experience. Such incremental improvements are then usually paralleled by other more radical and discontinuous ones, that could allow the formation of parallel and alternative payments systems—such as in the case of the much-hyped block chain or "distributed ledger" technology.

With payments becoming more cashless and (process wise) invisible in the future, new challenges but also new roles are potentially on offer for banks and for other "traditional" financial intermediaries, if they can capture and actively manage and mine a large amount of data and information and develop intelligent platforms able to engage with corporate and retail customers in new and more value adding ways—increasing usability and reducing costs. But before thinking of the potential role that the "synapses bank" could play, it is useful to recollect the major innovation trends that are changing the competitive landscape in electronic payments.

5.2 Breaking up the Payments Value Chain

From a business perspective, the payments value chain covers three major components, from acquiring, to processing and issuing. The value chain usually starts with the payments solution being provided to the merchants and other business owners—enabling them to execute electronic payments transactions and receiving further potential Value Added Services (VAS) at their Point of Sale (POS). In this first phase, the acquiring business is developed by banks—they sign up merchants to accept payment cards, handle the transactions once received from the gateway, facilitate the authorisation requests and bear the full risk of a customer's default or of a non-fulfilment of the good and services being exchanged—therefore becoming responsible for the underlying transactions with the merchant and helping the development of commerce.

Following the value chain, the acquirer's processor provides then transaction processing services for the acquirer, for example acquiring the transaction and routing it for authorisation, clearing and settlement and processing charge backs and retrievals, or conversion among different Countries. The payment network scheme is then providing the infrastructure over which transactions are routed—asking for authorisations, clearing and settlement between the merchant acquirer and the issuer, and establishing and enforcing the rules and regulations for the smooth functioning of the transaction flow. The networks scheme or owner provide then appropriate memberships and licences and develop new products and marketing initiatives for partners.

In the following phase, the issuer processor provides then payment processing services for card issuers, including account and customer interaction management, PIN code, plastic cards and statement generation and management and few others. Banks are then the typical issuers, with cards bearing their own brand and relying on their current account, but working mainly on the technology already provided by third parties (but for the banks fully integrated and owning also most of the processing capabilities). In a final stage, the card issuer (typically the bank) holds the agreement and manages the relationship with the customer, authorising the transaction and confirming future settlements. The card issuer receives then payments from the customer and remits funds through the network, and is responsible for the marketing and distribution of cards to customers.

With the advent of digitization, the payments value chain is now being disrupted by a number of new entrants that are putting traditional revenues at risk. The traditional players (as shown in the following Figure) are attacked by new FinTech companies, also highlighted in the Figure, that—across the value chain—are now offering new value added services. In the merchant solutions/merchant acquirer first

5.2 Breaking up the Payments Value Chain

phases they are now, for example, offering omni channel solutions and a greater digitization of the customer experience, and even introducing new ways of buying and of getting instant credit lines (as in the case of the Klarna).

In the acquirer processor bit, they promise to reduce fraud, improve the quality of the information provided to acquirers and minimize transaction costs. Then, in the payment network phase they offer third party solutions and integration and, finally, in the card issuer phase they are introducing innovative payment products and card dematerialization (e.g. finding ways to pay without the use of plastic cards). Ultimately, they are also introducing a new phase of "digital wallet/authentication", where they try to manage the overall wallet and drive value added services to enhance customer experience (as for loyalty programs, later discussed).

This "break up" of the payments value chain (as shown in the Fig. 5.2) can be analysed following a bottom up analysis, or with a more top down, strategic overview of the changes now undergoing. Following this second approach, we could identify four major innovations as key drivers that could potentially change the competitive landscape of payments, attacking both the front and back end component of the system and of its value chain.

On the front-end side, new players from the digital and shadow banking space are entering the sector and increasing its competition, ultimately to the benefit of the consumer. Also, new payments rails are being developed, as an extension or as an alternative to the existing payment network schemes and, finally, new technologies are opening up the system to almost limitless opportunities in terms of data gathering and mining to get a better understanding of the customer and, ultimately, an higher share of wallet of what she/he is going to spend or save or invest in her/his every-day life—with many up and cross selling opportunities available to the owner of the customers intelligence produced. On the back end side, the potential obsolescence of the traditional technology (by no mean "analogic", as most of it is

	Merchant Access Point/ Solutions	Merchant Acquirer	Acquirer Processor	Payment networks/ schemes owners	Issuer Processor	Card Issuer	Digital Wallet/ Authentication
Traditional players examples	• Verifone • WorldPay • Ingenco • ISO (Various)	• Worldpay • First Data • Tsys • ISO (Various)	• WorldPay • Elavon • First Data • Intessa Sanpaolo	• MasterCard • Visa • MutiBanco	• Worldpay • First Data • Tsys	• Retail Banks	• Paypal
Fintech disruptors examples	• Clover POS iZettle (POS) • Stripe (APIs) • Klarna	• Square • iZettle • Bitpay (Accept Bitcoin) • Stripe		• MasterCard MasterPass • Visa Checkout	• Apple Pay (digital wallet)	• Mondo (new bank) • Bitpay (pay with Bitcoin) • Pingit (P2P)	• Apple Pay • Android Pay • Google Wallet • Starbucks • Klarna
Digital focus area	• Omni channel solutions • Digitalization of the customer experience • Introducing new ways to buy (e.g. Klarna post delivery) • Value added service to merchants		• Reduce fraud across transaction • Improve quality of MI to acquirers • Reduce per transaction cost	• 3 party solutions • Integration	• Reduce fraud across transaction • Improve quality of MI to issuers • Reduce per transaction cost	• Innovative payment products • Keep "top of wallet" placement • Card de-materialisation	• Manage "top of wallet" • Drive added value to customer experience (reduce friction, add loyalty etc.)
Revenue drivers	• Transaction fee • Gateway fee • Terminal rental	• Transaction fee • Gateway fee • Terminal rental	• Merchant service charge (managed and per transaction)	• Scheme fees (per transaction)	• Issuer service charge (managed and per transaction)	• Interest income on balances • Interchange • Other fees and commissions	• Transaction fee

Fig. 5.2 Payments value chain and the disruptions from digital

already digital, but with new super-digital standards that are making this obsolete nonetheless) is coupled by a potentially paradigmatic shift in key infrastructure solutions, such as in the "distributed ledger" block chains example.

The first discontinuity is driven by new intermediaries entering the competitive field. Payments is in fact one of the most capital light businesses in banking and very much driven by technology. New players are thus entering the sector by adjacent ones (e.g. telecom, as in the M-Pesa case) or just as a start-up often not even requiring a regulated license to operate. They can enter the market by offering "open loop" payments solutions, such as in the case of mobile wallets; or they can start offering streamlined payment solutions for merchants; or they can offer "closed loop" mobile payments solutions to capture and dominate some markets.

In the open loop development, the new players (like Apple, Google, Amazon or the "old FinTech" companies like Visa and MasterCard) leverage the existing payment networks, but improving as well the service by way of new technologies, for example offering NFC (Near Field Communication) and one-click payments. The immediate effect of these "open loop" competitors for incumbent banks is to increase the competition to be the "default card", as many new players will push transactions that ultimately settle on a single registered card (as in the case of Amazon or for the Apple Store). Also, as shown in the Fig. 5.3 (Front end innovations in electronic payments) even if the loop is "open" to everybody, it is the flow of information that matters, and the ability of the owner and manager of the loop to read through it—similarly to what broker dealer investment banks have done for decades, facilitating the flows of buy/sell orders for a small commission, but being then able to read the trends and swings in key financial markets and main players to facilitate their advisory capabilities, not to mention their principal trading business.

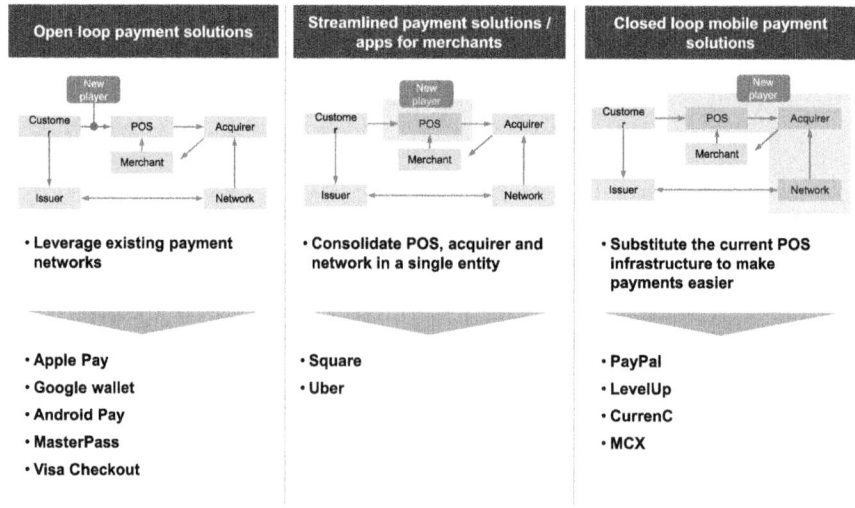

Fig. 5.3 Front-end innovations in electronic payments

For the streamlined solutions, the immediate effect for banks is instead the loss of relevant market share with merchants, as they find new propositions that are cheaper, faster, easier to implement and often characterized by a number of compelling value added services initially offered for free. These new streamlined solutions tend to substitute the current POS (Point of Sale) infrastructure to make payments more compelling, either as part of their core business (as it is the case for Square) or just as an ancillary part of their core business (Uber). In both cases, the impressive rate of development and specification of tailored solutions has hardly been matched by incumbent banks that in some cases have tried to ally and co-invest with innovators.

Of significant relevance is the case of Apple, that has launched its Apple Pay mobile payment and digital wallet service, that lets users make payments using an iPhone, Apple Watch, iPad or Mac. It does not require Apple-Pay specific contactless payment terminals and can work with existing contactless terminal. Therefore, it is aiming to digitize and replace a credit or debit card chip and PIN or magnetic stripe transaction at a POS terminal. Also, the service keeps customers' payment information private from the retailer by replacing the customers' credit or debit card Primary Account Number (PAN) with a tokenized Device Account Number (DAN) generated for each transaction. Hence, Apple retains further information and the power to create intelligence out of it, and is pushing for global acceptance via the EMV standards form the major payment networks.

5.3 Closed Loop

The closed loop mobile payment solutions try instead to consolidate the POS, the acquiring business and the network into a single entity, so as to dominate some alternative form of payment and for a circumscribed, well defined perimeter. PayPal is one of such closed loop solutions, and maybe the most internationally well known. It basically allows people to make financial transactions on line by granting them the ability to transfer funds electronically between individual and businesses and in 25 different currencies and onto its system. It was initially meant as a mean of exchange to support payments in the context of online auctions or to settle online purchases of goods and services, or to simply donate money in a P2P or institutional, on-line context. It then offered from 2009 to 2016 student accounts as well, to allow parents to set up accounts outside the traditional banking system, to send money for their sons as students, or to get a debit card for them.

PayPal, initially operated as a closed platform, opened then to third parties, allowing them to get access to its code and to use its infrastructure to enable peer to peer transactions. In its acquisition spree, PayPal acquired then the online credit product Bill Me Later (now rebranded into PayPal credit) to then offer shoppers access to an instant revolving line of credit that is available at vendors that accept PayPal, thus further reinforcing the network effect and its adoption rate.

More recently, PayPal has introduced a "one touch" service that allows for the payment with a one-touch option on participating merchants, and then "PayPal Here", a small business mobile payment system that includes a combination of a free mobile application and a small card reader that can be plugged into a smartphone. In its new, updated application for iOS and Androids, PayPal has then expanded its mobile app capabilities by allowing users to search for local shops and restaurants that accept PayPal as a mean of payment, to order ahead at participating venues and to access its dedicated credit lines.

The aggressive strategy of PayPal to both acquire targets and to develop organically new capabilities is showing how a mix of the two can actually be employed in parallel to invest and build capabilities than are progressively spanning across the entire consumer journey for critical segments (e.g. students) or spend categories (e.g. restaurants). In the following Fig. 5.4, some of the main acquisitions of PayPal are mapped across the different stages of the consumer's value chain, and encompassing online, mobile and even in-store payments. This development strategy has followed another one, famously commented by former CEO of eBay Meg Whitman, where "First, PayPal focused on expanding its service among eBay users in the US. Second, we began expanding PayPal to eBay's international sites. An third, we started to build PayPal's business off eBay".

The initial development of payment services by niche and start up players (like PayPal, or Square) as then been followed by the competitive moves of established digital leaders like Apple (ApplePay), Google (Google Wallet), Facebook and Amazon, now worldwide leading companies in terms of market capitalization, growth rate and number of customers. But several new FinTech players are still

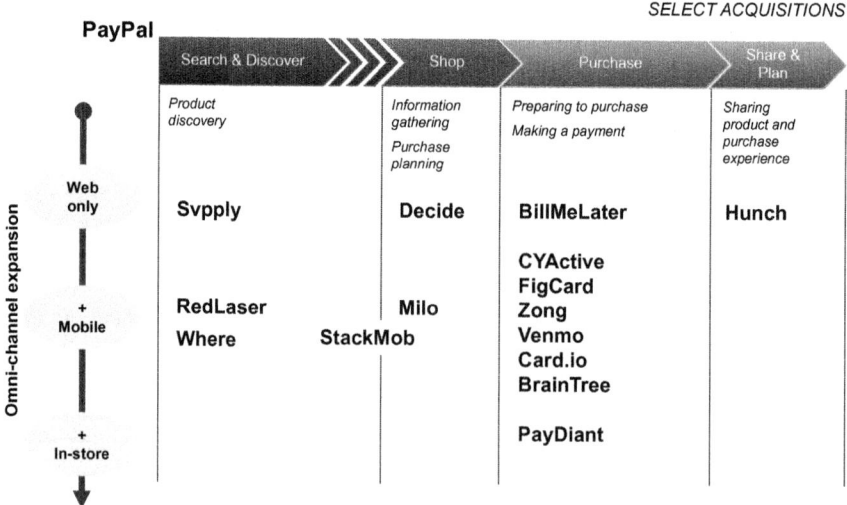

Fig. 5.4 PayPal is investing aggressively to build out capabilities across the full consumer journey

5.3 Closed Loop

challenging these big companies, by focusing on P2P payments, or specific services and technologies that could then be acquired by or developed in alliance with traditional banks—or be kept as independent if it acquires the critical mass to compete.

And as "old FinTech" companies like Visa or MasterCard have been trying to reinvent themselves as digital challengers, a consistent stream of payment businesses "carve outs" from traditional banks have been bought by private equity funds, willing to invest in their digital transformation to earn a share of the pie of the payments business where an increased competition is now offering opportunities to the new and old challengers, but also passing through most of the gains to the end customers.

The closed loop payment solutions are also a main part of the discontinuities happening because of new payment rails. Whatever the solution in the closed loop, or in the crypto currency being created to pre settle most of the transaction within the "loop", it all has the effect of reducing the usage of credit and debit cards and of any "traditional" payment mean (wires, bank notes, checks, coins etc.) and therefore the role and business of traditional banks—the Law limiting the inter-banking transaction fees is just making things worst.

Even the current account could become much less utilized, and with "collapsed" information regarding multiple transactions getting through it once a week or month that are just saying what is the net settlement of that many transactions that have already been cleared within the loop. Also, the entry point to offer other financial products such as loans, insurance coverage or mutual funds are lost by banks to the advantage of the new players that tend to act as "black holes", e.g. attracting all the business within the closed loop.

Further to the digital disruption introduced by FinTech players, regulatory changes are also going to contribute in a critical way, to the potential transformation of the payments value chain, potentially away from the fully bundled, bank captive current business model. As summarized in the following Figure, on one side, the MIF interchange regulation already mentioned has been compressing the profitability of the sector, curbing the anti-competitive effects driven by the interchange fees and sponsoring alternative practices.

On the other side, the Payment Service Directive 2 (PSD2), has fostered a revision of the existing payments directive to encompass new payment services and sponsor a more open and transparent competition. And finally, the General Data Protection Regulation (GDPR) is also promoting open data but also focussing on the potential risks posed by cyber thefts and other malpractices. These three regulatory changes are then converging and being integrated into the Single European Payments Area (SEPA—see also Fig. 5.5 on overall regulatory requirements), an EU lead initiative to integrate the European retail payments system, with focus on electronic payments, already near completion for direct debits and credit transfers and pursuing a vision of "any card accepted at any terminal" (still requiring significant effort and with no certain deadline set).

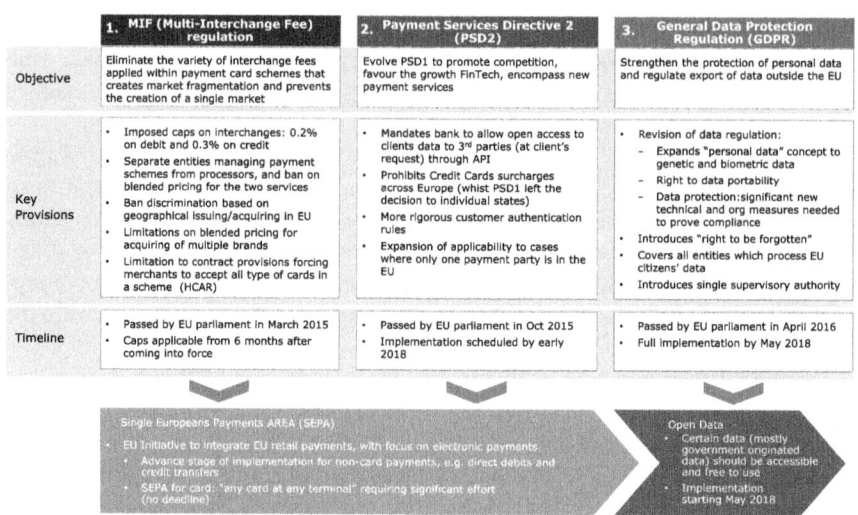

Fig. 5.5 Regulatory Impacts in Europe: introduction of new regulatory requirements will require digital innovation in response

5.4 The Opportunities for a Synapses Bank

Whatever the end game scenario coming from this mix of digital innovation-led disruptions and of regulatory-driven discontinuities, a useful interpretation of the competitive disruption to come can be derived applying the "five senses", to understand how a "synapses" bank could react and potentially profit from them.

As a starting point, as digital wallets consolidate on multiple digital payment platforms, or proliferate across many of them, financial institutions will inevitably risk to lose some or most of their control over their customer transaction experience —particularly so if better ways to execute payments, in real time, less expensive, more seamless and safer are devised by new Fin Tech players. However, the more data rich environment can allow a better capitalization of the current relationships with customers, also to the benefit of banks, if they are able to capture, store and manage the new data abundance—with regard to retail but also merchant clients, and potentially coupling the payments information with other ones more focussed on the understanding of the customers' behaviour on-line or inside the physical shop (as later described).

A synapses bank should get future-ready in payments not just by capitalizing as much data and information as possible, but also being able to produce new serviceable intelligence on its customers, derived by the use of applied analytics and self-adjusting algorithms produced by machine learning/AI—on their current and future behaviour. It could all be used to gain and solidify the bank's market share on the wallets—and offer the bank the opportunity for promoting further goods and services, of a financial and non-financial nature, potentially enlarging its role on the basis of loyalty programs (also discussed in a later paragraph).

Banks, and other financial intermediaries, would not get to a sustainable competitive positioning just by competing on the digital wallet only, but will also need to think about ways to play their traditional "intermediary" role in better ways, interconnecting the relevant players of the payments system in novel and value adding ways. The payment business is also favouring an enlarged role played by banks, as they could smooth the transactions among suppliers, merchants and end customers, also helping them in creating more efficient and effective value chains, from the original producer of a given widget to its final user.

As new Fin Tech players have been particularly effective in defining and tackling a specific use case (or very vertical component) of the payment value chain to then derive a radically better economic solution, so banks could identify one or more specific use cases to be addressed with a "sand box" approach—developing a fully digital and innovatively superior solution first, and then re-implanting this into their old business model—progressively overcoming all the constraints and limitations of their current set up of IT legacy systems.

In turn, once the solution-driven new use case is set and functioning, an extended approach to leverage this to develop new interconnections and junctions with multiple players in the system could be derived backward. In this case, leveraging the much more extended commercial platform the bank has vis a vis a new digital player with a very limited service offering and few clients, with a limited story of penetration and fidelization.

In other words, the bank could augment and densify the value introduced by the new use case and economic solution identified and implemented (our fourth "sense") by extending its applicability and relevance with regards to a much larger number of potential and relevant interconnections and junctions, on the basis of the final critical factor. That is the trust and credibility that can still command on current and prospective clients, reducing the time of adoption of these innovations and extension to new parties and relationships, therefore moving away from a battlefield limited to the quest of dominance in the digital wallets space alone.

5.5 Distributed, Therefore Exists

Digital wallets, seamless solutions allowing better convenience, greater accessibility and a full all range of new value added services completely mobile and "on the go" will shake the competitive dynamics of the global payment system, potentially leading to a cash-less society where the control of the payment fundamental functions minds even more—to banks and to other financial intermediaries, if they don't want to be displaced as the traditional choice of preference within the set plumbing system, e.g. taking into account of the payments rails in place as still representing the so far prevailing and unchanged fabric of the system.

Following these accelerating incremental drivers of change, we have argued, banks could adopt a "synapses" strategy, leveraging on their traditional strength whilst digitally innovating (potentially following a "sand box" approach) to compete on the new use cases and economic solutions introduced by the FinTech players. Reaching a dominant position in digital wallets (whether following the consolidation or fragmentation scenario), and beating the challengers that have chosen to fight the banks on its very same competitive turf.

But what about if a new competitive turf—radically different from the prevailing fabric of the global payments and overall financial system—is introduced? Challenging paradigms almost as old as money itself—e.g. a centralized power setting the rules and running the system, requiring some role, in any kind of financial settlement, for the global financial systems and for its set of actors, markets and products/services?

In fact, the current, centralized financial value transfer system, built on central banks and secondary wholesale/investment and commercial/retail banks, on clearing houses and payments systems run via formal, structured, closely controlled rails could be approaching a tipping point—where revolution takes place, and the central authority of the bank of banks (the central banks) is challenged by "distributed ledgers" systems.

In these systems, the rule governing the creation of money is inherent and embedded into the system itself and defined once and for all, and the clearing and settlement of any kind of transaction—spot or forward and potentially regarding any financial products traded across any kind of market and among any kind of counterpart—can happen independently, without a formal, centralized, governing role for the global financial system. Not, at least, following the traditional definition of its key components.

The block chains technology and the advent and potential adoption on a large scale of crypto currencies could just lead to that, and on the basis of quite sound economic rationales: allowing almost real time and inexpensive transfer of money and related risk/return profiles across people, geographies and time horizons, potentially offering more certainty in the system, with less mistakes and reworks needed and more protection vis a vis the worst cyber risks—as the all-decentralized system is run in parallel, on a huge number of distributed servers that close a transaction when a majority agrees it has happened, in this or that way.

The crypto currencies are potentially destabilizing the overall set of traditional monetary economy tools and objective as well: how is it possible for Central Banks to control the quantity of money supplied by independent third parties, or the interest rate of reference, if new currencies, almost anarchic in nature and "minted" and put into use in the economy without any possibility of monitoring, controlling and governing the process?

These crypto currencies are in fact providing compelling alternatives to the incumbent payment and settlement systems—challenging the competitive role of banks and of other financial intermediaries and bringing them into a new, fully decentralized battlefield that breaks loose with regards to the definition of Country or jurisdiction as well, being fully intangible in nature and run on the world wide

5.5 Distributed, Therefore Exists

web by... no central authority, but with distributed efficacy—fugitive even to most stringent supervision of international regulators.

The future of the payments and settlements function could then develop and unfold onto new "rails"—more global, faster, transparent, cheaper and decentralized: actually making of their "distributed" component the critical one justifying their existence and potential prevalence versus the traditional un-distributed system.

Decentralized payment schemes leverage in fact cryptographic protocols to transfer value virtually—in a secure, low cost and near instantaneous way—most decentralised payments schemes use then a single distributed ledger and denominate payments between users in a native "currency", minted by the relevant technology—the BitCoin being the most notorious example, and far from by being the only one!

This crypto, highly mobile currency can then allow transfer of value between people, with no further intermediation required on the side of the financial intermediaries—globally and even in underbanked or unbanked regions. Not only margins on the current payments and settlement transactions tend to collapse, with potential global implications, given the related opportunity to develop these alternative and hyper efficient rails at international levels, overcoming (bypassing?) the regulatory complexity of local jurisdictions. But also, as highly accurate and efficient alternative rail designs are implemented, the role of traditional financial intermediaries (not only banks, but credit card companies as well) as trusted party diminishes.

These distributed systems could therefore end up competing directly with the existing financial ecosystem, with new financial products and services, denominated in new crypto currencies, and with new intermediaries.

This existential threat, by no means obvious to get through, given the extraordinary technological complexities of the distributed systems and the still relative fragility of some of their structural components (e.g. starting from the critical flow of transactions they could master at regime, still far from what required to fully substitute the current "plumbing") could force the banks and the other intermediaries to develop new solutions to fix quickly the most relevant pain points in the current payment system, potentially leveraging some of the digital innovation that can nonetheless be nurtured and grown in a "controlled" environment—whilst regulators (themselves at risk of being disintermediated) could find ways to red tape and constrain the development of the distributed ledger movement and limit its legal adoption across the globe.

Alternatively, banks and other intermediaries, and regulators as well, could choose to facilitate the growth of these "alternative" payment networks—as a complement to existing networks (also given their lack of proven reliability under stress and given the low critical volumes handled), and allowing the launch of their financial products into these new rails—closing effectively the loops between non-distributed and distributed schemes.

Eventually, they could even be forced to concede victory to the new "anarchic" system based on the block chain technology and on distributed ledgers, and they could in turn concede victory to new technologies and to even more digitally distributed ways of managing the interconnections and junctions within the global financial system. Whilst the payment/settlement function is the first most obviously impacted function, by all means the adoption of such distributed systems would then also impact all the remaining fundamental functions.

If such is the case, should we worry about the traditional "unbearable lightness" of banks as being replaced by an even more structural one, relating to a new system, where banks have simply no reason to exist? Or would a "synapses" bank still be able to have a viable positioning and critical role—maybe adding stability to the overall system? In a distributed system of ledgers continuously generating and clearing data and information, where data and information actually become embedded into the system and impossible to delete or alter, the advanced management of such an intangible capital would become even more critical, as more critical becomes the ability to derive serviceable intelligence, on economic phenomena that can be acted upon to define a better business and operating strategy to cope with a more distributed and complex ecosystem.

Whilst much of the current discussion is still on the block chain technology itself, and how it could operate, and be adopted at large scale and disrupt the prevailing rails, it is also reasonable to assume that commercial and financial interrelations among multiple parties will also change in nature, potentially allowing the introduction of new ways of interconnecting economic agents in a distributed, and therefore more anarchic (or democratic?), system, better able to devise new ways of creating synapses via junctions and meiosis.

These new ways of interconnecting and collaborating would then need to identify new opportunities and devise innovative use cases and economic solutions that are shifting the isoquant of the prevailing risk/return trade-offs—somehow allowing a greater and more stable creation of economic value, given the scarce resources available at global level, starting from what we described as "cyber trust". It should all follow if the hypothesis of the new distributed system being more transparent, real-time, cheap, reliable and cyber secure holds true.

Whatever the development of this or other distributed market scenarios, there seems to be hope for the "synapses" bank, well away from its principal balance sheet business and real estate based false certainties. This hope of "synapsezation" and survival of the traditional bank would again be driven by the superior design and execution of the five emerging competitive invariances described, with trust and credibility being again the last, but not least critical component to consider. As in a more and more distributed (anarchic, or loosely democratic) world, trust in institutional counterparts will become even more at premium, and the credibility of an intangible brand—corroborated by consistent behaviours and by the fulfilment of subsequent commitments, even better reflected in a brand equity value that stands still and grows in value through time.

Finally, it is also worthwhile to remember that, whilst on one side the potential challenges brought about by major technological discontinuities like "Block chain" seem paramount but so far have not materialized in a meaningful way, a more practical, urgent challenge for the industry and for the synapses bank would be to ensure that an almost real time clearing and settlement of transactions is achieved.

5.5 Distributed, Therefore Exists

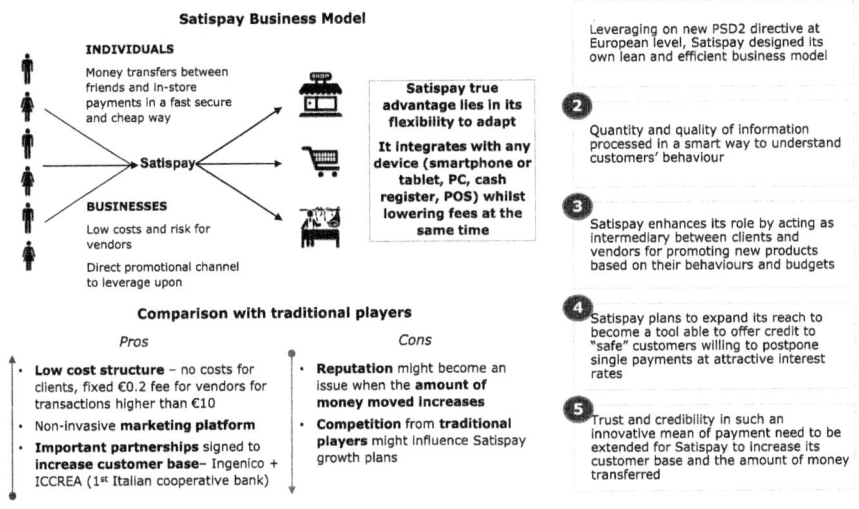

Fig. 5.6 Satispay business model: a five pillars analysis

The Block chain, should it gain large scale adoption, would (as of today) require a very long time to clear and settle anyway: therefore, offering a "real time" service on the "old infrastructure" could actually help delay the distributed ledgers breakthrough and leave more breathing space for traditional banks to change and transform.

If not, other smaller and nimbler FinTech players will do, as it may be happening in Italy with Satispay (Fig. 5.6), that is offering an almost real time clearing and settlement on the basis of a very old infrastructure—and introducing along the way a further disruption in the business model as the merchants, the ultimate "historical funders" of the value chain, that have been charged as a percentage of the volumes transacted for no particular reasons (the cost for clearing and settling a 10 Euro transaction is similar to the one sustained for a 10 million Euro ticket), are now charged a fixed amount per transaction (and getting services for free if the transaction is below 10 Euro), to promote the switch from cash to electronic payments and the disappearance of coins.

5.6 If the Bank Wears Prada

It is notoriously said in finance that whoever is able to follow the money can also make money. Because of this, banks, and other payments institutions, should be in a very good position, given their control—so far—of the physical and digital railways that make possible the clearing and settlement of most of commercial and financial transactions. However, as margins of this traditional business are progressively wearing thin, incumbents and new digital players are looking at non-traditional ways to monetize such privileged positioning. And so should banks do, and quite consistently with our "five pillars" approach to "synapsezation".

The technological innovation and digital transformation of payments as fundamental function of the global financial system is actually stimulating new ways for banks to become even more profitable. These business model changes could in turn impact, in a more fundamental fashion, on the other functions now performed by universal banks, starting from a holistic evolution of its core intermediating role in asset gathering and lending (buying and selling money at a spread).

They could also impact on the overall brand equity positioning of the bank that could become more of an advisor on consumers' lifestyle and, ultimately, a facilitator and influencer of the way the different production-to-distribution-to consumption value chains operate, across all kind of goods and services.

End buyers are quick in thinking of money, and of the payment system, as a dumb component of their everyday life, when they decide on their consumption patterns based on some economic rationale (e.g. price comparison, compatibility with a financial budget) and on their emotions and passions. Banks are, in this view of the world, almost utilities, powerless with regard to the critical decision making of the rest of the economy, and just able to influence consumers (and producers) on the basis of their lending decisions—relaxing or tightening the financial budget for consumption or investment of the main actors in the competitive market.

In fact, banks could end up ultimately playing the role of Miranda Priestly (played by Meryl Streep), the powerful editor of a leading fashion magazine in "The Devil wears Prada" made-in-Hollywood notorious movie. Following our example, end-users may feel, as Andrea (Andy) Sachs (played by Anne Hathaway), not interested in fashion and really in charge of their own everyday consumption decisions. But in reality, most of their choices are not only influenced but also controlled by people like Miranda.

Even the dull, unfashionable blue sweater that Andy wears represents a choice made by other at the top of the value chain—the manufacturers, the designers, the trend setters and the Devil itself, e.g. Miranda Priestly that famously tells Andrea how "you (really) think this has nothing to do with you. But what you don't know is that that sweater is not just blue. It's actually cerulean, showed up in the collections of eight different designers. And then it filtered down through the department stores and then trickled on down into some tragic Casual Corner where you, no doubt, fished it out of some clearance bin. (…) that blue represents millions of dollars and countless jobs, and it's sort of comical how you think that you've made a choice that exempts you from the fashion industry when, in fact, you're wearing the sweater that was selected for you by (… me)".

Banks could end up playing such a role, influencing the customers' behavior and driving the local economies made up of small businesses and merchants, and the global manufacturers and wholesale distributors as well applying the "five senses" that can help them in creating a "synapsized" competitive positioning, expanding their business from the simple brokering of money to one that includes any category of goods and services.

For a start, they can accumulate and master all the data and information they already have access to, via their key role in the payments systems and by offering new value added services that can help merchants and consumers (and in turn manufacturers) in gathering, analyzing and utilizing all the relevant intelligence that could be produced out of them, by mining them and by deriving, via the use of machine learning/AI, patterns of behavior for consumption and investment, and in addressing potential pent up demand.

For example, the access to payments data and the gathering and analysis of other unstructured information via specific digital devices, video cameras and satellites can allow the monitoring of the traffic flows of a certain commercial area or shop, and the efficacy of a given lay out or the efficiency of a certain inventory of final goods or services. A "synapses" bank could offer to its merchant clients not just a digital-based, fully convenient POS offering, but also the technological set up to monitor the footfall of customers into its shop, their average time and path across the different shelves and even their perceived level of "happiness" (derived by video of how they behave and by pictures taken at point of payment, analyzed by psychometric software).

Other information could then be taken from social webs (on the number of "likes" of that particular shop, or on qualitative comments on that shopping area), or from the satellite (in terms of traffic, illumination of the streets at night, weather conditions etc.). All these data and information could allow, via systems powered by machine learning/AI and run by the "synapses bank", to better analyze the customers' behavior of the merchant and how this can be affected by specific marketing decisions and then reflected in a better commercial and financial performance of the merchant (and with an higher satisfaction for the customer).

These produced "intelligence" would then be used by the bank ("the bank wearing Prada") to suggest different set ups for the shop, or a different pricing campaign or few temporary promotions (in case of a restaurant, where the food and related services is dependent on the moment of consumption and the level of occupancy should heavily drive the interplay between supply and demand in setting the price). Banks could therefore end up suggesting commercial and marketing strategies to small business and merchants, if not directly, by offering them a "behavioral" Tableau de board on their sales effectiveness and by managing digital loyalty programs that allow them an indirect flexibility in pricing, via cash backs or other sort of fidelity gifts.

5.7 Loyalty for the Public Good

By designing and mastering different kind of loyalty programs (such as the MFO—Merchant Funded Offers, where the gifts and loyalty schemes are specifically designed for any given merchant and for any targeted clients' cluster, and funded by the merchants themselves; or such as the CLO—Card Linked Offers, where the loyalty is registered and accrued with a use of a specific card and paid as "cash back" at the end of the month), banks, or any other financial intermediary doing this from the starting point of the payment system, could change the nature of their "intermediation", augmenting the valuable components of their interconnectivity and junction playing, among multiple stakeholders: from the global and local manufacturers (designers and assemblers), to the wholesale distributors, to the retail point of sales and many other.

In doing this, the "synapses bank" is not only helping merchants and customers in matching their supply and demand, leveraging on the data, information and intelligence that they can build playing smart, but it can also help in defining a more tailored merchant proposition for any given target cluster of clients: helping on the merchants' side in setting up the best lay out, reducing their inventory and utilization of time sensitive services, and cutting short on any generic, broad band advertising or middle man almost wasted expense.

The synapses bank could end up helping the customers in finding their personal best proposition and "value for money" (also by way of the fidelity program itself), as they receive very tailored offers on their next best product that take into consideration not just the history of their past purchases, but also the trend in their lifestyle and future consumption ambitions and dreams. Not to mention the manufacturers, that will know better and in advance what to design and how much to produce and deliver by when (and to whom).

Via these new strategies of interconnection and junction playing driven by the design and management of intelligent fidelity systems, new business solutions can be derived, helping to optimize the overall economic system, as global manufacturers know better, and in advance, what the merchants are going to sell more in the local markets and for the better enjoyment of the end customer, thus reducing waste in used materials, energy and processes and increasing the productivity (and predictability) of the different layers of capital put at work.

This last point is extremely critical, as superior data and information management is relevant, but is powerless without a derived superior intelligence to be put at work. And this needs to be acted upon and become serviceable enough to derive new, more sophisticated and efficient and effective ways to realize commercial interconnections and junctions and allow a "synapsized" competitive positioning to the bank.

However, the ultimate litmus test resides in proving how all of this is creating more "overall" value into the ecosystem, allowing the best allocation of resources in the global economic system and not just via the formation of prices—something the financial functions have traditionally supported—but also via the creation and sharing of further, more intangible, "integrated supply and value chain management intelligence", that leads to new ways of interactions among market participants and new equilibria where all can be better off.

Even starting from this simple example of the bank (or of any other financial intermediary) leveraging its role in the payments system to design and manage loyalty systems at almost no costs (being not more "bank funded"), it gets obvious how being able to sit in the middle of this new "interconnection/junction" game, potentially covering all kind of products and service categories can become very profitable in itself, as it lends to potential rebates (or value sharing, more justifiable than the traditional interest rate spreads), advertising and advisory fees, and potential cross selling of other financial products such as insurance protection on the goods and services being sold, not to mention the know how being created on the creditworthiness of each counterpart—end customers, small business merchants and global, large corporate manufacturers, as traditional historic data based statistical approaches are being substituted by more innovative, real time machine learning techniques—able to better foresee the future by not just looking at the rear-end view mirror.

It is also obvious how the current positioning of the financial institutions in payments can allow them some kind of time advantage that needs to be solidified by their trust and credibility at the eyes of the different counterparts—the last of the five competitive invariance of the "synapses" bank. This could actually end up dominating in the commercial ecosystem of local markets "without" extending loans and "without" taking any principal position on its balance sheet or in its physical distribution capabilities deployed in such a market.

How fitting then the parallel with Miranda as the "fashion synapses" between designers and manufacturers, merchants and customers and along the full value chain, till the last tragic casual corner and clearance bin. By rethinking its extended mission and its historical stronghold across the global payments system, the "synapses" bank can harness the power of digitalization at the local and global level, and radically alter its approach to balance sheet, lending and even to its distribution strategy. Following a very light business and operating model, it could end up developing new products and services, reinventing the way it relates (or interconnects) with its corporate and retail clients—helping the former to customize offers to the individual latter, thus optimizing production and distribution costs and the productivity of the wider economy.

Payments would therefore, in a way, play the Trojan horse opportunity to allow to new players a rapid disruption of many other fundamental functions—to almost become a fully-fledged retail and commercial bank. Take the example of Klarna, the Swedish Fintech leader that has recently obtained the full banking license[1] to try to become a Ryanair-type low-cost disruptor of the banking sector (in the words of Sebastian Siemiatkowski, Klarna's CEO), attacking established lenders across the continents. Value at more than USD 2 Bln, Klarna has started as alternative payments company, then offering short term loans, allowing customers to buy and receive goods before paying for them, taking on the credit risk for retailers.

It has then ended up capturing most of the market for online payments in the Nordics and Germany (with 60 Mln customers and Euro 13 Bln in transactions volumes processed in 2016) and it is now ready to offer bank cards and salary accounts and to expand into the US, being already profitable and targeting traditional banks that, in the view of Klarna's CEO, are offering poor customer service at inflated prices. Interestingly enough, Siemiatkowski has also stated that the banking

---

[1]Swedish fintech leader Klarna wins banking licence, Richard Milne, Financial Times, June 19th 2017.

license was required as it provides a level of confidence. It's about legitimacy and trust—and building specialized customer offerings that are global at the same time.

Following this kind of strategy, the "unbearable lightness" of the inverted pyramid business model could be greatly reduced and potentially become mostly redundant and a legacy of the past—if the synapses bank can move fast, in its new role of market enabler via payments system—before other operators (whether pure play, FinTech digital companies or other non-financial ones, such as telecoms), will do it first, with payments becoming the first "digital battleground" between challengers and challenged, and with the other functions to come. That is why payments mind now, even more than in the past: just follow the money to see why.

Transformation in Funding

Abstract

Digital transformation in banking is promising to turn upside down the function of funding, in both retail and wholesale worlds. It will also bring about social discontinuities and changes in the way we live, contribute to, benefit from, the current prevailing capitalistic system—with many people at risk to be left behind. On one side, new web-based funding initiatives are promising a new "cyber capitalism" that will be open to many people, if they just have few pennies and a good wi-fi connection. On the wholesale front, greater transparency and liquidity should allow greater and better opportunities of funding for small and medium businesses. And in retail banking, new solutions could be built around the core deposit-taking business of banks, with great opportunities to create new value but also impacts on unemployment and inequality.

Keywords

Crowd funding · Broker dealer · Artificial intelligence · Self-learning machines

6.1 People's Cyber Capitalism

The global financial system and wholesale, investment banks played a major role in the accelerated development and international dominance of the capitalistic model, after the second world war and in the last few decades specifically, often spurring and exacerbating phases of booms and busts in the developed or developing economies, or both. Capital raising has been, in fact, traditionally facilitated by specialized institutions, that grew to became global behemoth, with institutional coverage sometimes able to influence the economic policies of sovereign Countries, if not their economic cycles.

As major capital raising for multinationals or for large, indivisible infrastructure projects have become the preserve of an handful of global investment banks, their power broking relevance and critical support to this or that economy (from the same Country to its major corporates and commercial banks) has grown so rapidly to qualify most of them as systemically important for the global economy—and "too big to fail" at the eyes of the market participants, at least until Lehman just did so, on October 15th of 2008.

These wholesale, investment banks, whose coverage power was and is still born out of very strong personal relationships with senior officers at governmental institutions, corporates and banks, have always been dominated by elites, working for further elites, either political, industrial or financial—in a very secluded way from the common man and the "remaining 99%", as the anti-Wall Street movement that developed after the great crisis came to be known.

In this traditional model, large amounts of capital were made rapidly available, but for very few, as economies of scale and scope, and of brand building, were required to pool funds internationally, in a matter of few weeks. It was in a way a capitalistic model managed by a few, and for a few people, able to tap into the pockets of everybody through an origination channel that was connecting retail, commercial banks, insurance companies, asset and money managers and even governments with the wholesale "originate to distribute" operators—taking large amount of risks themselves, but usually for a fraction of time and able to flip the "hot potato" quickly and back to the hands of more patient (or stupid) holders of last resort.

This traditional model of capital raising is fulfilling a fundamental function of the global financial system, as scale and scope (the ability to reach many pockets around the globe to fund a big company or an indivisible project somewhere else) do matter. But it is also increasing further the inherent instability of the banking system, introducing new "unbearable lightnesses" derived, as we have seen, by the increased velocity (via securitizations and their "originate to trade" business models) and by the principal investment risks they are in any case taking: from their proprietary trading activity in liquid financial instruments, or in illiquid assets such as real estate or NPL, or commodities (often building synthetic positions via futures and options contracts, but also, in some cases, assuming long positions in the physical assets themselves, stored in some remote warehouse in the countryside, far away from Wall Street in New York and the City in London).

This traditional model poses also a number of challenges, which are constraining the ability of the system to fulfil an optimal allocation of the scarce capital at risk that can be put at work in the global economy. Access to capital is, as said, limited to elite counterparts that are large, global, with a brand recognition and a track record to allow them to tap into diverse, more or less deep and liquid, equity capital markets.

6.1 People's Cyber Capitalism

The capital raising process is then usually lengthy and subject to a number of regulatory constraints, risks of manipulation and still very much relationship driven, e.g. far from being fully transparent. Also, the tailoring of the capital raising proposition can be limited, as the segmentation of the best holder of the equity piece of any single company and of its related risk/return profile can go up to a point. And finally, the power implicit in the advisory/intermediation role poses questions regarding the conflict of interests that the all-mighty investment banks can be facing, given their continuous search of cross selling opportunities and their double role as public and private, e.g. as principal investors and as independent advisor/intermediary in the financial markets (no matter how high is the internal "Chinese wall" built, somebody of the bank has to sit on its top).

As for the lending business, this traditional approach looks likely to be disrupted by the increased connectivity, the digital capabilities and artificial intelligence available on on-line, independent (non-bank) platforms able to act to democratize markets and allow, in principle, to fulfil a people's capitalism—where everybody can have access to some equity capital, provided their risk/return profile is of some appeal; and where everybody can invest into different opportunities, no matter what their available money is—even pursuing alternative investment opportunities in illiquid ventures like start-ups, or second/third funding stage companies.

In a people's capitalistic model, the crowd—the remaining 99%—are getting more opportunities, as individuals are getting more empowered—on the sources and on the uses side, ideally spurring a better return on investment and more opportunities to launch entrepreneurial initiatives and innovation in the economy. As these opportunities develop, power is then taken away from the business model of global investment banks, long in senior coverage, balance sheet, "smart" intermediation and… conflicts of interests.

Alternative digital platforms, similarly to what lending platforms could do, provide an "investment of one" potential value proposition, connecting the specific individual, as small capitalist, to tailored entrepreneurial opportunities of other individuals, advising and facilitating the equity underwriting using, again, all available structured and unstructured data and information, applied analytics/machine learning techniques and new ways of interconnecting people—with better profiling, more extensive and democratised taping of funds/uses opportunities and potential solutions that are making the overall economic system better off, on the basis of a common trust that needs to be even stronger than the one required to develop the traditional lending business.

Let's take the example of crowd funding platforms that offer to "would be customers" the opportunity to finance and buy something, with small amounts, usually equivalent to the market price of the end product being produced in a novel way, plus additional venture capital like returns. By adding these different dimensions of people as customers and shareholders, they allow their resulting crowd to vet a product even before starting its production. If not enough people (e.g. customers) are committing, no potential shareholder is actually called to finally commit capital. Vice versa, in the worst case, people as customers are getting the product they wish being realized at a fair market price, with no additional returns as small venture capitalists.

This interconnection is different from the mere intermediation happening when equity sales professionals start calling professional investors that are putting others' money on products they could not like or understand at all. The intelligence being created by analysing the social "noise" on the web regarding a specific product launched by a company is in fact different from the equity research report written by a financial analyst reading structured, financial data, mostly trying to extrapolate from their past what could be their behaviour in the future, as driven by the commercial acceptance of the widget they don't wish to own.

And the overall impact on the ecosystem is also rather different, as everybody can turn out to be, easily and just with the tip of a mouse, a (small) venture capitalist or an ("in fieri") entrepreneur.

A new kind of trust is then built, on the basis of greater transparency, velocity, access to data and information, valuable and less obvious intelligence continuously updated and coming from the social (and not just financial) realm... and mostly conflict of interest-free, as the platform works for the crowd on both sides of the capital raising equation. And it is neither trying to cross sell anything else to the would be companies or investors, nor is taking any direct or indirect principal interest in the primary and secondary equity markets they are just about to disrupt—in a cyber capitalistic world that could potentially do without investment bankers.

6.2 Artificial Investing and Real Life

In a digitally transformed capital raising process, alternative platforms, run by new, non-bank players, could act as marketplaces themselves, doing without both bankers and regulated stock-markets. They could act across the full life cycle of a company, acting as an incubator of seed-stage companies, for which a peer-base funding approach, were peers are potentially both shareholders and end clients, works particularly well, as they enrich the screening process based on the view of the end customer, whilst reducing the financial risk per se (they will get a poor end-product for consumption, in the worst case).

Alternative equity platforms can also work well to provide funding to lower return investments—for cohorts were the prevailing investment rational has motives that go beyond mere financial return (e.g. pursuing the development of communities linked to these cohorts, or other ethical or ecological considerations), and where the community bonding among these angel investors is potentially a part of the investment value proposition.

And can also work well where alternative, creative ways of funding need to be considered, with a "club-deal" like approach, given the specific issues the recipient companies or indivisible projects need to overcome and resolve—as an example, well known larger consumer companies could engage and raise capital from their customer base. In this case, the synapses approach would add value by creating new ways of interconnecting stakeholders (e.g. providing future discounts as consumers to new shareholders, or free warrants linked to how much you spend—leveraging the commercial marketing and customer loyalty associated to strong brands).

Whatever the focus, these alternative, on-line marketplaces for equity capital can more efficiently and effectively facilitate the "price discovery process" in real time, and on the basis of machine learning/AI applications, as most regulated stock-markets already do, but augmenting the value of the price discovery because they express the wisdom of the people, and not just of few financial analysts, and this wisdom is informed by the intelligence derived by the analysis of all kind of data, quantitative and qualitative, financial and non-financial or "social". Price discovery gets therefore more social and less "financial".

The disruption, that we have seen starting from the capital raising process, can then extend to the larger world of investment management, as individual investors (interpreting the "capitalism for everybody" principle) gain direct visibility and self-control (albeit guided and supported by independent advisory) over investment target selections and allocations—without paying hefty commissions to low value adding middle men, and getting the opportunity to a more direct exposure to the risk/reward profile of the companies they choose.

The support of "AI investing" tools gets an even more profound meaning in the money management function of the global financial system, as data and information are increasingly getting available and new, different intelligence is produced and potentially made available almost for free to everybody (most of the current equity research is also kind of free, but mostly based on financials and produced by elite analysts working for elite institutional investors—professional, very large and with deep pockets, but no keen interest in becoming client of what they buy: e.g. buying the food company but even considering to ever eat the fries made by it).

The exploitation of unstructured, social and extended data sets, and of other unobvious information, e.g. the level of happiness of consumers, after they buy a new key product of a given company, as analyzed by the psychometric analysis of their implicit and explicit behavior, is promising to also increase the bar of the accuracy of any given investment management analysis, whether done top down (from a strategic allocation perspective) or bottom up (from a stock picking perspective, with regard to both asset selection and timing). And all kind of machine learning/AI intelligence, producing alpha algorithms not new to the hedge funds industry could also become available to the crowd, democratizing the hedged "alpha" opportunities—and automatically arbitraging them away, as no easy trade is left then available for financial elites.

Apart from the "alpha" component, the extended, social intelligence—then incorporated in the crowd's wisdom, is also promising to deliver faster and cheaper approaches to asset allocation and picking, easier ways to get to an increased set of opportunities and diversification and better risk management and monitoring—as it can also create diverse interconnections, profiling and ways of linking providers of funds and uses, but also potentially suppliers of insurance coverage on certain tail risks, and customers that are turning into shareholders and vice versa—to ensure a better connection between the financial and the real economy, and the behavior of consumers—putting the investment money where the commercial wish is.

It all then translates into the most fundamental objective played by this function at global level, e.g. ensuring the best and optimal allocation of equity capital across sectors, geographies, companies and down to the level of any single new product/service or specific feature attached to them—where the end solution of "investment of one" turns then into an ideal "production—consumption of one".

In a way, it could all help in reconnecting the artificial intelligence driven investment process, with the real life way of doing things, where emotions are choices and a strategy to cope with life, and where every consumer is voting every day with his feet, in every single act she/he is doing as an aspirational reflection of her/his lifestyle. Digital becomes emotional, and the best way to read the customer's state of mind.

As they do this, these alternative digital platforms for capital raising will keep adding further competitive pressure on wholesale, investment banks and even on the more traditional private equity and venture capital counterparts, whilst offering an increased number of alternatives in the asset and wealth management side—extending the FinTech battlefield to the money management industry.

6.3 Dealing Digital for Digital Dealing

Alternative platforms to raise equity over the web are however just part of the transformation story that could significantly change funding, that very fundamental function of the global financial system that is also comprising debt—over short to long term maturities and raised through wholesale markets and the international capital markets and also funded—mostly via deposits—by retail and commercial banks.

Debit is, at the end of the day, what really fuels the many booms and busts of the economic cycle, and contribute in a critical way to the maximization of its sustainable growth rate. Without debt, investment resources would be halved, and even consumption patterns would be constrained by our ability to closely match what we want to buy now with what we can immediately afford (usually we need a lot when, at younger age, we don't have much money to spend, and we have no time, when we have money, and vice versa).

Let's start to consider in this paragraph the first "wholesale" part of debt origination and trading as done in the international capital markets by investment banks, with the critical involvement of mostly long only professional investors (in a following paragraph we will assess instead the "retail" component and the impact on the overall retail/commercial banking brought about by artificial intelligence).

Bond issuance, for a start, is still mostly driven by "high touch" investment bankers, backed by teams of financial analysts, where main technological innovation can still be traced back to the introduction of excel. Not much has changed in the analysis of mostly financial, structured data, and in the production of the issuers' business plans. Even credit rating models used to grade the creditworthiness of the bonds are relying on traditional financial analysis, of structured data and applying traditional statistical regression analysis.

We could maybe have expected the trading side of the value chain, for the well-functioning of secondary bond markets, to be much more sophisticated and "electronified"—as much as equities already are, or even more, given the larger volumes and the scope for addressing the investment needs of international investors that—as a rule of thumbs, tend to follow a 60–40 to 80–20 allocation of bonds versus shares. Far from that, corporate bond markets appear still astonishingly archaic,[1] with even basic data that are proving hard to come by.

Whilst shares and derivatives are now mostly traded electronically—using digital applications and opening up to "social crowd" initiatives, and becoming more and more the preserve of fully automated and robotized management approaches, that use machine learning/AI and self-adjusting algorithms to select and execute trading strategies, corporate bonds are still pretty much "high touch" and very manual and "analogic". As of today, more than 80% of trading in US corporate bonds takes place with a dealer, usually over the phone—e.g. on analogic[2] based connectivity, with obvious consequences on the transparency and efficiency of the market.

Digital innovation is now starting to challenge the overall value chain. On the origination and primary issuance side, allowing for more sophisticated applied analytics, that can leverage as much structured data as unstructured ones (including "behavioral" and "social" information on the issuer, on its core business and key product/service offerings and any other data and information that could be helpful in deriving a better business plan to prove the serviceability of that debt, or to assign a given credit rating—based not just on hard to quickly update historical information, but also on continuously refreshed, real time further data points).

But it is on the trading phase, the most traditional core business of "broker—dealer" bond houses, that new, long overdue, disruptions are starting to emerge and potentially alter the structure of bond markets. Tradeweb is, for example, now offering "all to all" trading in European corporate bonds—and not on analogic lines. Any participant to the market venue can trade with any other, as it has already been done for Government bonds (60% of European ones are now traded electronically), but not yet for corporate (just 25% of global trading volume for investment-grade and 13% for high yield ones). These corporate bonds in fact tend to vary extensively in maturity, typology of issuer and in the relative juniority/seniority vis a vis the issuer's hierarchy of other issued debts—in a word, because of these many peculiarities, they have resisted liquidity and frequency (they tend to trade over an average of five times per year) and hence transparency and efficiency.

This has favored a more traditional way of matching buyers and sellers, operated by traditional brokers that also act as dealers, e.g. taking on risks, as they commit to always name a price and buy the bond, holding it in their inventory until a buyer

---
[1]The Economist, Broken dealers, April 21, 2017.
[2]The Economist, Click to trade, April 21, 2017.

emerges—this in turn has led to a competitive position where dominant broker dealers have been able to capture significant value, whilst limited transparency and efficiency has been further added to the market, and not even ensuring sufficient inventory capabilities when corporate bond markets are on a "risk off" position (as they just name prices that are too low for a seller to accept).

With digitization, and the development of stable, safe and fast interconnecting platforms, even the broker dealers competitive positioning in corporate bonds is going to be challenged, as all-to-all trading venues can change bond market dynamics fundamentally and in favor of users (the buyers and sellers), taking out profits from the low value added intermediaries (the broken broker dealers).

6.4 Everybody Is a Dealer Now

For example, MarketAxess as can be seen in Fig. 6.1, pioneered in 2012, allows now to any user of a network to trade with another directly—in direct competition with traditional broker dealers. Its business model now makes it possible for asset managers to move from being price takers (having to accept quotes from dealers or just accept not to trade) towards being price makers, proposing their own prices to anybody active on the platform—with the platform just offering information and infrastructure services (but not taking on any more risk, thus also avoiding any potential conflict of interest).

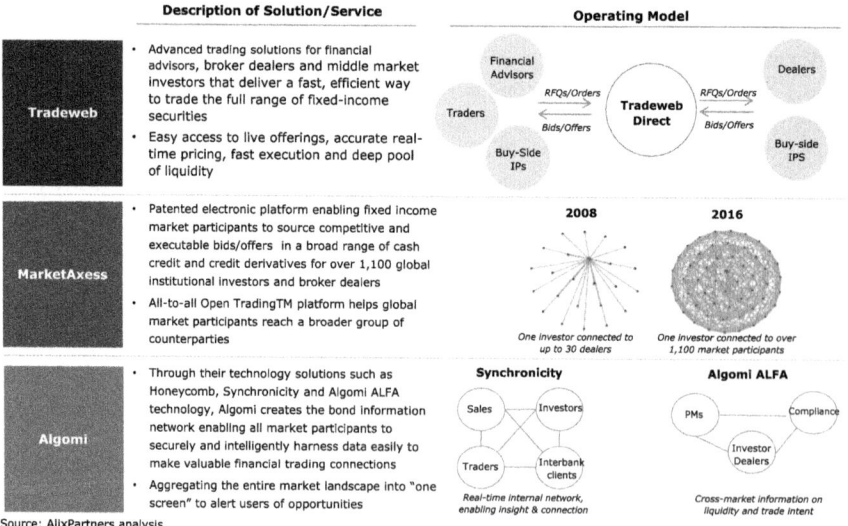

Fig. 6.1 Tradeweb, MarketAxess and Algomi: advanced trading and data network solutions in broker-dealer corporate bond market

6.4 Everybody Is a Dealer Now

In this scenario, dealers are dead or, actually, everybody can become a dealer now, as it can quote a bid or ask price on all the bonds that are traded in the system —hence increasing liquidity, frequency, transparency and the overall efficiency in the system—with previous oligopolistic rents disappearing and with funding costs for corporates that should decrease through time (because of the lower illiquidity discount).

True, this was maybe possible even in the analogic era, with few phone calls among multiple counterparts and, it may be argued, the issue of not finding any willing buyer at a time of market swings (when the risk is "off") still looms large. And finally, how to make sure, given the very fragmented state of the products being traded, that the system is always going to find a match? Adding many-to-many counterparts helps, but also increases the level of complexity in match making.

Algomi, a bond market data firm is actually addressing at least part of this "match making" issue, as it seeks to reduce the time lapse, by matching buyers and sellers across time—keeping track of enquiries for each specific bond, and suggesting similar ones if not available, and with no inventory held, as business model is purely reliant on facilitating match making—on the basis of superior data management and derived intelligence.

Again, considering our five pillars "synapses" model provided below in Fig. 6.1, it is easy to understand how this framework applies to these and to other disrupting innovators to come in the broker dealer world.

Apart from accumulating multiple data and information, and including unstructured ones on the hubris of the market and on the behavioral "risk on—risk off" aversion of buyers and sellers, these new challengers use extensive applied analytics to understand and predict the trend in the market and facilitate the best "match making" across multiple criteria—thus playing a much more effective and efficient interconnection game, lowering the spreads involved in the transactions and their time to close, as they get paid on the basis of volumes and not of risk taking, and they can potentially create few global venues that are able of pooling a much larger number of counterparts together, then squeezing margins out of thousands of broker dealers.

Also, the better, faster, cheaper match making results in a greater wealth creation for the ecosystem and—as a result of the greater liquidity, transparency and efficiency and efficacy created—funding costs are also lowered, as volatility is lowered as well and therefore the risk borne by the ultimate buyers and holders of these bonds: more intelligence is known on the market trends and on the state of the creditworthiness of the bonds' issuers (as part of the value added services these corporate bond trading venues are progressively offering to participants), hence a lower cost of risk is born and priced.

Similarly to the PSD2 in payments, a new regulation is also helping this disruption in the broker dealer market. In fact, from January 2018, the MIFID 2 (a wide-ranging European financial market regulation) will require participants to report prices and volumes of all completed transactions, adding further accessible data to the synapsezation game to come. Transparency will weaken dealers' market power and push more trading onto electronic platforms and all-to-all trading venues. And their operating model will then be revolutionized by automation and robotization—from repeat trades to algorithmic activated ones.

It is then easy to understand how a further revolution could come about if similar principles were applied to the world of the collaterals of such bonds, or loans that, via portfolio securitization, could also start to be traded in a many-to-many fashion as an extension to the synapses business model we just described—of course, as long as the fifth pillar (the trust in the digital platform) is also secured, and credibility is built via repeat, successful execution and delivery. Matching the name and reputation that was once of the best broker dealers.

6.5 Artificial Retail, Banking on Intelligence

Leaving aside the wholesale component, funding in banking—and specifically in Europe, it's done mainly by banks that get financed through the deposit taking activity—a core business for retail banking, as much as lending is. Funding through deposit taking, we have just seen, is also promising significant changes, and so it is for the overall retail banking business, because of the greater data and information and of the more powerful applied analytics systems available, to produce intelligence and help transform a business that, notwithstanding the many calls for "revolution" (when it started offering on-line trading and accounts, or when it promised a total convenience based on an omni-channel distribution strategy), it has so far not really changed a lot. It looks now that change could get "real", as retail banking gets "artificial", adopting more and more machine learning/AI applications, not just to do things better and faster, but also in a cheaper way.

For a start, it is worth to consider at this point a more extensive definition of "artificial intelligence" (AI) as cognitive, computer based solutions applicable to banking, and built on three key principles. As a first, AI should have natural language processing capabilities—e.g. possessing an ability to understand human language, to then potentially be able to produce or modify a meaningful text, or audio signal (i.e. voice recognition), or text by advanced search. Already, such kind of applications is available even on smartphones.

Secondly, AI should have machine learning capabilities to learn from situations without prior programming and without requiring too many principles and updates. Machine learning has in fact the unique ability to aggregate multiple sources of data and to integrate them all the time, so to have a continuous dialogue and (self) learning process that truly starts from the voice of the customer. Thirdly, AI should be able to generate meaningful hypothesis, with powerful predictive capabilities—validated by evidence through back testing and continuous present and future testing, as new information come available. Finally, best answers should then be able to show, open box like, their main root causes. As shown in the following Figure, AI computing really develops by mimicking the working of neural networks

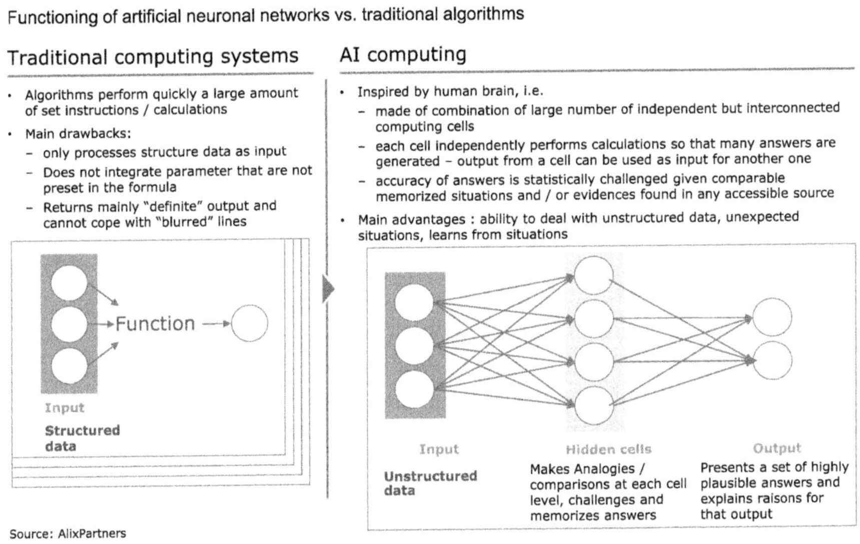
Functioning of artificial neuronal networks vs. traditional algorithms
Traditional computing systems
• Algorithms perform quickly a large amount of set instructions / calculations
• Main drawbacks:
– only processes structure data as input
– Does not integrate parameter that are not preset in the formula
– Returns mainly "definite" output and cannot cope with "blurred" lines
Function
Input
Structured data
AI computing
• Inspired by human brain, i.e.
– made of combination of large number of independent but interconnected computing cells
– each cell independently performs calculations so that many answers are generated – output from a cell can be used as input for another one
– accuracy of answers is statistically challenged given comparable memorized situations and / or evidences found in any accessible source
• Main advantages : ability to deal with unstructured data, unexpected situations, learns from situations
Input
Unstructured data
Hidden cells
Makes Analogies / comparisons at each cell level, challenges and memorizes answers
Output
Presents a set of highly plausible answers and explains raisons for that output
Source: AlixPartners

Fig. 6.2 From traditional computing to machine learning/AI

and the synapses of the human brain, and specifically its ability to learn dynamically through reconciliation of information (Fig. 6.2).

In retail banking, this machine learning/AI capabilities can be exploited in a number of ways, with potential use cases encompassing the main value chains of key products and services. As an overview, a number of applications are already in use in distribution and back-middle office management in retail banking. In branch network distribution, AI applications are already working as processing assistants, doing email management and specific tasks that are either routine or more sophisticated. They also work as commercial assistant, scheduling activities and offering support (preparing brief ex ante presentations and ex post briefings), and as "virtual expert" available for support via PC or audio (e.g. in supplying scripts to the personal financial advisors on asset allocation strategies to discuss with clients). In online banking, they can also offer the execution of basic information and (in few years) they will be able to answer directly to simple questions of customers.

On the back-middle office side, these AI systems can support a lot of the compliance and audit processes, with an ability to spot potential issues (and quickly discharge the inevitable many "false positives") with an efficacy that is already surpassing the ability of best trained employees. They can also support and therefore streamline most of the credit approval and underwriting processes, and (as for the front office activities) offer online virtual expert support to employees—on almost any topic, from legal to IT, with further efficiencies to be gained by the parallel utilization of AI and other "robotization" systems, that could allow one day to make away of most of the people working on the non-revenues producing activities of the bank.

With most of the talk of the digitization happening on the online channels, the opportunity for the retail banking business could thus end up coming from the "traditional" branch network and back-middle office activities. Leveraging the first two of the "five pillars" synapses framework introduced, it's easy to see how most of the current employees of the global banking sector could be made redundant, but also how the remaining ones could be made much more valuable, focusing more on the advisory and relationships making value added activities. In a way augmenting the meaning of their work along with their efficacy/efficiency.

The issue with machine learning/AI could thus become its heavy impact on the "social engineering" side of banking—with a fraction of people employed in the future by the sector and a greater and greater divergence between the highly value, more creative, advisory based, personal-touch kind of jobs and the few remaining. That would be an issue for the science of politics to address anyway, as economics and business management is all about creating more and better sustainable wealth for the overall ecosystem, whilst its redistribution (via the tax system and other "social buffers") belongs to the realm of a democratic political discussion.

The real opportunity for machine learning/AI in retail banking comes anyway from the deployment of the third and fourth pillars of the "synapsezation" model, e.g. leveraging the new intelligence available not just to do things better, faster and cheaper, but also, and more importantly, to do things differently, moving away from the traditional intermediation retail banking model and designing and implementing new solutions, with specific use cases that are making unique, incremental contributions to the value originated in the system. If machine learning/AI will end up solving real problems, then real value will be delivered and potentially captured by the "synapses" retail bank—making "artificial" looking a less contentious, if not positive term.

Trust, our fifth pillar of the "synapses bank" model will also be relevant, for the full exploitation of machine learning/AI, but in a different way.[3] Trust, in this case, will need to develop starting from the senior management of the bank: they will need to start "believing" in the machine learning applications themselves. Technically a subset of artificial intelligence (AI), machine learning systems excel at finding patterns and at making predictions—and despite the fashion and maybe hype now surrounding the topic, real applications are still minimal, and managed with skepticism by middle managers (not surprisingly, according to the principle "turkeys are not looking forward to Christmas") and top managers alike (mostly "non-native digital").

If trust is not developed and warranted by strong cases and related back testing, incumbents are potentially going to miss maybe one of the most significant of the shake ups to the modern world of finance. Other, more innovative FinTech and nimbler and faster challengers, have started applying the technique to everything from fraud protection to audit, and from trading strategies to credit work out. Machine learning is actually getting a first in-road on much utilized and cost-heavy tasks such as compliance, audit, legal and risk management—examples would

---

[3]Unshackled algorithms, The Economist, 26 June 2017.

include Intelligent Voice, a company selling machine learning driven speech and transcription applications to help investment banks in monitoring traders' phone calls for signs of wrongdoing, such as insider trading or collusion (as for the LIBOR or FX "ring" cases). Other specialists like Xcelerit or Kinetica offer banks and investment firms near real-time tracking of their risk resources, allowing them to monitor their capital requirements in real time, and adapt the reactionary, contingency plans accordingly.

But it is in the retail space that machine learning tools are now potentially offering more promising applications. From start-up digital companies like Feedzai (for payments) or Shift Technology (for insurance), to behemoth such as IBM, they are now all offering services to spot unusual patterns in transactions—Monzo, a banking start up on payments, has stated to have been able to reduce the fraud rate on its pre-paid cards down from 0.85% to less than 0.1%, in just 6 months.

Natural language processing—powered by machine learning bases unleashed on the transcript text, are also starting to make an impact on the back office of banks and of their branch network and, as already commented, other applications are also being applied to support decision making on on-line and off-line credit applications. Wonga has for example been applying this to the pay-lending business and on-line. Whilst other players like Zest Finance has rolled out a machine learning underwriting tool to help lenders in making credit decisions, even at the point of sale and for people with little structured information available as well. Psychometric analysis, including applications on facial recognition and analysis can also help to understand when an applicant is lying: studying is tone of voice, perspiration, breath and eyes flickering.

It is therefore natural to ponder whether the branch strategies of banks will be further revolutionized, not as much by the further disappearance of branches attracting deposit holders (this is already a well-known trend, but with several customers still looking for a physical place to stop and buy and recognize as "concrete" and "real" and made of bricks and mortars), but by the disappearance of tellers within those branches. Important implications seem therefore in waiting even for customer management and relationship building—albeit new machines learning on how to enjoy wine and dine appear still a bit in the waiting.

6.6 Understanding Customers' Customers

Retail banking is not, obviously, just about individuals and families, as it tends to comprise small businesses—mostly merchants (in a more extended definition, a typical retail/commercial bank will also cover small medium enterprises). For this kind of counterparts, several new applications coming from digital can be offered to them by a synapses bank that is regarding them not just as clients, but also as a potential business partners, with end customers that can be better managed, to ensure their greater satisfaction, and a greater economic benefit for the suppliers (the merchants and the bank).

Managing customers on-line in a more interactive, data richer ways, leveraging all kind of machine learning/AI techniques to get a better understanding of their current behavior and to build predictive capabilities on their future ones is already a well-established art, if not fully fledged science, mastered by the likes of Amazon, Google and Facebook. Building a similar intelligence on the off-line funneling of customers in the bricks and mortar world is however a less established practice: there is no real-time detection of how customers walks by the street, decide to enter and spend time and walk across the shop, staring at showcases and express their willingness to buy, happiness at point of sale and an attitude to come back as they walk out to the street.

A new range of analytical solutions are now being developed for the "bricks and mortar" component of the retailing industry, with established, traditional merchants facing the increased threat of the likes of Amazon, now also building aggressively physical shops, to complement their already dominant presence on-line. As small business merchants cannot have the investment capacity and sophistication required to build similar real time tracking approaches, it comes as an opportunity to the synapses bank to offer such capabilities as a service, complementing its traditional offerings on payments, lending and deposit taking—in a consistent way vis a vis the five main pillars (or criteria to match) of the synapses model we have described.

The solution on offer could be to build capabilities to track in real time the off-line customer flow, leveraging external unstructured sources of data and information (satellites monitoring traffic and parking slots in the area, work in progress and even weather, and social websites "like" on the specific shopping area, typology of shop and main merchandise on offer). But also other IoT applications coming to fruition by leveraging digital devices able to track the smartphones of the customers (walking outside and in the shopping, as first time or recurring clients) or to analyze their facial expression as they walk by a given showcase or set of products, or pay at the point of sales—banks can then also easily match all these customers' behavioral data with the transactions data and with the cash flow generated by the shop at close of business and per week or month.

From a merchant standpoint, such a commercial dashboard and its related applied analytics on their customers' behavior would offer them the opportunity to try and test different marketing strategies almost daily. A change in color or style in the street facing window could increase conversion rates of people walking by (as they decide to stop and stare for a certain—tracked—number of seconds in front of it, and eventually walking into the shop). A new lay out of corner points, or products' selection inside the shop or even a different color for the refurbishment of the point of sale could instead increase the funneling of people asking to try something, or their footsteps and time spent with pleasure into the shop (excluding then the queue time, also being monitored, but to optimize logistics and staffing coverage through the week).

In short, they would get access to a real-time off-line analytical tool, to understand the commercial and financial performance of the store in a mark to market way, with the possibility of testing new management and marketing approaches and immediately assess the impact on profitability—understanding the whole conversion funnel—from the customers walking along-side the storefront to the customers that close a purchase inside the store.[4] Over a longer period, merchants would also get automated insights, maybe in the form of short, simple sentences—received by email or as voice messages and generated by machine learning/AI applications supplied by the bank, on how to run best their shops, so to increase commercial and financial performance, hence optimizing their creditworthiness as well.

The retail bank, as partner of the merchants, would benefit in several ways, if it were able to build and deliver such digital capabilities, in an economic way and before other FinTech or sales support companies will do it, making a serious inroad in their previously protected relationship. As a first, as it would be the case for any other services of such a solution, it could access and build a new revenue stream—as merchants will start paying monthly fees for the pay per use/pay per time service received—a kind of Bloomberg for merchants.

Further, they could develop cross and up-selling opportunities based on their new understanding of the customers' customer behavior and of course of the merchants themselves. Finally, they could also get a deeper and more dynamic, timed, future-ready understanding of the credit scoring of the merchants, developing new ratings that would be less reliant on opaque, outdated financial statements, and more on holistic information and forward looking intelligence—continuously mining new data as they come available.

A synapses bank offering such a solution as a service, providing then advice on better financial and commercial management, and greater and cheaper access to funding, would right-click on advanced data and information management and on applied analytics based on machine learning/AI. And it would position itself for a new, more extended intermediation game, interconnecting merchants with end customers, and potentially with manufacturers and other retailers, as more efficient and effective paths to consumptions for cohorts of customers can be built, then leading to a more tailored optimization of the overall supply chain. It can all bring greater value for the ecosystem. More satisfied customers, more profitable merchants and manufacturers, and wholesale distributors, and with less waste of scarce resources and pollution in the ecosystem.

Also, as banks walk away from their traditional branch model, they can now potentially explore new forms of "merchants banking", opening small corner point on the merchants' shops premises, to offer new products and some very simple technical support for their on-line platform—from brochures to i-Pad available to do transactions on line, maybe with the help of a consultant for the IT-averse people. The banks, using the same tools built for the merchants, would then know, in real time, how end customers would react and feel about their products and services and marketing mix, even without entering a branch and without consulting a teller (see Fig. 6.3, on how banks can better leverage existing information and collect new unstructured data).

---

[4]White paper in collaboration with Paolo Dotta, Altar Technologies (Altar.io), 2017.

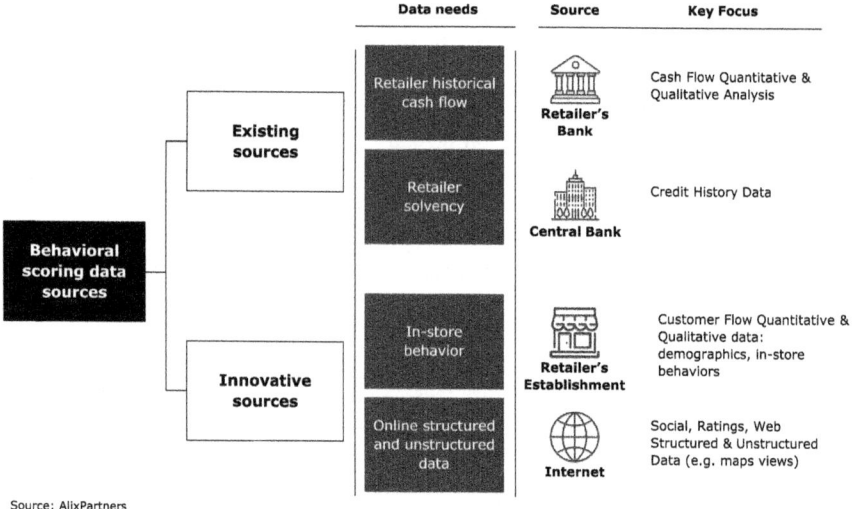

Fig. 6.3 Banks can better leverage existing information and collect new sources of unstructured, proprietary data

An obvious question could then be "why should a bank offer these services to merchants and not, say, an Amazon or a Salesforce?" Of course, the most simple and maybe reliable answer could be: they could do it, as well, and maybe better, and possibly they are already working on it, to displace banks from this opportunity and further away from their customers (once there, Amazon and Salesforce could also start selling loans and payments services, as we will later comment). Still, banks have a chance to play, driven by relationship and trust. Trust, is indeed one more reason to support the choice of the synapses bank over an Amazon (that could be perceived as a competitor) or a Salesforce (too global and for large corporates, with no history of relationship), with the payments, deposit and lending relationships working as a glue, at least in the short run.

6.7 Shifting Channels

Whether branches will still be run by human beings or robot employees, it is a safe bet to assume that the overall distribution strategy of "synapses banks" and channels preferences of customers will keep shifting—following the shifts in generational readiness to the adoption of new technologies, always-connected lifestyles and even new financial products and services (e.g. with the decrease in mortgages expected on the side of the "generation rent", always looking to rent in an increasingly socially and geographically mobile society).

6.7 Shifting Channels

Shifts in channels' preferences are not new in banking, and a few times there have been premature talks on the "death of the branches and middlemen" and on the triumph of on-line banking. With all the hype that surrounded the development of the New Economy and the following DotCom bubble and subsequent burst and economic crash in the early years of 2000, still a number of macro trends have shown to have survived the worst of the cycle, creating few on-line banking champions and many others in retailing, entertainment and technology—with enough cash to spare to buy the entire banking system in Europe and change.

As of today, there is no global champion in on-line banking that has been able to establish market shares worth noticing—also because of the many constraints posed by global and domestic regulations. Still, other on-line companies like Apple, Amazon, Facebook or Google and Alibaba have flourished, with market caps approaching the trillion mark: they could buy the entire global financial system, if regulators would allow it. Would this time around then be the right one for the creation of the Google or Alibaba of the banking on-line?

In the last few years, the more recent wave of innovation in digitization have manifested in a number of distribution strategies emerging across primary account providers. Direct banks (a kind of fad name in itself, as it was first used in the '90s for "telephone banking", analogic banks) have further evolved into "virtual" banks, relying heavily on online and mobile (via smartphone) banking. Initially established as subsidiaries of traditional banks, targeting price sensitive customer segments, have now evolved into pure players, like Simple (a brief overview provided in Fig. 6.4), mBank or Zuno—and offering new and compelling value propositions that go beyond lower costs and higher convenience.

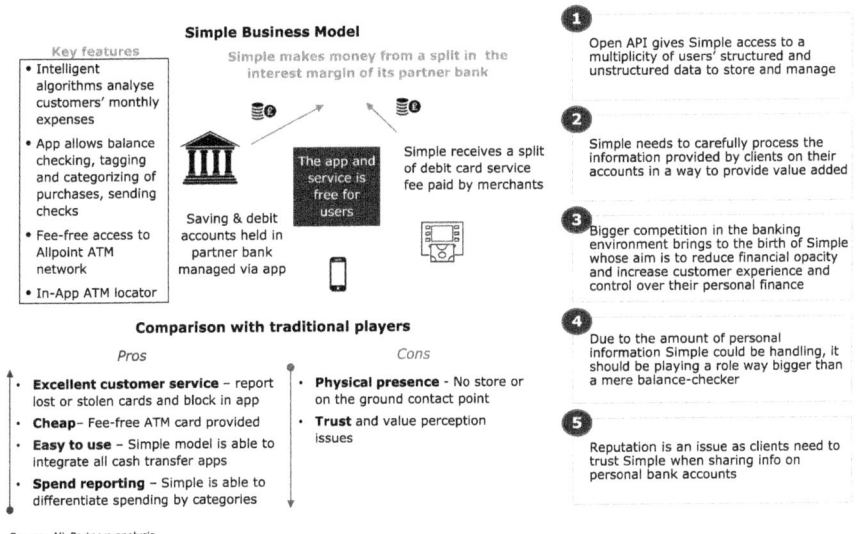

Fig. 6.4 Simple reduces complexity through its online-only services and advanced budgeting and saving tools

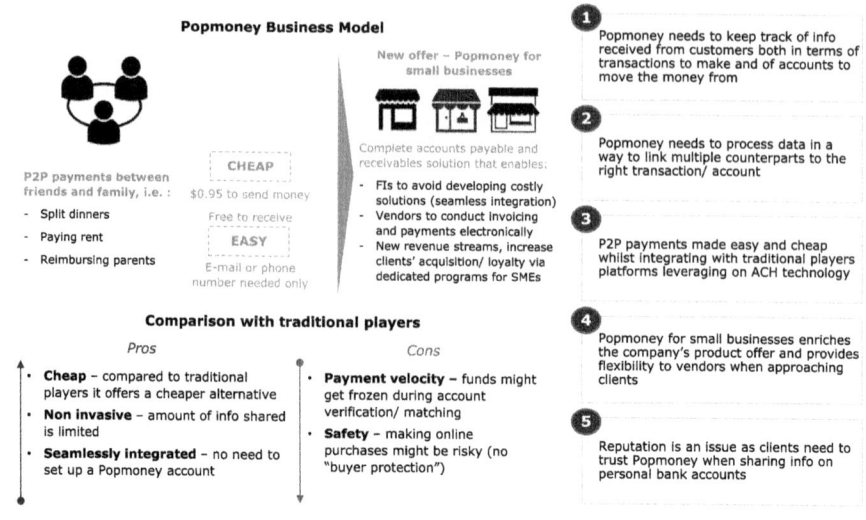

Fig. 6.5 Popmoney allows people to send/receive money held in several bank accounts at low cost/fore free

More importantly, in the last few years, mobile banking only operators like Popmoney (as summarized in Fig. 6.5), Mitek and USAA have emerged, following the rapid adoption of smart phones, more and more powerful, with larger video and simpler to use even on the move. Free of legacy systems, these non-traditional players are emerging to offer mobile apps that makes for effortless financial transactions, sometimes soon even activated just by voice recognition and security —for P2P money transfer, payments of bills or simple money management.

Finally, as consequence of the PSD2 and open data regulation and movement already discussed, other players—both traditional and non-traditional, from Credit Agricole to Yodlee, have developed "banking-as platform" initiatives, aimed at standardizing API across financial institutions and allowing third party developers to easily build and integrate customer-facing enhancements to the legacy driven core offerings—thus limiting or avoiding altogether the constraints to richer and faster innovation introduced by legacy IT systems.

Whilst it is unclear which one of these business models, or some hybrid or a new one, will prevail in the future, the adoption of a "synapses" approach seems to underpin the strategies of the potential winners, as they seek to follow and meet the continuously changing needs of customers—more and more interested in a "full virtual experience" (including, one day, augmented, virtual reality), tailored to specific communities and for the individual (addressing the evolving behavior of the customer and his/her lifestyle needs) and characterized by an even more seamless integration with the other realms of digital interactions the client has online.

6.7 Shifting Channels

Data aggregation and optimal management, of richer, less obvious unstructured information can then help in shaping offerings and channels strategies that are able to better understand the personal side of the customers, apart from his/her financial health—with the help of machine learning/AI applications that create intelligence on who the target client really is, now and more importantly, could aspire to become in future.

Even more importantly, virtual, mobile and banking-as-platform players are trying to address the third and fourth pillars of our "synapses" bank model, e.g. designing new, richer ways of interconnecting multiple stakeholders and offering them new use cases and solutions which are adding incremental value into the ecosystem. Multiple scenarios are then potential arising for the funding function and for the retail banks of the future—again, mostly driven by the shifting customer channel preferences and related needs.

In a "disaggregation" scenario, new FinTech players, on the basis of the trust they have been able to develop and capitalize, will get more direct control of customers' relationships, on the basis of their superior digital ways of interactions, so good to even overcome the inertial reticence from customers to swap from their old traditional banks (if you ever thought swapping your current account to another bank, just try: the load of bureaucracy, time required, potential mistakes and re-run of wires and Iban to consider is just incredible).

In this scenario, traditional banks can either evolve in parallel and, acting on all the synapses levers, can still try to compete on the customer relationships piece, or be destined to a less relevant and capital heavy role as products manufacturers, being interconnected by smarter and brainer new challengers sitting in the middle. Theirs would not, however, be a typical intermediation game—as they should be able to aggregate many other non-financial suppliers to fully deliver the customer's targeted "intentions" or "life projects"—as we have described for the loyalty programs and the potential role of the bank "wearing Prada". And they should be able to provide new use cases that truly add value to the system—again, as we have already commented, optimizing for example the overall supply-chain and real time production-delivery cycle of one.

In a "disruption" scenario, new FinTech would instead start competing on the manufacturing side, with light, virtual financial institutions focusing only on client management. These "light banks" could then offer a comprehensive set of financial products by partnering with a range of alternative providers of financial services—from P2P lending, to crowdfunding, to payments etc. and competing with old, traditional fully bundled retail banks. The disruption would then be limited to the back end of the value chain, with an interesting role maintained by the banks that would be able to fend off the offensive on the front end.

In a third, more negative "disaggregation and disruption", scenario, incumbent banks would be challenged both on the front and back office/manufacturing side of the value chain, ultimately losing both battles, as they would be crowded out by trusted, more technologically advanced FinTech players on the client management side; and by alternative digital providers of financial products on the manufacturing side (from payments to lending, from funding to investment management), with little competitive space left to survive.

In a fourth scenario, the "synapses" retail bank would play tough on both dis-aggregation and disruption, embedding even closer into its customers' daily lives. The synapses bank would leverage advanced data management and last generation applied analytics to stretch all kind of new virtual channels and augmented reality to offer frequent interactions with customers, above and beyond today's needs-based transactions, to strengthen customer relationships. Virtual channels would then allow to the synapses bank to beat the digital challengers at their own game, offering not only financial but also non-financial value added offerings, leveraging the manufacturing and capital structure of other players, without increasing costs and investments, but actually augmenting the content of intelligence and tailored value added embedded in any offering.

As they will evolve their core offerings to stay more relevant in their customers' daily lives, synapses banks will have to expand into unfamiliar and less well defined areas, with new risks and compliance requirements to be considered and proactively managed. But still worth to consider vis a vis the potentially unsustainable and certainly less profitable other scenarios, not to mention the anachronistic one of the "inverted pyramids".

Transformation in Investment Management

Abstract

Digital transformation is shaking up investment management at least on four fronts. It allows the extended participation of people to the international world of capital markets, further pushing the limits of the concept of a "(cyber) capitalism" open to everybody. Secondly, it further contributes to develop the trading battlefield into a war among machines and AI-powered algorithms. Thirdly, it changes the world of advisory in money management, as robots are becoming better and nicer at this job. Not to mention, finally, the impacts on the back and middle office activities that are becoming more and more "industrialized by digitization". Very large pay offs are at stake for markets and societies alike, but also new risks, as algorithms tend to think alike, even more than human beings, with potential effects still not fully understood and just partially addressed. Successful transformation will rely on this optimal relationship between men and machines.

Keywords

Cyber capitalism · Robot advisory · Artificial intelligence · Self-learning machines · Algorithms

7.1 Money Management, Power to People

It seems a truism to state that wealth management is for rich people. As uncontroversial this statement appears, it looks set to be challenged soon, as wealth management, even the most sophisticated one, traditionally offered by a variety of financial institutions, including universal banks, private banks, family offices and even broker-dealers and insurance companies is now potentially going to be made available to everybody—from the higher to the lower end of customers as measured by investable financial asserts.

Everybody will have the potential to play at the investment management game as even the most privy club deals could be opened to everybody, as a new form of "capitalism" for the people—leveraging data and information, applied analytics and AI and new forms of digital interconnections and junctions, as all of these is made cheaply available by the use of sophisticated technologies and the ultimate robotization of the financial advisory and related execution and post trade reporting that are forming the basis of money management.

The wealth management industry has in fact suffered from the loss of trust since the financial crisis—related to the negative performances that have remembered how "alpha" is difficult to attain and almost impossible to ensure through time, and how diversification (one of the key rationales of the value added ensured by investment management professionals) tend to collapse in the worst of times, as things tend to get nastier when markets are bad, and even the more robustly negative correlations break down. It has then suffered from cases of fraud and embezzlement (that also tend to rise when markets go down) and from episodes of miss and cross selling—where the next best product cross sold was basically a tax avoidance scheme or else.

But apart from all of these partly extraordinary critical issues, the real loss of trust for this industry—more structural and harder to recover—has come from the deal achieved with customers and from the value that it really delivers. It is arguable that fixed fee commissions, and entry or exit ones, should be charged to customers, given the expectation of incremental costs approaching zero in the mere administration of money. And the level of these fees "all-in" has been so high not be justified by the "other than extra performance" services offered to end customers. Finally, success fees have been set sometimes arbitrarily, with no symmetry driven by negative performances and on the basis of a delivered "alpha" that could be disputable under a number of common methodologies used to assess a risk/return relative and absolute performances.

In this context, a number of new FinTech challengers have started to play on a number of disruptive propositions, offering everything from automated wealth management services, to trading platforms cum social website, to low-cost but still sophisticated solutions to support optimal portfolio generation and investment strategies selection, down to the automated generation of "timing" and "picking" recommendations. The example of Spacehive (in the following Fig. 7.1) is showing how a target offering could be created to focus the investment platform to support local communities' projects.

All of these solutions have the effect to appeal to a broader customer base and empower people to have more and cheaper control of their investments and of their "investment lifestyle". In doing these, they have not just lowered the bar to allow the access of many of the people previously left behind, but they are also eroding the "core business" of private, wealth and asset managers—offering new and maybe greater investment intelligence, high tech services and at a much lower cost than

7.1 Money Management, Power to People

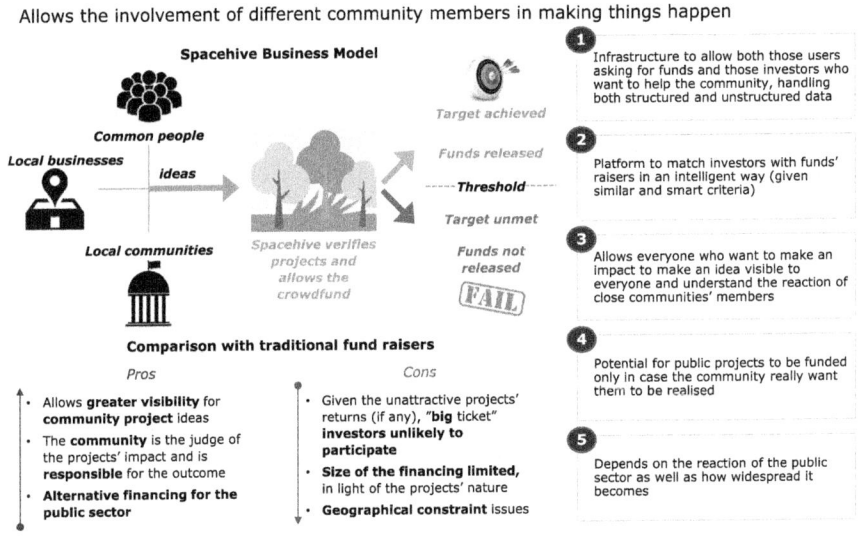

Fig. 7.1 Spacehive socially responsible investment platform supports funding for local communities' projects

traditional "wine and dine" offerings. A cost that could potentially decrease further, as their technological proposition runs at near zero incremental costs.

Whilst it is becoming obvious how the pressure for the next big wave of cost cutting will focus, after the investment banking and the retail/commercial banking, on the wealth management business, it is also clear that taking out costs and reducing the price point of incumbent players will just buy time to incumbent players, as their digital challenge and the transformation to come is much greater than that and entails this "power to the people" proposition, sustained by the social dimension of investing and by an artificial intelligence one that is promising to displace the best investor professional, Warren Buffett included.

As a number of purely quantitative, algorithmic driven hedge funds are already popping up and developing in the global ranking of best performer, a potential scenario where our investment needs are advised, executed and reported by robot investors and machines are becoming more and more likely, risking to displace one of the few remaining fees-generating, capital-light business of the global financial services industry.

7.2 Better Mouse Trap

A number of FinTech digital innovator are rapidly building a "better mouse trap", aimed at the billions of customers not yet reached by a basic banking proposition (the 2 Bln + that don't have yet a current account, but could get now to a sophisticated investment management in just one gulp). This "better mousetrap" is also targeting the much fewer, fat cats (the VIP and Ultra High Net Worth Individuals), already carefully cared by "high touch" private bankers and financial planners, that are however increasingly unable to justify the commissions they are commanding, and with an increasingly challenged value proposition.

The FinTech are acting on a number of dimensions in order to build this "better mousetrap". They increase access, with sophisticated wealth management services once available to a few people and now made economically viable for a broader customer base, including the mass affluent and the mass market customers.

They also increase transparency and control, as end customers—with any kind of "AFR—available financial resources"—gain greater visibility into their financial planning and risk/return optimized portfolio, and with a larger and larger accessibility to a number of new investment opportunities. They then increase convenience, with online and mobile channels being increasingly leveraged to interact better and promptly with customers, delivering sophisticated financial analysis in real time and with a near zero marginal cost.

They then offer personalized services and hyper profiled investment strategies, as they mine new social and behavioural data as they become available over the web or through the IoT applications that will increasingly accompany us in our private life. And they will offer all of these at incredibly low price points, as advisory and other investment management services are reaping the economies of scale and new isoquant of productivity now allowed by digitization, machine learning and cognitive automation driven by robo-advisors and traders.

The improvement of both the reach and richness dimensions of the wealth and investment management propositions operated by these new FinTech players happens in a number of ways. They ensure, for once, cheaper and faster online tools and automated services, offering risk appetite analysis, the creation of efficient portfolios on the basis of this, and of the matching of the global investment opportunities mapped, to the automatic execution of the trading strategy and reporting. Most of them started from the reach dimension, targeting non-served or underserved mass market customers. They are now then moving upwards, offering more valuable content and addressing affluent and private clients, with more personalised, relationship-based interactions, still done pretty much on line, therefore allowing to steal market share from traditional banks, and then—once the new richer offering is in place—going back to even address the mass market, as the incremental cost tends to zero as indivisible IT investments are made and scale is further developed.

The move from reach to richness and then back again, in its virtuous development, is promising not just to offer much more to everybody, democratizing in a way, if not money itself, the access of best in class money management advice, execution and reporting tools. This kind of innovation is therefore acting in the interest of the larger society in another interest way, as it does allow much more than a "capitalism for everybody", as it also supports the development of the investment expertise, culture and overall awareness of people, with intuitive and affordable tools that—via social trading platforms—allow to share the individual

7.2 Better Mouse Trap

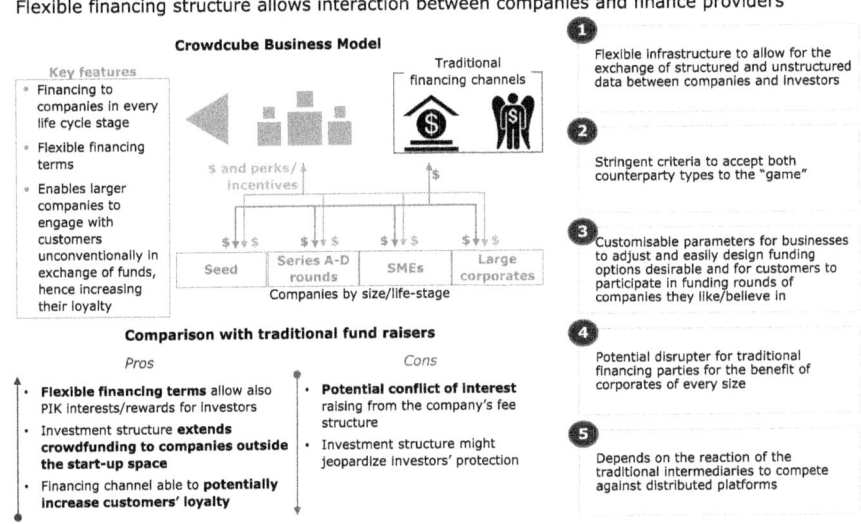

Fig. 7.2 Crowdcube aims to extend crowdfunding as a credible alternative financing option to all corporates

spikes of most talented people and enrich the common wisdom of the globally extended investment community. In doing so, the aggregation of very diverse providers of investment capital can then help in developing alternative sources of lending to SME—positioning crowd funding as an alternative to the traditional lending by banks—as in the case commented in the following Fig. 7.2 on Crowdcube. Or even as an alternative provider of equity capital to SME, as shown with the case of Seedrs in UK (Fig. 7.3).

In an extreme "populistic" scenario, crowds of mass market people and even previously unbanked people will end up getting together online, organizing and coordinating themselves in a structured way, following the charisma of some of their lead contributors to the social trading platform investment thesis. In such a scenario, even the governance and management of blue chips global companies could be forced to change, with the all too powerful CEOs that will have now to reckon the voice of the mass market investors: the proverbial remaining 99%, able to influence their decision making as just key institutional shareholders—such as asset managers, pension funds, insurance companies and the like—have been able to do in the past.

Looking at an initial taxonomy of FinTech disruptors, we could then segment the emerging players into three buckets. A first bucket would include players that are entering the arena by offering highly automated management and advice. Companies like FutureAdvisor, Personal Capital, WealthFront, MotifInvesting are offering high value added services on portfolio allocation and money management at low cost, based on automated analysis—where the automation on a personalised

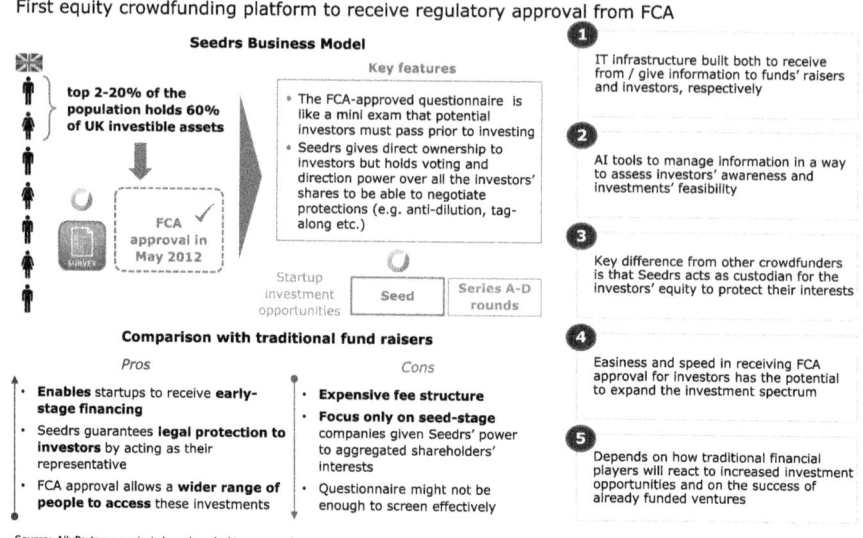

Fig. 7.3 Seedrs is one the most active equity investors in UK SME

investment portfolio is based on the client's needs, with integrated views of the overall risk/return performance and across multiple client's bank account.

A second bucket would then include players such as Covestor, Estimize, StockTwits, TradePop and SprinkleBit—all focussed on social trading, empowering individuals to build and share investment strategies and portfolios with other investors, and share their opinion as well, to gain market insights from the crowd. Finally, a third bucket would focus on an offering of algorithmic trading, to enable even retail investors to easily build, test and execute investment algorithms even if they have limited technical knowledge and no owned IT infrastructure—CoolTrade, AlgoFast, Quantoplan, QuantConnect are FinTech playing in that space.

Such a non-exhaustive taxonomy is again focussing on few of the critical disruptions we have mentioned in the introduction, e.g. allowing to mass market clients to trade in international capital markets, offering them sophisticated (robo) advisory and the opportunity of networking with other investor crowds, offering them sophisticated algorithms to trade as a service and—underpinning all these—allowing a much cheaper and more efficient running of the back-middle office activities required to operate in the investment management space.

The combined effect is telling: lower barriers are democratizing the international world of trading and wealth management and each and every one of us can become, on the cheap, a sophisticated trader—globally connected and running her/his own alpha strategies on built-for-purpose algorithms, or a well-served VIP client: maybe missing the wine and dine component, but potentially getting the best asset allocation strategy and long term planning—with limited risks of human error, fraud and embezzlement by a private robot-banker.

7.3 Investment Synapses

Many different incumbent cohorts of the global wealth management industry will have to react fast, and not just by heavily cutting costs and by digitizing their operational model so as to be able to compete with more agile, flexible technologies and with more fast, secure, content extended and rich value added services.

A first obvious consequence of the disruption introduced by the new challengers, and a first tangible move towards a more synapses based business and operating model for the wealth management industry entails the externalization of "not more core" (or less core) processes. In fact, some of the previously considered "core" ones, could be now outsourced to third parties, or pooled together and re-platformed with other peers in club deals, to deliver more flexible, cloud based, technology—aiming at greater efficiency/efficacy and at new levels of process sophistication and excellence—given the greater affordability of shared investments.

As a consequence, as third party service providers externalize and consolidate processes previously considered core capabilities of the incumbent wealth manager champions, their core competencies truly able to differentiate them shift from the routine process execution to the high value added production of investment intelligence—potentially de-coupling the requirements of economies of scale from the chances of success of a certain operator: process scale becomes in fact attainable in the market and investment intelligence proves to be driven by "alpha algorithms" that require quality and deepness, not necessarily quantity and volumes. Outsourcing, or the pooling of IT and operations to get away from critical scale competitive constraints is just a further impact coming from the more radical disruption introduced by digital and technological innovation.

Traditional asset managers, the manufacturing and process plumbers of the wealth management value chain, either active, passive or alternative, will have then to face a major challenge in the competitiveness of their investment strategies: how they deliver alpha to their customers, having gathered all kind of structured and unstructured (mostly social, behavioural) data and information on the available assets and investment strategies, and having generated the best possible intelligence on how to get the next one up on Wall Street.

As the gut feeling and statistical analysis leave space to artificial intelligence, we may expect to find an higher and higher ranking of "algorithms driven" investment funds in the coming years. And, as algorithms are intrinsically easier to share over the web and across people, we can expect that markets will get more and more efficient, with any minimal arbitrage opportunity being cleared away in fractions of seconds (as the knowledge of the algorithm becomes rapidly absorbed by the market price and therefore common knowledge).

Private and wealth managers, focussing on the advisory and relationship management part of the business, will also need to master at best data, information and the generated intelligence. Moreover, they will have to develop their business and operating model to define and address new opportunities to deliver better value by just "sitting in the middle". As in the past they were intermediating clients and investment products by way of a mere brokerage model or with a more sophisticated investment/portfolio management advisory service platform, in the near future they could support and influence the emergence of these social trading platforms, becoming the best channel to voice the emerging "investment populism", but also posing common sense rules and some minimal technical constraints to help these social platforms in coordinating themselves and act to maximize their objective functions and for the best of the extended markets and of the society at large.

As this "synapses" wealth managers gather all kind of structured and unstructured data, generate new investment intelligence with machine learning/AI, create diverse interconnections (getting together professional research analysts, crowds of small-money investors and supporting the formation, coordination and acting of social trading venues), they can eventually deliver an extra value to the rest of the economy as companies, their boards and top management will have now to answer to them, e.g. to the common will of the social network, with greater transparency, completeness of information and sharing of power.

Most of the information failures of the markets should then theoretically disappear. The principal-agent dilemma could be significantly reduced, as all data and information will be immediately available and understood by everybody, and a consequential input would be given by the social trading platform "principal" to the CEO "agent". No hidden secret agenda would then be safe from the snooping of the web—as even employees and partners and the clients of the company at large would be heard and analysed by the system.

Similarly, no moral hazard behaviour would go un-noticed and un-checked, as boards and CEOs would be forced by an extreme populistic vetting process to behave and adhere to the risk appetite and targeted return profile that the democratic investment management process of the main social trading venue will be deciding and commanding—basically assuming, over time, the role of the Blackrock of this world—with a few new Investment Social Networks (ISN) gaining unprecedented size, on the basis of a competitive set of services potentially offered for free and of barriers to entry that they would rapidly establish given their growing scale.

Even adverse selection would be strongly reduced, and with it its quite high related costs to the overall economy: as everybody knows everything, the social investment network will know even better—better than the CEO as well, and it will judge whether a given sub-performing credit is correctly marked, or whether a new car model is worth the price is budgeted for in the business plan of an automotive company.

Ultimately, if the best investment management solutions would be made available to everybody, it could then even be assumed that, via the global financial system, the process of polarization between the hyper reach few magnates and the very poor billions of people should be contained and reduced, as most of it is driven today not as much by the initial entrepreneurial drive or managerial prowess but by the elitist access to superior, privileged investment opportunities, that are delivering then more returns to the richest people that need less.

7.4 Wine and Dine 2.0

A number of scenarios are opening up, as a consequence of the disruptions mentioned above, allowing a greater access to the international capital markets and to most people, offering them high quality robo-advice at very low price, built-for-purpose algorithms and a new level of efficiency and efficacy in most of the back and middle office services and shared backbone infrastructures (most of which are ripe for consolidation across peers, as we have seen). Some scenarios are more extreme, and worth to consider as reference point.

On one extreme, the "capitalism for everybody" movement supported by digitization in the field of investment management will imply that, empowered with intuitive, affordable and accessible tools, some individual investors could potentially gain a sufficient level of sophistication to act as investment professional—sharing data, information, intelligence and ideas across social networks of non-professional, retail investors that still could act as "virtual" asset management companies, directly competing with traditional investment managers, if not on performance, certainly on the competitive value offered by the virtual network, given the level of fees required (almost zero, as just the infrastructure and algorithmic services will be paid "as you go").

On another extreme, the "wealth management for everybody" movement also supported by digitization could also imply that, served by cheaper and faster online tools and automated services, also underserved and one day even unbanked clients will be reached by a mass market advisory offering. Paradoxically, as incremental costs will be very low, and indivisible investments high, larger numbers of mass market clients could provide an even more interesting niche than the high net worth individuals one, characterized by the high sophistication and strong bargaining power of the counterpart. FinTech players will be better placed to run this strategy, as they will not be constrained by existing branch networks and expensive financial advisors and private bankers.

A more interesting scenario, for the incumbent banks, could however gain relevance, as they react with some efficacy to the digitization of the investment management sector and take advantage of most of the five pillars of our previously introduced synapses model. In this mid-ground scenario, incumbent wealth managers could be able to revamp their own value propositions, commoditizing them and then automating the most routine components of the value chain and squeezing costs. Some value-added components could also be robotized and automated in digital investment platforms, allowing to the wealth manager to gain bargaining power vis a vis the financial advisors and private bankers—the real winners of the last decades of competition in this industry.

Whilst "industrializing" most of the wealth management services that do not require high touch personalization, they could still further leverage data, information and the intelligence provided by machine learning/AI, to then offer bespoke advisory and new integrated investment use cases and solutions, at an almost behavioral if not psychological level, caring for families across generations and across the typical issues that a large family can face, from fortune to disgrace, from health to death, from marriages to break-ups.

7.5 Ex-Ex: Extended Externalisers

Whatever the scenario that will set the scene for the evolution of the investment management industry and of its landscape at global level, an emerging trend that should be reconfirmed and spurred by digitization entails the extended definition of what is "non-core" to this business. A new breed of process externalization providers are in fact using highly flexible platforms—typically based in the cloud and built on new web technologies and philosophies, to provide investment managers with increased efficiency and new levels of process sophistication and excellence. Without the burden of the in-house management of IT and back-office.

A number of innovations are now potentially enabling this new digital breed of process externalization. On advanced analytics, companies like Ayasdi, utilize advanced computing power, algorithms and analytical models to not only automate existing manual processes but also provide a new level of sophistication. Cloud computing—offered by companies like Fundapps or Redkite, leverages instead cloud technology to improve connectivity with and within institutions to facilitate data sharing, streamline implementation and maintenance of processes and getting them down ideally to an almost "real time".

Finally, natural language applications, offered by companies such as Duco and Kensho, integrate natural language technology into processes to make them more intuitive for end-users and available in multi-languages applications, reducing the need for deep technical backgrounds. And many others are popping up, as behavioral analysis tools are digitized and deploying the larger and larger volume of unstructured information, to create a better psychological understanding of the risk/return appetite and regret profile of the investor—to again be offered as an external infrastructure able to complement the internal analysis of the company.

As multiple innovations keep emerging, these new breed of extended externalization providers tend to get structured according to few typologies. Technological platforms, such as Novus or OpenGamma, can act as real-time databases and expert systems, leveraging automation to help user in completing tasks faster and with fewer resources. Other providers, like Fundapps, offer instead full externalization of entire capabilities and processes, priced as-a-service model, hence minimizing the infrastructure investments required.

Finally, a capability sharing solution is also on the offer, by companies such as eCo financial technology, building on the IT "clubbing and pooling" trend we already described in previous chapters, to facilitate institutions to work with one

7.5 Ex-Ex: Extended Externalisers

another to share capabilities or easily integrate with new external providers, acting as cleaning rooms and constructing new legal and technical standards and vehicles that they could also end up managing as independent partners. In a way playing the cleaning and steering room of the alliance.

Different scenarios of extended externalization could end up transforming the investment management industry, and in the possibly most impactful way across the global financial system, albeit the same principles could apply, as we have seen, to the payment function, or to the funding and lending ones and to many others.

Following a first incremental hypothesis, this new breed of "extended externalisers", or Ex-Ex, could use advanced technologies to carve out and then consolidate and commoditize processes previously considered "core"—in more efficient and effective way—building sophistication on economies of scale and know how. For this incremental scenario, banks' winning core competencies would shift from superior process execution to more qualitative and strategic decision making—whilst developing the ability to offer great soft skills and bundling. A synapses bank would also benefit, as it could keep focusing its core business and operating model on the "intelligence building, solution design" critical part, and getting away from most routine process needs.

Because of this, a second scenario could develop as complementary to the first one. As external services are made available in a competitive way to all kind of players and of all size and nature, a new breed of challengers (either small traditional banks, or new FinTech) could also more easily develop, overcoming the barriers and constraints driven by critical volume and scale—in short creating a more level playing field. Also in this case, the synapses bank could have greater chances to flourish, and make alliances with new challengers, or beating them in their own turf, as they are also trying to explore advanced data management and applied analytics/AI and ideally exploring ways to introduce new use cases for specific components of the chain.

There is finally a third scenario, where these Ex-Ex players are not only ensuring an higher competitiveness into the system and greater value creation, given the larger economies of scale and know how attainable, but also greater and faster compliance by financial institutions to upcoming regulations and even more stability to the system, as they act as centralized communication touchpoints for regulators—ensuring for example a single AML (Anti Money Laundering) platform to access most of the correspondent banking and currency markets at scale and with the greatest level of reliability and consistency. From this point of view, and on the basis of an even more critical trust (required to convince potential banking partners to join and carve out, contributing to the platform their own processes), these Ex-Ex could also play across all of the dimensions of the synapses model, interconnecting multiple peers across business models and geographies and creating incremental value for the overall ecosystem, potentially shared by incumbents, new entrants, regulators and end customers.

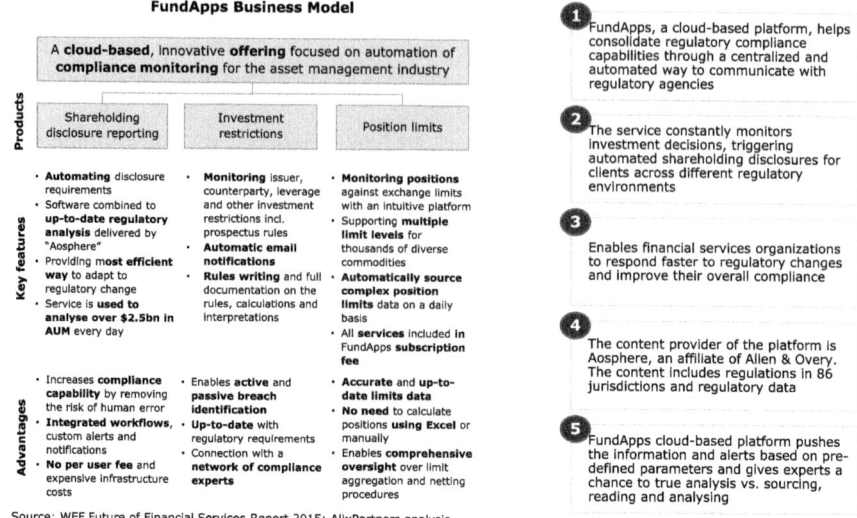

Fig. 7.4 Fundapps specializes in automated compliance monitoring and making regulatory disclosures for investment funds

As shown in the Figure below, Fundapps is, for example, already offering organized regulatory information, delivered on a cloud-based managed service way. It can therefore offer automate shareholdings disclosure and investment monitoring (and checking of restrictions) across more than 100 regulatory regimes and on a daily basis. The Fundapps partners then work with a global service provider to monitor and translate changes in relevant regulations into rules daily—hence sharing the costs and required its investments (Fig. 7.4).

As regulatory compliance with investment management companies becomes more closely integrated with Ex-Ex providers, some regulators could choose to collaborate directly with them and even to the point of issuing regulations in programmed code rather than as policy documents, limiting uncertainty in the interpretation and multiple, single institution investments—ultimately ensuring a faster and safer implementation of new regimes, almost on real time as the new code is released on the few Ex-Ex regional hubs.

Eventually, an ultimate end-game scenario could also consider the opportunity to "rule by machine learning", i.e. leveraging artificial intelligence to come up with the new set of rules that make more sense given the objectives pursued and assigned by human beings (for example, ensuring a most liquid, transparent, competitive and hence efficient market and preventing any manipulation on prices and unappropriated investment styles for certain customers or behaviors that could damage end customers in an unfair way). In this way, the synapsezation of regulators looks an even easier bet, and promises strategic venue to explore—and not just in terms of data and analytical tools to drive tactical e-discovery of fraud and wrongdoings.

7.6 Trading Machines: Faster, Smarter, Richer?

As the popularity and profitability of high frequency trading picks up (based on super faster connectivity and automatic, simple rules-driven decision making used to derive and monetize superior price discovery and order execution), the next evolution in the history of asset picking will probably depend on the use of unstructured data and information advanced management and of algorithmic based applications derived by machine learning/AI powerful capabilities developed by rocket science analysts and with a stint in quantum computing.

The quest for "alpha" (the over-performance attained in a consistent, sustainable and uncorrelated way versus the market) is as old as the history of money management. But new digital applications are now opening up to a new world of possibilities, potentially leading to a trading battle field where super quantum-computing powered algorithms compete with each other, with little breathing space left to gut feeling and hunches—with machines one day taking over even legendary investors such as Warren Buffet.

These machines will get faster and faster, but their key attributes will become "smarter" (as they are built on more and better data and information and best applied analytics) and then "richer" (as they will drive a greater and greater portion of the "alpha" delivered by the investment management industry). These machines will be able to process all kind of available data and information, getting news feeds through algorithms in real time and with little human interpretation required (if not for the training phase). These info-crunching could allow them to discover major events faster than the market, getting the best of social media and sentiment and behavioral analysis—real life events will get incorporated into investment strategies, in an even faster way than they will appear on media channels and before being fully understood by people and professionals.

A number of FinTech companies like SNTMNT, or SemLab, and established ones like Thompson Reuters and MNI (of the Deutsche Borse Group)[1] are already able to process news feeds through algorithms in real-time and—more importantly—without requiring human interpretation, hence discovering major events faster than the news via social media and sentiment analysis. On the basis of this extended access to "unstructured" information, even the price formation in the market (one of the old-time key functions provided by the global financial system) will become more and more driven by real-life events—with lower and lower time latency, as new events are getting mined and interpreted by the machines in faster and more meaningful ways.

Other companies, like Teradata, Ayasdi, Hadoop, Palantir and SAS are also serving the access and capitalization of these new huge amounts of real time data, in order to uncover, through cloud-base analytics, predictive insights on market movements, on the basis of correlations mapping. Whilst further companies like Sentient, Opera, Rebellion and Portware are further developing and offering machine learning/AI models that are able to ask questions, discover and test

---
[1] The future of financial services, World Economic Forum report, June 2015.

hypothesis and make decisions automatically—leveraging the advanced analytics and the extensive data sets that are also captured with the help of other applications and companies.

In their most sophisticated development, these machines, also dubbed "deep learning", will self-correct and continuously improve their trading strategies, with minimal human interaction through machine learning and prescriptive analytics, hence requiring less and less human intervention even in the design and training phase.

These deep/machine learning techniques are not, however, entering on the trading floor just from the new FinTech companies' doors, as UBS, the global leader in wealth management by stock of assets under management and one of the top international investment banks recently showed.[2] The Swiss-based global SIFI is already using artificial intelligence systems that can help traders perform better—and not just on automatic manual, repetitive manual tasks to save costs. According to the new mantra, artificial intelligence can in fact work at the heart of investment management operations, to help the bank's star traders in allocating funds and analyzing data to develop better strategies: in a way, with robots moving from the back to the front office.

One such application scans for emails sent by clients detailing how they want to divide large block trades up between funds—it then processes these and executes the transfers—saving times along the way: from 45 to only about 2 min—freeing time for traders to more value adding things such as calling clients. A second application goes even further, with a machine learning application used to develop new strategies for trading volatility on behalf of clients. It examines vast amounts of trading data to build an "adaptive" strategy based on learning from market patterns —at the service of the bank's portfolio and of third party clients. And JP Morgan Chase has developed a similar system, based on machine learning for its equities business, which helps to analyze the best way to execute a big block trade by reading market conditions.

In a trading environment, further and further dominated by faster and smarter machines, the ownership of these "learned machines" will determine who the "richest guy in town" will be next—with new oligopoly potentially arising from this. On a positive side, the price discovery function played by the market will become more and more efficient and effective and less prone to errors—as trading activities will become mostly automated and with little intervention of people. Also, investment management strategic allocations and tactical stock picking should also improve, as machine learning/AI should do a better job in adhering to the targeted risk profile of the investor and in translating this into consistent trades.

On the negative side, this arising oligopoly will tend to perpetuate itself, with the owners of the faster and smarter machines (hence richest) increasing their performance gap because of their ability to keep investing in technology and in originating, capturing or buying and then mastering larger and larger quantities of data

---

[2]Robots enter investment banks' trading floor, Financial Times, Martin Arnold and Laura Nooman, 7th July 2017.

and genetically superior, self-adapting algorithms (with new branches of science, such as the "genetic algorithms" one, taking further prominence and building increased barriers to competition).

This would also pose new risks as "herding behaviors" (not uncommon to human traders, to tell the truth) could arise as well, and be supported by the explosion of superfast, computer powered, robots managed trading outfits—as these machines could potentially converge and "think the same" and "flash crash". As the emerging players will tend to access the most complete sets of data, their analysis could start converging into a single view of the market that, for a period, it will be self-fulfilling (if most of the traders wants to get long on a stock, its price will increase because of the excess of demand on its supply), and then turn into a crash, as they need to sell at some point in time, at deep discounts, as the market will get cornered around few remaining buyers. Diversified trading strategies, making use of alternative data, or using diverse methodologies of "deepest learning" or "unconventional AI", and maybe a bit of human gut feeling and creativity, could then resurface and infer different strategies used to then profit from this machine-lead market failures.

Few simpler rules will still however hold true in the future in international capital markets, no matter how sophisticated is the technology and the "synapses" that artificial intelligence systems will be able to develop: in trading, some parties will gain and some others will lose, in a "zero sum game", with the net, sustainable gains in financial markets converging over the long period to the ones achieved by the real economy.

7.7 Capitally Connected Markets

The development of machine learning/AI powered trading strategies, should not, however, in the short run, be able to address the all too many illiquid markets where financial assets are still traded by old fashioned broker dealers—as we have seen in the paragraph dedicated to corporate bonds. These and many other markets will remain dependent for some time on intermediating Institutions to discover and connect buyers and sellers—in a network game where personal and institutional relationships will still be very relevant.

However, following the financial crisis, even these remaining incumbent intermediaries have had to reduce they risk appetite to play on the principal side, to act as dealer and offer a price to any potential transaction requested by market participants. As an answer to this lack of supply and to its related market opportunity, and leveraging the electronification of the trading value chain, and the automation by digital applications and robots, new FinTech platforms are emerging, with an aim to make even the most illiquid segments of capital markets better connected—making the price discovery function work in a better way, for the benefits of buyers and sellers and with the erosion of some of the value now captured by traditional intermediaries.

New information platforms are for example emerging, offering connectivity and access to data (structured and unstructured). Based on the economics allowed by a digital platform, they can offer these services almost regardless the size and volume of the transactions mastered by its counterparts. And they can act either for the supply or for the demand side—thus aggregating a larger overall volume and helping in the price discovery function for any given vertical sub-segment of the debt or equity market.

They could act, in this way, as an alternative to the largest broker-dealers. Their competitive move would play based on the data/information pillar and then add further value added via applied analytics and on top of the connectivity offered. But they would mostly play on the third "synapsezation" pillar—offering a different, more exhaustive, many to many, evolved interconnection model. And they would also potentially compete because of new solutions adding incremental value to the system, arranging for example club deals on line, or profiling at a very detailed level for the client counterparts the access to sale or investment opportunities, or arranging for build-up of fragmented demand through time and geographies, with complementary alerts and monitoring/reporting systems. And all this because of the required, extended digital and cyber trust.

Other platforms could instead work for larger financial institutions, to create a more liquid network and potentially realizing an alternative infrastructure potentially posed to then challenge regulated (and already highly efficient and liquid) capital markets. These FinTech platforms would in effect position themselves as a potential competitor to the most well-known future, bond and stock exchanges—with applications serviced over the web and transactional data stored in the cloud—again eroding value out of these players. Their super-connectivity on offer would still rely on most of the five pillars of our "synapsezation" model, and try to answer to the question "what extra and better data/information, intelligence, interconnection and solutions could be offered to institutional investors vis a vis, say the NYSE or the Deutsche Borse?".

Finally, a third kind of platform could also develop, extending the information and connectivity services to small businesses and individuals, in a way further realizing a vision of capitalism open and ease to use for everybody—where even the smallest investor can have access to opaque, seldom traded, traditionally illiquid assets, with maximum flexibility and certainty of a transparent way-in and out to invest and divest in some of these assets. They would increase the potential customer base and thus the price efficiency, and offer as a complement the necessary, almost required training that non-professional investors would surely need.

Overall, improving the flow of information, intelligence (and in this case even financial culture) among a larger base of investors would end up creating tangible benefits to the global financial system and to the underlying economic sectors served—further incrementing the information value embedded in the price formation process happening in competitive markets. And they would end up eroding pots of value now captured by traditional banks, retail and commercial and even by wealth and asset managers, as they could again leverage on the five pillars and progressively move from data/information to intelligence services, and from

7.7 Capitally Connected Markets

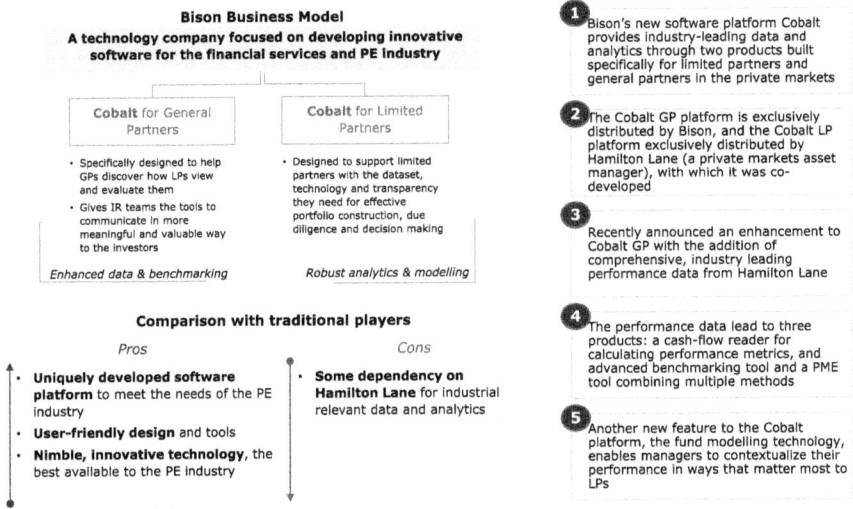

Fig. 7.5 Bison, an innovative technology company focused on private markets, offers proprietary, market-leading software solutions

interconnection and hyper connectivity to new solutions offering, designed and placed on the basis of their undisputed trust.

Different players (the FinTech platforms) are now arising, and covering specific market segments, from fixed income (Algomi), to mutual funds and fund of funds (Novus), to venture capital and private equity (Bison as in Fig. 7.5), to private company sales (Liquidity) and tenders (SecondMarket), to commodities and derivatives (ClauseMatch in Fig. 7.6).

In a show of the potential disruption to come, they all offer some common social element in their competitive positioning—as they embed the elements of social network required to facilitate the interactions among buyers and sellers and to improve how buyers and sellers are evaluated. And they all compete on standardization and automation, from the data and information collected to the segmentational criteria to evaluate buyers and sellers and proceed to their best match making and to price discovery: faster and more efficiently.

In summary, in the full digitization scenario depicted, not only the trading and investment management world will get more and more dominated by intelligent machines and super-efficient robot, with the casual exception of few "synapses" banks able to play at the new FinTech game; but the very same logic of competition will change, with blurring boundaries among broker-dealers, retail/commercial banks, investment/wholesale banks, wealth/asset managers, and even insurance companies, pension and endowment funds and the like... and even regulated spot and future markets. In short, as products and players, and fundamental functions will become more and more digital, so will prices, ensuring a better accuracy and transparency along the way. As they are the best proxy that we have for the "true" value of things, this should not be a bad outcome at all.

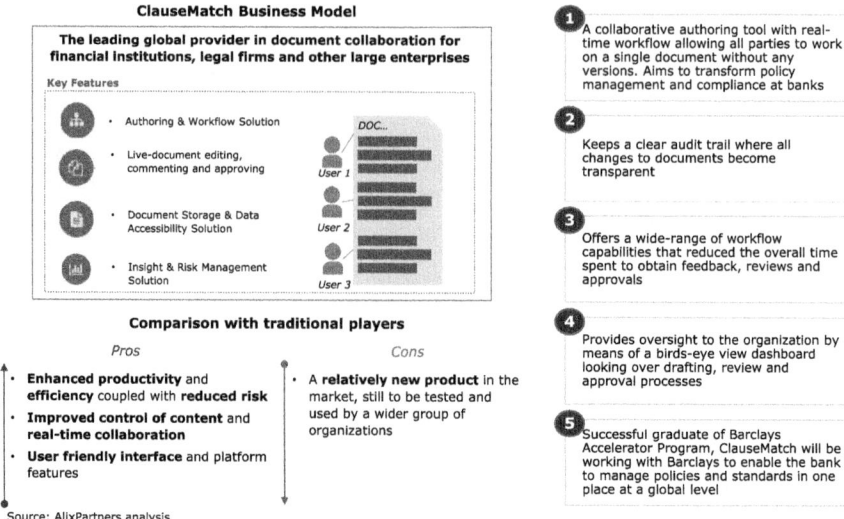

Fig. 7.6 ClauseMatch provides a software-as-a-service platform for smart document management, specifically for financial services firms

7.8 Market Utilities: Clubbing Together

Not only the capital markets' front end will get connected and enriched with data, information and intelligence to a much higher extent. But also, the back end of the infrastructure will be ripe for change and transformation, as digitization kicks in and allow to do this faster and better; but also more effectively and efficiently "together". The attack to the "plumbing" supporting the global financial system comes as new digital technologies become available, making the most of current information, whilst related operating systems become progressively obsolete and potentially unstable. We have seen how cyber risk can impact its main players and markets, whether regulated or OTC (Over the Counter), domestic or international—with the very notion of space becoming blurred in the virtual reality on which codes are written and operated.

The issue of the main sectorial capital markets (e.g. trade finance, or asset management, or fixed income currency and commodities) and of their supporting infrastructure being in urgent need of technological upheaval poses then relevant consequences on their governance and operating model of reference, calling potentially for new approaches that overcome traditional competitive boundaries among peers.

As new non-banking players, or no-players at all (as in the case of the block chain/distributed ledgers technology), could take charge and control of the ownership of some critical "rails" of the system, innovative business and operating model could be designed to redefine the profitability curves impacting on most financial products and services. And, before that, the issue of keeping developing the internal infrastructure (the IT and operation backbones) of banks could turn to be a too heavy duty one, potentially mining their ability to change and transform in a digital way, not to mention the efficiency targets that could be achieved by aggregating more volume across players and for given specific commoditized, less competitive, bits of their value chain.

Financial services are already a big contributor to the outsourcing industry, with IT (more than operations) having led the way in the last few years, and—with regard to IT—with a very strong focus on application development and maintenance and system integration. In many instances, after the start of the financial crisis, global and domestic banks ended up selling their own IT unit to infrastructure provider, ideally better suited to exploit the benefits driven by scale and specialization (with banks ready to monetize on a quick capital gain).

Still, the overall BPO (business process outsourcing) market has since been in decline, particularly for large sized buyers and with the number of deals decreasing over time and some "re-insourcing". This trend as however been counterbalanced by the increasing number of Global In-house Centres (GIC), where the bank establishes its own, well defined legal entity and self-contained service unit that supplies, ideally at arms' length, the required IT and operations services as required by the (one and only) captive client.

A more radical approach is now required for copying with the disruption happening at the level of the external and internal plumbing and of the rails of the system, where the "sell" option is now substituted by the "pool" (or "club") together one, and the "captive" is taken over by an "open market" approach, where the proof of its economic rational leading to a better performant IT and operation system is tested with real clients, ready to pay an adequate price, or to just walk away. In this "market utility" approach, banks are in fact considering which kind of vertical slice (e.g. vertically with respect to a specific component of the value chain, for example, for the post-trade services functions, like clearing, settlement or tax reporting) or horizontal component (e.g. regarding the generic IT and operations capabilities of banks sitting in the same location and serving the same geographical market and client segments), or—ideally—both.

Let's follow for a moment the example of post-trade services, with specific reference to the processing IT and operational capabilities required for any major global bank. From clearing and settlement, to custody and asset management, to fund administration, to the issuer and trustee functions, to middle-office and reporting services... it is possible to map a total of at least 15–20 macro activities that could be more or less apt for carve out—as new regulatory requirements and market evolution are driving new significant investments; as most processes are still reliant on manual work and would benefit from standardization and robotization, requiring major investments to act but then driving almost negligible marginal costs; as the management of specific regulatory or operational risks would benefit from an industry-wide approach that ensure consistency (Fig. 7.7).

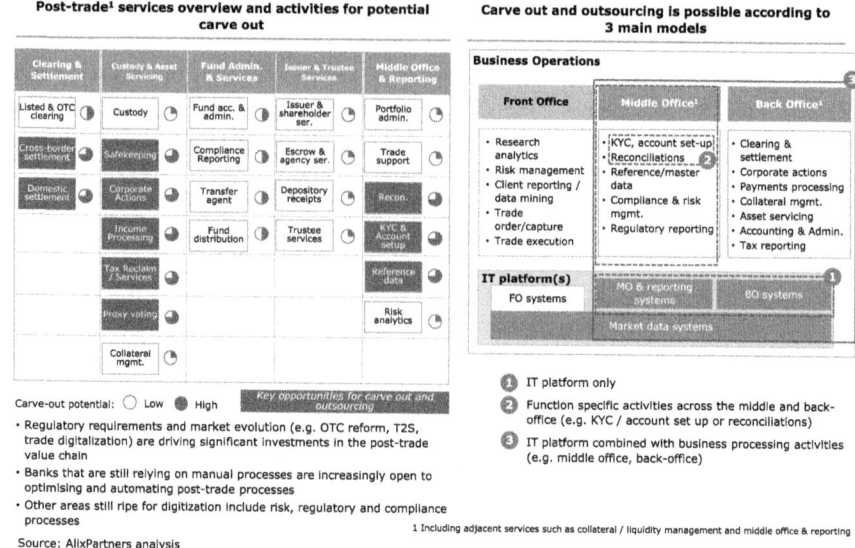

Fig. 7.7 Low-value added activities can be carved out and transferred to market utilities

The "carve out" operating model for one or more verticals of the post trade services could then be set in different ways, addressing just the IT platform only, or combining this with business processing activities (e.g. middle and back office), or functional specific activities across the middle and back-office (e.g. for the KYC—Know Your Customer—account set up and reconciliation).

In any case, one critical component in the design of the carve-out would entail the identification of common features and maturity levels in business operations across different banks and their different business divisions and geographical locations. Other key factors to consider for the carve out would then include, as mentioned, highly standardized products (e.g. equities and fixed income), more homogeneous market structures (e.g. UK and US) and standardized and commoditized functions (e.g. market side settlement processing).

This pooling of IT and operations capabilities, being executed as a carve out of tangible and intangible assets, and including some people and a related long term service level agreement (SLA) with the parent company, is then crystallized via a contribution to an SPV, that can be co-owned by the contributing banks, or by a third party, either industrial or private equity fund, that can drive the multi-parties lengthy negotiations and stir the digital re-platforming of the new combined entity, most likely in need of more efficient and effective integrated systems that can allow the agility and flexibility required to keep the contributing companies happy—but also to hit the market to serve third party clients and develop a profitable business per se.

The old logic of the front-to-back fully bundled bank is then overcome. As well as the one of banks competing with each other on anything, including basic back office functions such as purchasing or payroll management. Whilst "co-opetion" could be too big and hyped a word to spend for this, it is obvious that the sense of urgency to find new ways to further reduce the cost base of banks is leading them into unchartered waters, where the threats of a FinTech taking the lead on some key infrastructural component is even bigger than the worry of being fouled by a traditional outsourcer or than the risk of "opening the kimono" to a peer.

If this will happen in a major way, digitization will have successfully delivered another revolution, of a more industrial sort. And even more than that, it will revolutionize the ways of working, having overcome so much greater challenges in the governance and culture of banks, than the ones linked to mere bits and bytes.

Transformation in Lending

Abstract

Lending is at the core of banking, and has been determining its fortunes and misfortunes—over the cycle and across Countries. Digitization could however even change this more traditional of paradigms, as banks could be successful (or not) in the future, on the basis of their decision on what digital lending model (if any) to have, and on what risk screening and underwriting process will determine their future origination, pricing and management strategies. Whilst impacts on non-banks originated lending volumes has been so far limited, the impacts introduced by alternative credit risk scoring and rating models are already impacting the credit market, potentially bringing to a better management of the inherent trade-off between risk and return.

Keywords

P2P lending · Credit scoring · Credit rating · Self-learning machines · Risk adjusted pricing

8.1 Lending: A Social Business

Lending has always been the key pillar on which banking developed, since inception and through history, at local and global level, and with regard to retail and corporate clients as well. It has since been driving the fortunes (and misfortunes) of this and of that other sector, as lending policies have the power to shape the overall setting of the economy, accelerating (sometimes towards a final crash) its growth, or stabilizing and spurring it when in peril of a recession, and helping allocating the scarce resources (not just lending) among the many opportunities available: sometimes feeding almost without limit—without any apparent economic reason—

some industrial vertical and specific counterparts, whilst almost starving others to death. Lending has in fact the power of extending the lifetime and power of industries, companies and people, and vice versa.

Provided an unlimited access to credit, even the most troubled and unprofitable company can keep going and growing—with an hard landing when it stops. And not having access to credit can seriously limit the chances of going and growing of profitable companies, as equity and profits are usually not enough to cope with the increased competitiveness of global markets and with their required investment plans. Being credit-worth is not always, however, synonymous with having an easy and cheap access to lending. Nor is often, being credit-unworthy, an impediment to get easy money to waste, as many cases in the banking history could testify.

Plenty of academic books have been written on the well-known hypothesis that credit is available, as a set of financial products and as a sector per se, and mostly managed by banks, to provide an efficient and effective mean to transfer resources across time, geographies and people—on the basis of a thorough economic analysis —performed by banks on behalf of its shareholders and debtholders, of the risk/return profiles associates with the net takers of financial resources. Still, less documented is the dimension of credit as a tool and as a strategy to broker, influence and develop economic power—i.e. ultimately associated with the right, for the lenders, to grant an option to borrow, develop and perform: given to industries, companies and individuals.

For this very reason, the "unsustainable lightness" of the banking business model has been put to further risk, as lending has been interpreted as a "personal" business, often managed under the influences of a relationships-based capitalistic model, not to mention the suasion (moral or un-moral) exercised by politicians, regulators and the like—to feed friends and starve foes, to extend good credit and pretend it is still so.

No matter what the quantitative background of the analysis, and the so called "credit scoring" performed by the chief credit and risk officer, the ultimate decision making in terms of lending policies and related pricing has always been influenced by a significant degree of qualitative analysis and by the good (or bad) will assigned to the counterpart, often on the basis of very personal relationships. The emerge of the all mighty "power broker" banker has too often been the result of this—with sometimes catastrophic implications on the misallocation of resources at the level of the domestic and international economies.

8.2 Creditworthy: A "Witticism"

A "witticism" that could have been worth of Oscar Wilde could have stated that, since time immemorial, "the ones that have credit, do not ask for credit" (and vice versa). The core business of banking (hence its sustainability continuously "at risk") is instead built on the opposite principle, e.g. that the people that have less creditworthiness are asking more credit extensions from the banks and vice versa.

It all gets balanced via the credit underwriting capabilities of the bank, via the risk pooling, transformation and diversification principle (it's more difficult, albeit not impossible, that all things go bad at the same time—not impossible because, as we have seen, there is indeed some correlation among bad events at times of crisis). It is also ultimately stabilized by the buffer equity capital and subordinated debt provided by the bank's shareholders. Still, as we have seen, this imbalance continuously at risk persists, with the occasional bank going bust and with likely know-on effects on the extended economy, not to mention the usual systemic risk.

The digital transformation of the global financial system is potentially promising to redefine not only the essence of lending as the core business of banking, changing it to become less of a "personal" and more of a "social" business, but also making this potentially more stable, and less prone to the risks introduced by the paradox outlined by the above-mentioned witticism. As a start, lending is getting less personal and more social (therefore less prone to individual meddling) on at least three quite different but still critical perspectives.

On a first dimension, the analysis of "personal", official data of a potential counterpart, to assess her/his creditworthiness is becoming more of a social business, as more unstructured data, available from all kind of social sources and mostly through the use of the world wide web, is now complementing and extending the set of structured data coming from financial statements, personal income accounts and the like—with a shift on the relative importance of the quantitative methods of analysis being used, e.g. less reliant on backward looking, historical series driven conjoint statistical analysis and more reliant on present-sensitive, forward looking "black box" machine learning/AI techniques—now applied also in risk management.

The "social" view of the borrower, embedded in the billions of unstructured data available on the web will therefore become more and more important to assess how worthy this is, offering intelligence and views (to be mined and derived with applied analytics techniques) almost in real time and continuously updated. In a way, offering an almost perfect democratisation of the credit selection process—from underwriting to pricing, moving this away from the relationships-based capitalism that has informed (and crippled) so many relevant parts of the economy and for such a long time, also contributing to the 2008 and successive "crashes".

This introduces the second dimension of lending becoming more of a "social" business, as "power broker" incumbent bankers are progressively disintermediated by other, alternative players—starting from the ones acting in the "shadow banking" space: private equity funds willing to go direct in underwriting credit, insurance companies doing the same on the unfunded component of the tail risk associated to it and even regulated capital markets than are less in need of the support of investment banks to originate opportunities and to screen and underwrite the available counterparts. They all do this leveraging the digital lever.

As more data and information are made available by the web (pillar one), it becomes less relevant to own a branch or a sales people network, as greater transparency exists on the borrowers. Their creditworthiness is also becoming more transparent via the use of applied analytics to understand the available data and get credit scoring intelligence. The "personal" dimension of decision making in banking is therefore potentially challenged by other more innovative players, with power moving away from banks and with the lending allocation process becoming now potentially available to new shadow, mostly digital, competitors.

The "social" dimension of the lending business introduced by the digital transformation can then extend, on a third dimension, on the liability side. Not only banks get progressively disintermediated on their asset business side (e.g. the origination, screening, underwriting and pricing, and then management and recovery of loans extended to retail and corporate counterparts), but also their deposit gathering and liability management business get progressively "socialized" by new liquidity pooling opportunities that are made available on the web—albeit with greater constraints coming from the regulatory supervision ensuring the protection of non-professional, mostly retail deposit holders (a banking licence is in many cases still required).

However, with no banking licence, in new P2P lending initiatives, digital players can act basically as a facilitator to allow counterparts that are long on funds to find proper opportunities for direct lending to other counterparts that are short on funds. And they can help this selection not just by matching the respective bid/ask on price, but also their risk/return profiles and many other subjective components (including which kind of project or initiative the individual lenders would like to endorse), potentially allowing a "lending of one"—any single lender can decide whom to finance, for what and at which condition, if available in the market.

In a nutshell, the transformation of lending into a "social business" could mean that all available data and information are utilized, in novel, more artificially intelligence driven ways, to better assess the creditworthiness of any counterpart and make the business more bankers-free and more independent, e.g. reflecting the social wisdom that gets analysed and utilized by machine learning/AI credit tools.

It means then that banks are losing their critical role in the asset allocation process, with the power deriving from managing the traditional intermediation process progressively moving away to a multitude of new players and ultimately back to the customers. Banks are therefore potentially losing their critical role on the asset gathering side as well—on their deposit taking business, as they have less return opportunities to offer and other intermediation channels can offer more tailored and risk conscious and cheaper ways to invest in lending.

But it also follows, as a consequence of the socialization of the credit risk scoring, underwriting and holding, that the overall global financial system can become more stable. As the collective conscience of markets and societies know better the creditworthiness of people, people are then more likely to get the credit they deserve, and at the economically fair price, with the remaining, occasional errors (of two types: of giving credit to the credit-unworthy, and of not giving credit to the credit-worthy) being also "socialized"—with no direct principal holding on the intermediating bank side—in the purest model, a synapses bank would hold a very limited balance sheet, with super safe assets to match the excess funds gathered and managed, following a "narrow banking" business design. In this way, even our starting "witticism" would hold true, with the most credit worthy banks holding (and asking) for less credit, or not at all, on their balance sheet.

8.3 Alternative Lending Models

The "unsustainable lightness" of banking, and the inverted pyramid that we described in the beginning, has been at least partially responsible for the global financial crisis that started from the subprime lending crisis of 2008. As a consequence of this, and given the following wave of re-regulation that has significantly increased the burden of the banking business (requiring more capital per dollar of risk weighted loans, more liquidity easily available and a reduced time lapse in the duration of assets and liabilities across all time buckets), in an increasingly risk-averse economy, the banks' business model of intermediating savers and borrowers by offering a "risk transformation" (with a buffered offered by the equity capital of the banks) has had the immediate effect to reduce accessibility to loans not just to subprime customers but, more broadly, to any other kind of customer, either retail or SME (large corporates may have greater access to capital markets).

This has in turn negatively impacted the investment and consumption cycles, limiting the growth rate of most of the developed economies, with greater negative impact on the economies, say in Continental Europe, where the relationships based approach to lending has been historically stronger, and—also as a consequence of this—the mark to market clean-up of the banks' balance sheet has been less timely and decisive.

In a market where lending has become less abundant and where still a number of banks are facing the challenge of a protracted balance sheet restructuring, the opportunity of going direct to lend to retail and SME counterparts on a very simple proposition and at interesting rates (and with a much reduced cost base, given the alternative distribution channels used) has been increasingly addressed by alternative professional investors, including private equity funds, insurance companies and other asset managers.

In a low interest rates environment, they have seen the opportunity to put their capital at work avoiding the heavy regulation of banking (as they are not managing the money of deposit holders, they can go long on credit without having regulatory capital to be set aside) and starting a disintermediation war with banks that is just partially fought on new technology and business models and mostly on the traditional finance camp.

The most interesting trend, spurred by the above-mentioned lending squeeze, has however indeed combined the appetite of alternative sources of funds with the power coming from new technologies and related business models. In the lending as "social business", new paradigmatic scenario, alternative lending platforms have started leveraging P2P models and lean operations to offer seamless services to a broader base of customers. Like other institutional investors, they have emerged to fill the funding gaps in the traditional lending model, but differently from them, they are also offering new technologies and business models, ideally promising to deliver the "lending of one" value proposition because of three main characteristics.

As a first distinctive component, these alternative, digital disrupters have leveraged online data and platforms to provide direct (e.g. not intermediated by the company's balance sheet and therefore not mitigated by its own equity buffer the way the banks are doing) matching of funds between savers and borrowers—truly acting a la P2P—therefore usually ensuring a much lower service and funding costs, as their cost structure is nimble and mostly driven by IT (no branch network, no regulatory compliance, risk management and underwriting advisory mostly done by automated machine learning/AI based credit scoring tools etc.) and they are not asking for any interest rate "spread", but get basically paid by an access and advisory, or deal driven, fee.

As a consequence of their set up, these digital disrupters are really lean and most efficient and effective in the way they re-do one of the most obsolete job of the world, e.g. buying and selling money. As they are free of regulations and physical assets (the branch network), with very few and technologically smart people, and with new IT systems that are built as digital and with no legacy issues, these players have as a second distinctive component their velocity, reliability and super automated (and partially robotized) processes. They can on-board and assess borrowers and lenders in a streamlined way, following predefined rules for fast, transparent and democratized processing—with no room left for "personal relationships banking". In the following Figure, the experience of the Funding Circle is analysed, using the five pillars framework (Fig. 8.1).

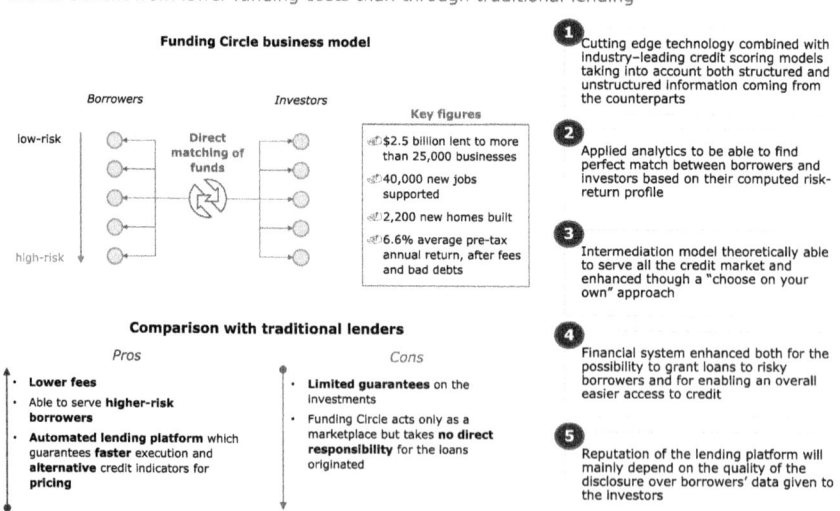

Fig. 8.1 Funding Circle enables direct matching of funds between savers and small businesses

8.3 Alternative Lending Models

These alternative digital lenders are however not just leveraging any kind of structured and unstructured data and information and applied analytics to produce new, superior credit intelligence and faster, cheaper and more streamlined processes. In fact, they also engage and interconnect in richer ways multiple counterparts (doing this in a smart way, and creating profiled, tailored junctions between lenders and borrowers—ideally pursuing a "lending of one" proposition). In this way, they are also transforming the way the overall economic system works, delivering new value added solutions and incremental value to the economy. The case of SoFi, targeting students, is shown in the following Figure, with his new approach to lending and wealth management (Fig. 8.2).

As a third distinctive component, they are assessing creditworthiness using alternative and more efficient metrics, and they use online adjudication processes (including auctions and reverse auctions) that make the overall asset allocation process more efficient, effective and competitive—ensuring maximum liquidity and transparency, where lenders have the flexibility to pick and choose a desired risk/return profile and corresponding loans portfolio. But there is even more than that, sometimes leading to further competitive advantages, and not just with regards to other banks, but even to the final (bad) borrowers. In the following Figure, a "five pillars" analysis of the business model of Kabbage is provided, as a direct lending business model also benefitting ecommerce players selling products and services over the web (Fig. 8.3).

Fig. 8.2 SoFi has followed a new approach to lending and WM, with more than $12 billion lent to date

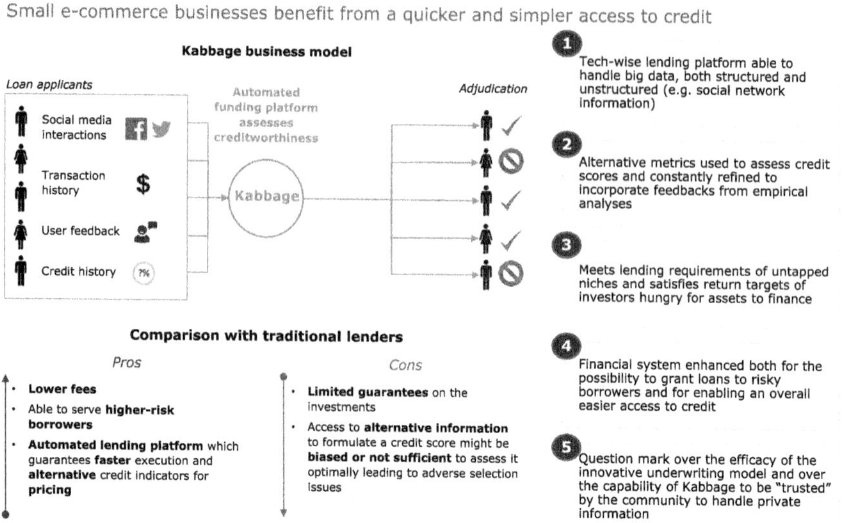
Small e-commerce businesses benefit from a quicker and simpler access to credit
Kabbage business model
Loan applicants
Social media interactions
Transaction history
User feedback
Credit history
Automated funding platform assesses creditworthiness
Kabbage
Adjudication
1 Tech-wise lending platform able to handle big data, both structured and unstructured (e.g. social network information)
2 Alternative metrics used to assess credit scores and constantly refined to incorporate feedbacks from empirical analyses
3 Meets lending requirements of untapped niches and satisfies return targets of investors hungry for assets to finance
4 Financial system enhanced both for the possibility to grant loans to risky borrowers and for enabling an overall easier access to credit
5 Question mark over the efficacy of the innovative underwriting model and over the capability of Kabbage to be "trusted" by the community to handle private information
Comparison with traditional lenders
Pros
Lower fees
Able to serve higher-risk borrowers
Automated lending platform which guarantees faster execution and alternative credit indicators for pricing
Cons
Limited guarantees on the investments
Access to alternative information to formulate a credit score might be biased or not sufficient to assess it optimally leading to adverse selection issues

Fig. 8.3 Kabbage direct lending business model is also benefitting ecommerce players

8.4 From Retail Banking to Retailers Banking

Amazon launched its own lending business as early as in 2012, with little fanfare and in a limited, selective way, offering to selected sellers playing on his platform instant access to loans for up to 12 months and at annual interest rates ranging from 6 to 17%.[1] After a total volume of over USD 3 Bln originated loans, it is now expanding its offer to more of the 2 Mln businesses selling on its digital marketplace—many of them pay Amazon to store, package and ship merchandise to customers on their behalf—accounting for almost half of Amazon's total units sold worldwide. There is a lot of "digital" in what Amazon is doing, as it leverages all the data that it owns on the businesses and on their commercial performance, but also more than that.

On one side, Amazon supplies funds from its own balance sheet within 24 h, then deducts payments on the loan every two weeks automatically from the sellers' accounts. If the balance of the account is going down, or if sales of a specific business suddenly dip, Amazon can put a freeze on any merchandise held in its warehouse until it gets repaid up. In this way, credit losses are not just better predicted, but radically avoided in a near perfect way—as Amazon sees the cash flow of the businesses, their commercial trends and even hold their inventories of

[1] Amazon to ramp up lending in challenge to big banks, Ben McLannahan, Financial Times, 7 June 2017.

goods as collateral it can quickly seize—a strong competitive advantage over bad borrowers.

Amazon's move is just a sign of a potential broader shift of power away from the traditional "retail bank"—that has pulled back from small business lending after the crisis also due to its high cost of risk and higher regulatory capital charges—towards smarter "retailers doing banking". These digital retailers a la Amazon, are even challenging new FinTech players like OnDeck and Kabbage, that have invested on lead-generation and marketing to find and address creditworthy borrowers, but without actually having already another established core business that serves them, as Amazon does—that also puts it into the position of being able to predict when money is needed and what customers are worth having on its high-quality balance sheet.

In fact, Amazon, or any other digital retailer, can already know what a business is selling, as they have an history and a marked to market trend in commercial performance and can project sales matching them with what they see in their inventory, hence knowing when they need to refurbish and reload it, with new money needed. Many other specialists in ecommerce are now starting making use of their commercial data as well, to get better, deeper insights into their customers and a superior ability to handle a loan—nothing a traditional bank could do, leaving aside the regulatory arbitrage as they lend their excess cash, in a way reverting the financial cycle (they get paid by retail end-buyers first, and then pay sellers, and they can lend the extra average cash flow capacity to businesses, to beef up their inventories, where they can hold as collaterals their own products). It is a better and almost perfect mouse trap, going much beyond the digital component.

Other players like Square (a payment processing company and its lending arm Square Capital), and PayPal (a money transfer company), are also addressing the potential informational advantage derived by the knowledge of how cash flow behaves, matching this, where they can, with commercial behavioural indicators—including returned goods and commercial complaints or the perceived happiness of the customers on the purchase.

Others are thinking to offer lending along with real time inventory monitoring tools and behavioural commercial dashboards—to analyse sales and, more importantly, customers' behaviours. In this way they are also contributing in serving better the best customers, helping to grow faster the businesses that truly deserve—and increasing their retention and cross sell over time, as these customers take up other services on offer.

It could even become more than that. PayPal, for example, via PayPal Working Capital, is supplying loans to businesses around the world. But it also runs PayPal Credit, a line of credit which customers can apply for and use at the point of sale—hence helping again the businesses, as they sell more, and hence become even more creditworthy and able to generate more business for PayPal Working Capital and for PayPal (the processor) (Fig. 8.4).

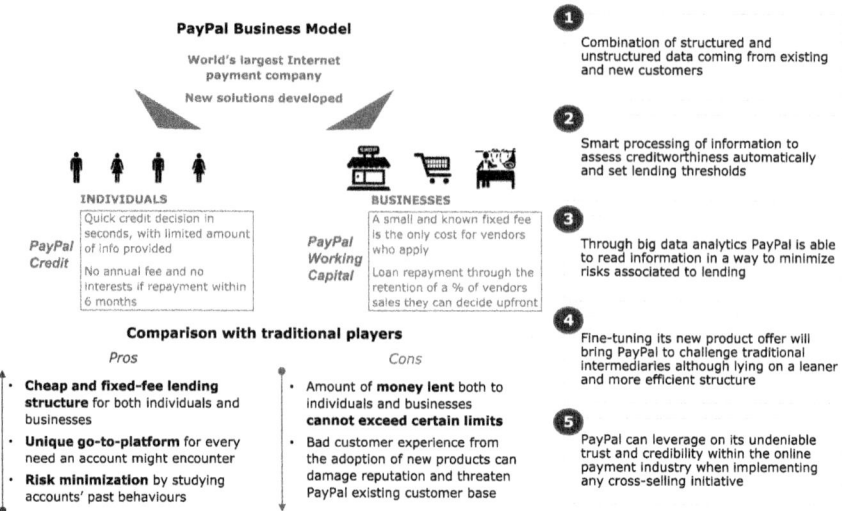

Fig. 8.4 PayPal is moving from being the biggest online payment provider to an integrated FS firm

Hence, via the products being sold, and the merchants and businesses being used, there will be a way to get to a better, instant credit rating for the retail end buyer as well, leveraging other information, coming from IoT and other devices, monitoring how a customer moves around the shop and smile at point of sale, if the sale is realized in an off-line context, or in how she flips across web pages, or moves a cursor, if it happens on-line.

In this move to "retailing banking", the synapses model is used in full, as it could be if traditional retail banks starts to react and innovate, playing the same game and harnessing data, information and intelligence from the customers' funnels, when they buy either on-line and, more interestingly, off-line. For once, on the unstructured data side, multiple new information need to be gathered, including how they move and look like being happy at the point of sale. And then, new intelligence can be derived and elaborated through the utilization of machine learning/AI techniques, thus moving towards new "interconnection" businesses.

In these models, the old intermediation game is substituted by a smart management of multiple counterparts that can act in more effective and convenient ways —and where the cost of credit risk could be reduced almost at will—take the example of Amazon, "owning" most of the digital business cycle of the seller, not to mention its physical inventory. But even more importantly, new, real value is created at the level of the ecosystem, as good businesses get instant access to more and cheaper credit and just when they need it—the PayPal example, going from consumer lending to the working capital one is showing just that. On the basis of a trust that is building in an accelerated way, and expanding well beyond the realm of retailing and ecommerce.

8.5 Alternative Models of Deposit Taking

The alternative digital models impacting on the asset side of the lending business are also promising to disrupt its corresponding liability side, impacting on the way savings are managed and put to a productive use. Whilst we have commented on the alternative lending models referencing mostly the first four pillars of the synapses model, for the deposit taking business it is obviously the fifth one that stands out as a critical one, as trust becomes critical to persuade retail customers, no matter what the extra convenience offered by fancy digital applications, to entrust their savings to a likely unknown, unregulated, web-based only player. And, whilst the trust on the lending side can be a fight that new competitors can fight with targeted advertising and aggressive pricing, what is really at stake on the deposit side of the business is not the potential yield offered on the savings, but the certainty of having them well protected and safe, no matter what.

The very definition of trust should therefore be closely considered by these alternative business models, to have a fair chance of succeeding. They are not in fact providing any guarantee with their own capital, as they act as mere (albeit intelligent) agents. And there is neither an explicit (insurance guarantee on banking deposits as provided by most jurisdiction up to a level of 100 k USD circa) nor an implicit (public guarantee of the Government to intervene in case of major banking failures to save the bank or at least cover most of its non-equity losses) assurance that somebody will step into protect their money if the company is failing.

Trust could however be built from the superior way these alternative players can manage customers' data and analyse credit risk on behalf of their clients on the liability side of their business models. Basically, the providers of savings are not required to make any judgment on the solvability of the company managing the platform per se, but on how effective it can be as asset manager, in helping them in selecting the best counterpart to lend to. It is therefore basically a trust that needs to be built via the reputation of the digital company as lending advisor and money match-maker—and it is independent from any regulatory requirements and statutory provision of capital.

A number of other pay offs can then be considered for the alternative model of deposit taking, to add to its attractiveness for potential customers, including the increased accuracy and customization of underwriting, the greater access to a pool of opportunities less geographically constrained (as the origination of loans will not be driven by a physical branch network), the reduced costs for access and management, the increased transparency and level of convenience and the better risk adjusted yield theoretically achievable.

More importantly, alternative, on-line deposit taking digital businesses can also develop a better commercial proposition and develop a brand equity for total convenience if, apart from ensuring a better economic payoff to customers and superior access to lending opportunities, they are better able to follow the emerging customer preferences in the way they want to interact with service providers—maybe offering them initially just one single financial product and then progressively extending their offering to a fuller range of products. As they develop and mature, and grow the number of customers they are managing, these alternative providers of deposit taking services can progressively develop into "depositories of trust", and serve as central platform for connections to niche providers' products—thus trying to hold customers tight via cross selling.

As in the past current account management and deposit taking has been traditionally the best place to start, this leg of liability management of the old "buy money and sell money" business looks like a promising basis for further disruption and the promotion of cross selling, further diminishing the competitive positioning of banks, as the "safe as a bank" statement loses progressively its meaning and new global and valuable brands (think at the likes of Amazon, Apple, Google or Facebook) come to dominate not just the consumer experience, but also their share of perceived security, in a fully digital financial world were cyber risk becomes a more relevant and dominant decision making criteria in the selection of the vendor you may wish to partner with.

8.6 Buying and Selling Money—Like a Brain

The very core banking business of "buying and selling money" could be progressively taken away by a number of alternative FinTech players, smart in bypassing and arbitraging regulations, in leveraging extended data and new technologies and in aggressively pursuing new approaches to better suit the changing pattern of the behaviors of customers. Whatever the scenario, of traditional banks ending up competing against these new incumbents, or of developing alliances with them, we could safely assume that the current ranking by total market capitalization of the top ten global banks will be quite different in a 5–10 years scenario—it has been quite different through time and even recently, with Japanese banks raising to the top in the late '80 and '90, with the American and European getting back afterwards and now with the Chinese ones taking over.

Next time could, however, be radically different—and not just because the ranking could change again and have few names listed that are not actually banks, but institutional financial investors or "shadow banks", but also because the overall size could be different, and actually lower, if the "buying money/selling money" activity will be increasingly funneled via digital, light, "synapsized" platform, without being stored and warehoused in a balance sheet owned by a third party, or into an all-encompassing fund.

A lending business which is increasingly social and "democratic" could potentially avoid forming large balance sheet intermediated by banks or management companies that broker power along money. A multitude of direct channels, via the web and the digital deposit—lending marketplaces being created, could ultimately end fulfilling the dream of a "lending of one", e.g. the ability to potentially connect the single lender to a well-diversified sub-portfolio of borrowers, geographically dispersed and neither intermediated nor guaranteed by a traditional bank

8.6 Buying and Selling Money—Like a Brain

(or investment management company for that purpose, as they would also be disintermediated by the machine learning/AI applications helping even the small investor on his/her credit underwriting).

Even leaving aside this extreme scenario, a profound revolution can be expected, as having a balance sheet becomes not only a costly regulatory burden and risky affair—no matter what the inverted pyramid is and how its unbearable lightness is managed by prudent and savvy senior managers. Lending could also become a less useful function and maybe an utterly avoidable activity—something heavy that cannot compete with the agility of the new digital ecosystem, where everybody can play the lending game, no matter what the scale and scope are, as they can be multiplied by the digital platforms, free of any space constraint and almost omniscient of the relevant information regarding credit risk in both its performance and solvency components.

Buying and selling money, as a business, could end up working in the future more like the human brain, and less as the muscles and bones underpinning and supporting the execution of the movements that the brain decides to impose on arts and legs. It follows that banks and the other financial players, traditional or new, will have to focus even more on the defining pillars of the "synapses" approach: to work more like a brain.

Data and information, on one side, are critical for all kind of financial functions and even more so in the credit world—for the provider of sources and also for the borrowers that need to get the fullest and most open and best access to the available forms of funds—to optimize the allocation of resources in the economy and further support its sustainable growth rate. Applied analytics on these data and information and the new developments of machine learning and artificial intelligence are promising to be the "next big thing" in lending—maybe ignored and not recognized by regulators and more traditional Chief Lending and Risk Officers, they could revolutionize underwriting and its related pricing—providing real time scrutiny based on superior intelligence, dynamically adjusted and modified as new quantitative and qualitative news become available.

These first two pillars of "synapses" are easy to grasp for incumbents, as they are able to accumulate and analyze unprecedented quantities of data, initially for marketing purposes and now also for risk quantification and selection. Traditional banks may try hard to fight, but they are starting from a number of disadvantages, including the lack of unstructured data, the regulatory, backward looking mindset that refrains bankers to accept anything that comes out of a "black box" approach, and a still strong attachment to the "personal" dimension of lending, e.g. the one related to the relationships based way of doing business and to the power broking dominant position gained by bankers because of their historical "stay-along" the money food chain.

The third pillar looks even more tricky, as it involves a move away from the traditional, low value added model of mere intermediation: the model that supported the profitability of banks for centuries via the "boosters" of the inverted pyramids key risk dimensions: e.g. with a lot of leverage, long duration mismatch and the supposed transformation (via the diversification principle and the extra buffer of the equity capital of the bank) of highly risky individual positions into a widows and orphans' investable portfolio. Not to mention "velocity", that introduced the "hot potato" game in an industry where smart people abound.

New synapses business models will be able to offer more, managing dynamic ecosystems that are able to profile the best match of lenders and borrowers, given the right risk/return profile and no matter what the scale and scope of the potential transaction and relevant counterparts. Lending as a "social" business could actually be sub segmented in different businesses, were other non-financial dimensions are adding further meaning to the "social" component, with all sorts of ethical, ecological, customer friendly lending players taking shape. The junctions could be played by the "synapses" bank like the brain works, and it would become easier the lesser the bank is involved from a capital perspective and worried about the management of its own balance sheet.

In the lending as "social" business there is therefore a value adding component strongly to the benefit of the overall economy and working from a multi stakeholders' perspective. In a way, more credit and better credit should become available and addressable, spurring a higher growth rate and adding more stability to the system—of course, if it all works and the other three pillars are producing better intelligence and business models to match supply and demand.

As an almost balance sheet free company, it follows that the "synapses" bank should also be getting on a higher and safer profitability path—being paid commissions for the technological service and the match making, and for the advisory (mostly done by machines that are independent and unbiased and less prone to errors, mistakes and wrong doings) on the credit underwriting and management of related risks.

How the change in the business and operating model, and—almost as importantly—in the balance sheet of the bank could be managed as a radical discontinuity whilst managing the current business is also going to be critical, and a matter of trust—our last but not least important pillar of our synapses approach. As customers will need to build trust on the new proposition, and the banks top management—maybe in an even more complex way—will need to build trust in a banking business that has not got money into its balance sheet—no more pyramids, no more full loads of coins and notes on their liability and asset sides, but just bits and bytes.

8.7 The Future of Buying and Selling Money

Following the financial crisis, a lower risk appetite among retail and commercial banks have significantly limited access to traditional bank intermediated lending—particularly so in regions, like continental Europe, where corporates are still heavily reliant on the banking sector to buy money, and retail clients are correspondingly very reliant on universal banks to sell them their money. The first reduction in lending has been visible in near and subprime lending, as risk appetite has decreased and regulatory capital charges have been made progressively heavier. But that was just the start of the story, and not the end of it.

In fact, over the same period, several FinTech lending platforms, leveraging P2P models, have been trying to address the lending supply vacuum to then get a foothold in the core business of banking. Their new, digitally empowered adjudication methods and lean, more automated processes used to offer loans to the riskier segment has now been tested and developed and looks ready to be extended to a broader base of customers—offering at the same time a new class of investment opportunities to retail and corporate savers.

In short, the newcomers are offering P2P models, where they leverage their online platforms and contracts to provide direct matching of funds between savers and borrowers—hence lowering funding costs via their online marketplace—as players like Funding Circle, Credit Ease and LendingClub have been trying of doing lately. They are also offering innovative adjudication mechanisms, to assess the creditworthiness of borrowers based on behavioural metrics that go beyond the traditional, regression analysis based, backward looking credit scores in use at traditional lenders—adding unstructured data, behavioural and psychometric analysis and new machine learning techniques able to beat the predictive capabilities of the internal rating based tools in use.

Companies like Lenddo or Kabbage are offering these and breaking new ground on price discovery and allocation of excess funds and uses. They finally leverage their FinTech, start up like, technological infrastructure to overcome legacy processes and old technologies, allowing them to onboard and assess borrowers and lenders in a more lean, fast and efficient fashion—also leading to more transparent decision making—as companies like Zopa, OnDeck and Prosper are already offering and showing in the market. It all therefore looks set to impact radically on the business of buying and selling money, introducing potential future scenarios—of fierce competition, crowding out but also potential alliances and coopetition.

In a first "fierce competition" scenario, digital lending platforms could successfully develop some market share and leverage their superior reach of unstructured data and deployment of better applied analytics and machine learning/AI. They could offer better service and a more extended, social-based, "interconnection" among multiple stakeholders. They could then offer superior solutions, to ensure better matching of counterparts willing to buy and sell money and in this way, add true, incremental economic value to the ecosystem.

But they could also end up competing on better underwriting and pricing on some small component of principal business that they could develop and build out of their capital base, and therefore increase profitability as alternative lender (and not just as alternative lending platform), better able to discriminate good and bad credit risk, and act accordingly. They would, in this case, try to displace and crowd out traditional banks and going upstream, into their core business of principal lending (banks are not mere, risk-free intermediaries as they ultimately take risks with their own capital, stretching it to get an higher ROE—Return on Equity).

In a second "alliance and coopetition" scenario, the new FinTech players acting in digital lending could just address specific sub-segments or sub-businesses, like the sub-prime clients or the money lending business. And traditional banks would keep catering for traditional segments of savers and borrowers, from mass market and affluent families and individuals to stable, almost investment grade small businesses and SME. Or they could play together in a more formal way, with digital lenders offering new origination channels aimed at, for example, millennials, or unbanked people in far-away regions not covered by the bank's branches and requiring more, complementary unstructured data and information to get to a positive underwriting decision. A more extended cooperation model could also consider formal joint ventures, or mergers, where incumbents would look at buying and absorbing alternative digital platforms (and lenders) as a mean to also transform their operating model, main processes and technologies. With the opportunity for the FinTech lenders to tap into a much larger pool of existing clients and on the basis of an equity capital more fitted for principal lending.

Whatever the scenario, it should be safe to assume that if not lenders, lending will not be the same anymore—as it develops into a social but also digital business, where cyber credit worthiness goes hand in hand with cyber trust, and is subject to the cyber risk that could alter, defect or completely annul the new capabilities being built in credit scoring, underwriting and pricing—a new revolution per se, built on new sets of behavioural and psychometric data, deep-learned machine credit officer and a new model for interconnecting people willing to engage in one of the oldest trade in international finance. All this will be further discussed in the next chapter, on the discontinuities introduced by digitization on the risk management function performed at large (in terms of assessing, transferring, holding, covering, insuring etc.) by the global financial system.

As it happens in every "revolution", sudden changes will give rise to few quick victories and multiple mistakes and disasters along the way. It is for the best credit-worthy "synapses" bank to design and ponder how to run this revolution, in its scope selection, level of sophistication aimed for and, even more importantly, with which adoption rate and overall extension time. It takes a lot to build a credit-risk savvy reputation, but just few hours to destroy this and much else, starting from the equity of the lender (digital or not) and the money entrusted to it by savers: they, even in a revolution, should consider how much they can afford the mistake of giving money to the wrong counterparties and platform, vis a vis the one of not giving it to the worthy ones.

Transformation in Risk Management

Abstract

Risk management is a quite critical, but less well known, function played by the global financial system. It allows for the valuation, pricing, transferring, holding, hedging, covering of risks—of a financial or pure nature. Whilst banks and other traditional intermediaries are running the "new" risk of being competitively leapfrogged by emerging digital players, even their risk management function needs to develop and innovate, to allow them to retain their competitiveness in their core businesses—starting from the lending one. Risk management has evolved in the past by quantum leaps: getting more quantitative, statistics-based, and then more holistic and proactive. It now needs to turn "digital", promising to revolutionize not just the world of banking, but the way corporates and individuals manage their own financial and non-financial risks, via the financial system—with a more augmented, meaningful and integrated definition of "risk management"

Keywords

Risk management · Behavioral and psychometric analysis · Credit scoring · Credit work out

9.1 At the Core: Holistic, Proactive, Integrated

Risk management is at the core of the global financial system and it underpins the working of its international capital markets, transnational, regional and local players and main products and services. Little understood until recently, risk is one of the least well known critical function that the system performs—when it allows for the evaluation, pricing, packaging, slicing, transferring, sharing, hedging, covering, insuring etc. of most of the risks we, as individuals and with our companies, face every-day, of a financial or pure nature. At the core of the global financial system, we have also stated earlier, sits "risk" as its main production factor and key driver of the successes and failures of its most relevant sub-industries (banking, insurance, asset management etc.).

On this basis, and given the impetus on the development of risk management methodologies and techniques by regulators, risk management has recently evolved from a mostly qualitative, gut-feelings based, reactive management approach, into a more proactive stance, based on a more thorough quantification (mostly based on conjoint statistical analysis) and on a more holistic definition of risks and potential risk factors (whilst credit risk still remains the main one in banking, further attention has been paid to such risks like market, liquidity, interest rate, foreign exchange, equity, operational, reputational, conduct, business, cyber… etc. etc.).

The development of a more scientific approach to risk quantification and management—on a holistic and proactive basis, has proceeded through quantum leaps, spurred by very significant investments from the side of the regulators and financial intermediaries—not always leading to great results, as shown by the huge investments done in the implementation of the Basle II Accord and of the internal rating based credit management approaches—just a few years before the outburst of one of the worst global banking crisis ever.

This latest crisis showed very clearly the limits of current risk management approaches, based on structured, mostly financial, historical data and on conjoint analysis, derived from "white box" statistical models. In a way, this could be the main lesson learned from the global financial crisis of 2008 onwards, when a number of holistic and proactive approaches to risk management showed to be in fact limited, if not flawed, because of their over reliance on the backward-looking analysis of the past (think of the risk underwriting in financial trading and in lending as done on the basis of regression analysis mostly developed on historical data).

A new quantum leap for risk management, as a science and as an art, is now probably in the making, driven by innovation in technology and spurred by the unprecedented development of the quantity and quality of data and information now becoming available to global financial Institutions and to their FinTech nemesis. We have already commented on the large volumes of "big data" now being captured and stored by banks and other financial intermediaries, not to mention FinTech players. And we have already showed examples of the augmented "quality" of this data, as structured information is also sourced in novel ways, from IoT, social websites, satellites, sensors and from all kind of other technological paraphernalia. But it is more than that.

In fact, data feeding now become timeless, as they are captured as they are produced, in real time and shared at high speed across a number of servers encompassing the world-wide web. Ultimately, a further characteristic is also characterizing the next transformation of risk management and its digitization—as it gets more and more dependent on new applied analytics techniques, more reliant on machine learning/AI and with greater weight of "closed box" approaches. In a way, a completely new way of thinking is potentially determining the approach to risk management in the global financial system—driven by the deep learning capabilities of machines and, in the future, by the automated, reactive/proactive policies enacted by robots.

In this scenario dominated by emerging forms of new "risk-intelligence", the "integration" component will also become more and more critical, as all these capabilities, old and new, will need to be strategically driven and embedded in the business and operating model of banks, financial intermediaries and new challengers.

The synapsezation of the risk management function will therefore need to happen in a horizontal fashion—with successful synapses banks being able to get the most out of the data and information available and of their risk-intelligence produced. But, again, the real challenge will be in identifying new, more sophisticated interconnection games where risks are shared, hedged, traded, covered or swapped… and with new use cases able to truly determine the creation of some extra value for the overall ecosystem of reference. On this basis, the synapses bank or its FinTech challenger will be able to derive a better productivity out of risk—with risk that will keep being one of the main production factor of this industry, albeit with a more digital nature.

9.2 Credit Scoring: Mind the Present

Marcel Proust famously wrote how people, buried by their past memories and worried by their future possibilities, tend to forget (and cannot enjoy at full) their present. Paraphrasing this, we could also say that banks—and other financial intermediaries, are so entrapped by their troubled past (the great financial crisis and the risk-underwriting mistakes and related scandals) and so worried about their future (being squeezed out by the heavy re-regulation of the sector and by the competitive challenges now posed by new digital banking players) that they tend not to focus enough, and stretch and leverage on their current present.

That seems particularly true about risk analysis, pricing and underwriting decisions. In fact, following the implementation of the "heavy duty" internal credit scoring techniques promoted by the Basle II (or BIS 2) regulatory capital adequacy accord, banks have become so focussed and almost obsessed on historical, structured data fed, statistically based analysis that they have become at times over reliant on them.

This has sometimes meant for them driving forward the lending machines whilst looking at the rear-end view mirror, with the unintended consequences that are now all too clear, as the monumental NPL/NPE stock in the continental European banking market, and its limited growth and innovation rate in the economy is showing: too many mistakes on the undertaken loans extended to unworthy clients, and lost possibilities on loans that could have been extended to clients with great forward looking creditworthiness, but with low profile past.

This BIS 2 sponsored approach to credit analysis, whilst grounded in data (our first competitive invariance: but in this case just past data of a structured form, e.g. not comprising qualitative, social sources but mostly relying on formal data—like financial statements for small business and corporates, all used on the heroic assumption they were "true enough" to be of some use), and on some intelligence derived by applied analytics (our second competitive invariance: but in this case with a very narrow recourse to statistically based, traditional multi-factors conjoint analysis based on historical series) has failed spectacularly to deliver the promised "objective, rational, open box" risk discrimination analysis, whilst it has helped banks to reduce their required capital—a trend now being reversed as a counter reaction to the many banks' failures that followed.

After that debacle, banks have so far reacted by being over cautious, relying even more on past analysis and going back to more traditional, paper based, people intensive credit scoring/rating techniques. The burden of the past has therefore just increased and the present has become further constraints on next developments.

The future challenges posed by alternative, direct (e.g. not intermediated by banks) lenders have then contributed to the worries of chief lending and commercial officers, that have answered by slashing the interest rates charged on (apparently) top quality clients, and moving away from (perceived) higher risk counterparts, that are now becoming the uncontested target of new players (see for example the case of the pay lenders in the UK), that have been able to charge very interesting risk-adjusted rates on those loans.

The worry of this competitive future has thus led traditional banks to re-trench in an even less sustainable competitive positioning. Their forward-looking lending policies have basically become an even more thorough and deterministic search for the "black and white" discrimination between the bad and the good ones—based on the formal, structured data they have, and on the statistical output of deterministic models, where almost no grey area and no risk-adjusted return trade off optimization is contemplated and allowed.

Digital and technological innovation are now promising to deliver concrete ways to revolutionize the way risks (financial and—per extension—"pure" ones as well) can be analysed, priced and underwritten, not to mentioned pooled or disaggregated and then distributed and transferred (at a price). A present looking approach grounded on unstructured data, behavioural analysis machine-learning driven and further digital applications is now available, for the potential benefits of banks, not to mention their end customers.

Let's take the example, already introduced in previous chapters, of merchants financing—e.g. lending to (mostly) small business companies whose financial statements' reliability is usually very limited and not usually up to date (there are published once a year), and whose volatility in commercial and financial success (closely interrelated) is often wide and sudden, with deep consequences given their usually thin capital structure.

An alternative way of measuring their credit risk, as already commented, would look at all the data that are, in real time, available, in a structured and unstructured form. It would also consider new applied analytics models, including self-learning

9.2 Credit Scoring: Mind the Present

and artificial intelligence that can make good use of these "big data" to derive better credit scoring models and risk-intelligence. On this basis, financial intermediaries could also create new ways to interconnect clients and systems (merchants to retail clients, and to their suppliers of end products) and value adding economic solutions that are just making the most of the integrated supply chain: increasing the overall productivity of, say, designing, manufacturing, marketing, distributing, selling and servicing.

In our example, the credit scoring could start from a POS (point of sale) value proposition, where the merchant is offered some advanced retail customers behavioural analysis application. The merchant is offered a "widget" (the size of a lighter) that, aggregating the analysis done via sensors, cameras and external social data, analyzes and predicts the behavior of the retail customers and their satisfaction with the merchant's offers. The sensors monitor their smartphone and how they move and where and how much they stay in different parts of the shop; and cameras take pictures of their facial expression when they pay, analyzing and monitoring via psychometric software their relative happiness or lack of it, and via the POS payment system, also cash flow data are made easily available, not to mention other unstructured data that can be tapped from the web, e.g. outside traffic and busyness of parking slots near the shop, the weather and lightness of the day, the comments on the shops or commercial area captured on social web sites and much more.

Recently, a French bookstore chain had video fed to a software that scrutinizes shoppers' movements and facial expressions for surprise, dissatisfaction, confusion or hesitation.[1] This has also provided real time support, to suggest clerks how to intervene for help or comfort, boosting sales by 10%. Estonia, a software from Realeyes, an emotion-detection firm based in London, has also showed that shoppers who entered smiling spent a third more than others. More than video, other more sophisticated and intimate ways of learning about emotions of shoppers are also on offer—it all looks like a new set of "agent 007" secret weapons, but it is not.

Thermal-imaging cameras, for example, are already in use. And they can detect the customers' heart rate. And wirelessly captured data from smartphone accelerometers can suggest when shoppers become fascinated (their movements often stops) or are fretting over prices (with phones being raised to check for cheaper products on-line). In even more intrusive ways (customers are convinced in agreeing to these by promising them a reward or discount), other retailers are trying wearable galvanometers—to measure moisture and electrical resistance on hand skin to reveal arousal. In short, a race is on to work out how best to collect and use "emotional data".

Emotional (unstructured) seem to offer new unlimited possibilities to get a better understanding on the decision making of customers that are by no means just mere "rational economic agent". Emotions are better able to express the urge to spend that drive most of our everyday life buying patterns. And they can be analyzed and understood to then allow the sell-side counterparts to improve packaging, displays,

---

[1] How retailers are watching shoppers' emotions. The Economist, 10th June 2017.

content and timing of sales pitches and of the products and services being offered... but also risk management—moving from "retail therapy" (with consumers driven to spend when they are feeling blue) to customer risk (psycho) analysis, where retailers work out how to spot mildly depressed (but safe) customers to sell more, and hoe to avoid fairly happy ones ready to buy at will, in their certainty they will not end up paying anyway.

If all new "emotional" and other "unstructured" data are mined and analyzed with self-learning machines/AI, a present-focused credit scoring can be developed—allowing the creation of a real time, self-learning, credit scoring for the banks on the merchants and on their end customers that, via back testing, should lead to demonstrable better credit selection, overcoming the backward nature of current credit ratings and their over-reliance on opaque financial statement data. These new behavioral credit scoring should thus be able to support the rise in consumer finance and related consumption and in the refinancing of the working capital of the merchants' businesses. Most of these loans to merchants and to their customers will be short term anyway—as emotions are flimsy, and so is the customers' behavior and hence the success of a merchant's business.

Better data, structured and unstructured, and better applied analytics to produce risk-intelligence can then be further leveraged in a new way if merchants gets, in turn, a very usable reporting tool on how they are performing commercially, on how their clients are happy about their offerings, and on why they should reconsider their marketing mix (pricing, promotion, location and shop's logistics) to be more effective.

In a nutshell, these digital applications would give them commercial intelligence to perform better and be more sales effective and operationally efficient, which in turn should improve their credit scoring and help them, and the bank, and their manufacturers and suppliers and wholesale distributors of finished products to better allocate their resources and to drive a higher productivity across they overall value chain. Hence realizing a much larger and more meaningful interconnection game, and creating new, tangible, incremental value for the overall ecosystem—that the parties can attain and enjoy, on the basis o trust... in the present.

9.3 Granting Education

If we think of the many opportunities brought to the traditional world of lending by digital innovation and by the mastering of advanced big data management techniques and machine learning/AI, we can come up with an almost limitless number of further use cases and system wide solutions. They are not just promising to dramatically increase the convenience of the product itself (now on offer from a number of new digital counterparts, from pay lenders like Wonga, to social web-based network managers like Tencent, AliPay and Baidu—all already able to process underwriting and answer to a new request of credit almost in real time).

9.3 Granting Education

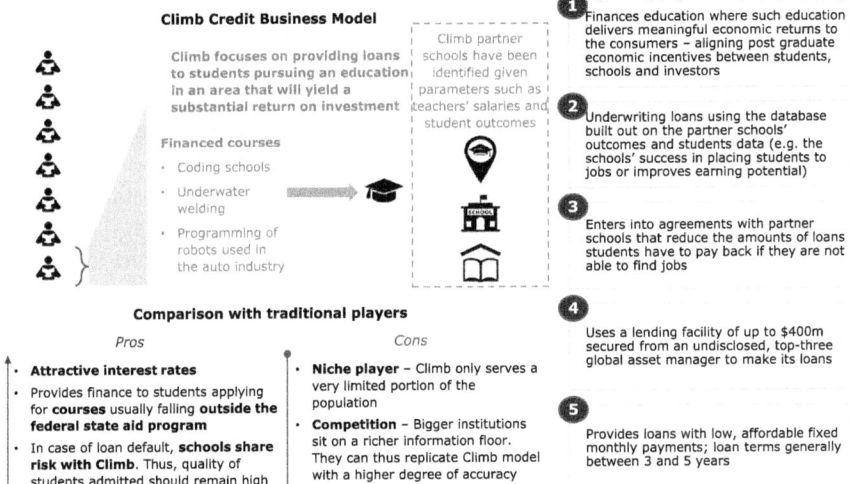

Fig. 9.1 Climb credit's mission is to fund high ROI education within the $1.3trn student debt market in the US

But they are also delivering a sizeable, increased, overall effectiveness on the risk selection and risk adjusted pricing processes. It could all mean that credit can become a new kind of co-investment, not just based on the current and backward set of historical information, but also quite tied to the forward performances of the counterpart—with the bank (or digital lender) investing on its client's future successes and then helping her/him to achieve them, with financial incentives that become vested to the lender as the client performs.

Let's take the business of lending to students, a large credit market in the US and in other Countries were most of the education is private and with very high costs and (maybe therefore) very skewed risk/return profiles. Using data, information and applied analytics, the "synapses" bank could, as a start, try to answer, in an objective way, the many questions regarding the (net present, financial) value related to a given education, program, course, teacher and even student, with the loans being then assigned and priced based on the composite expected return and related risks—with, potentially, dynamic adjustment mechanisms to reprice with lower yields the students that are doing better. A New York based FinTech, Climb (as described in the following Fig. 9.1), does just that as it focuses its lending decisions on sharp, quantifiable increases in the future earnings of applicant students.[2]

The average size of its loans is small (10,000 USD circa) and it normally finances programs of less than one year, focussing on what it should know better, e.g. education on IT development, coding, digitally-driven new professions like programming robots for car manufacturers—no matter what the formal education of

---
[2]The Economist, Grading education, 27th January 2017.

the students is at the start of the program. And the overall credit underwriting decision is driven by a business plan where revenues are defined as the uplift the student will likely get after the course of study, minus its costs (which include that of servicing the loan, and taking into account the foregone income sustained during the course), de facto applying a venture capital mind set to an investment hard to judge on the basis of the past.

In doing so, Climb is implicitly vetting and ranking educational institutions (the revenues of my business plan will change if I join a course of IoT at the MIT in Boston, versus a course of medieval philosophy at an unknown on-line institution based at the Cayman Islands). And is also strongly incentivizing students to perform, with tough contractual provisions aimed at both students and Universities—that have for example to give to students a drop-out period where they can leave without any loan obligation (in a way reducing the overall credit loss, as students should know better if the business plan based on the earnings uplift is working or not).

If a student defaults, the school is usually responsible for more than 20% of the unpaid debt—that gives to the University a good incentive to pick students carefully and train them at best, and with a specific objective function very much tied to the incremental revenues they could get out of it. Once the core lending service is supported and potentially created in a "light" way (as the digital FinTech could just originate, screen, price, underwrite and then pass over the loans to balance sheet players via securitization, or offering credit scoring as mere advice), a number of further utilities can be thought of, to incentivize the student to perform better and actually helping her/him in doing so, sharing for example the know how coming from social networks, and from the same institutions that have "skin in the game" and are long on the future success of the student.

Via a P2P lending utility, similarly to what offered for example by Tencent, the synapses FinTech (or bank) could then create a "digital wallet", or "virtual piggy bank", where parents or friends can contribute with few dollars sent via email or SMS, whenever the student succeeds in some exam, or produces a paper or some course work, linking the electronic agenda of the student with an alert system for friends and family.

Or, vice versa, whenever there is some failed exam, the FinTech could suggest some remediation work, or alternative learning tools and support the further commitment required by students to do better next time—interconnecting teachers, past students, parents, potential companies looking for hires etc.—maybe increasing a bit its potential exposure at default, but lowering significantly its probability of default and increasing the chances for the overall ecosystem to work (and for the students to succeed after all). In a way granting a further educational option to students, but also helping them in doing their best and in achieving their most.

That would introduce an even greater disruption to the world of lending risk assessment, pricing and underwriting, and in turn to the world of education as the implications would not stop to the realm of financial services. As for the use case just described for students and education, there are many further ones, potentially applicable to all client segments and products, with rating tools moving away from the "passive" or even "proactive" analysis of risk factors and drivers, to become drivers themselves of actual real risk minimization, for the benefit of the overall economy, as financial and all kind of other resources gets allocated at their best. For the sake of the present, unburdened by the past and with no worries about the future.

9.4 Credit Work Out: Getting Digital

Digital innovation and the mastering of big data and of applied analytics can have powerful implications not just on the credit scoring and underwriting, but also on the credit work out activities—when the loans become sub or non-performing[3] and some kind of restructuring, collection or liquidation needs to be done, following judicial and extra judicial approaches to remediate, in part, to the obvious mistake that was done on day one.

Credit work out (or credit recovery) is indeed one of the oldest activities on earth—as old as the credit business itself since, inevitably, bad creditors (and bad bankers) have always existed. And this activity, for years confined to the back-end of the banking business, with limited investments dedicated to the work out platforms and little attention paid by the top management to skilled professionals, motivating incentive systems, top quality data management systems and digital technology, have now become super-critical, as the global financial crisis that started in 2008 has left many regional and international banks clogged with NPLs (Non-Performing-Loans), particularly in the southern and eastern regions of Continental Europe, but not only.

Whilst a number of improvements to the servicing of sub and non-performing loans have come from traditional organizational and process front-to-back redesign, and by the application of "industrialization" principles such as "standardization", and "shared service functions", and by better HR management (including in this, investing in different skill sets and incentive models), significant further improvements could be brought by the digitization of its operating model, and by the transformation of some of its key use cases—from the segmentation of the overall portfolio of NPLs, to the organization and prioritization of work load and single dossiers, to the structuring of the optimal approach to the recovery strategy and active management of the underlings, to the selection of the best third party (including lawyers) to be involved in each single dossier.

For a start, the segmentation of an NPL portfolio is usually operated by considering as key driver several components such as the nature of the counterpart (retail or small business, SME or large corporate), the size of the file (the gross book value or the total nominal exposure), its aging (time in the recovery procedure), it is kind of collateral (real estate, equipment etc.) and legal status (with legal procedure initiated or not). Given a high level of sophistication and ambition, the number of

---
[3]Holistic active management of non-performing loans, Claudio Scardovi, Springer 2016.

possible permutations and therefore NPL clusters could easily get to a few hundred —a critical dimension in driving the best strategies to recovery for each of them, and dynamically trough time—a complexity hardly manageable with traditional spreadsheets.

Leveraging advanced data management approaches, and applied analytics based on self-learning/AI techniques could then allow not only to define and manage a very granular definition of clusters, but also to dynamically re-define them through time, as new data and information come available and new intelligence, on the best way to regroup and redefine NPL positions and clusters is developed. On this basis, the self-learning machine used to cluster can also proceed to develop interconnections and junctions, across the NPL portfolios and set of recovery strategies available, and the internal and external resources available (at a price) to ensure the maximization of the NPV (Net Present Value) coming from the work out activities —that will need to be prioritized and re-prioritized continuously, as new information come available.

In a dynamic way (e.g. adjusting the recommendations as new data/information are available and new intelligence is produced), the learning machine/AI application can digitize the overall strategic and tactical work out decision making process, giving indications on the best recovery strategies to be pursued, cluster by cluster; and on the optimal prioritization of dossiers (as resources are limited and, in many cases, there is an issue of "how much work the work out unit can actually cope with") to also optimize the recovery returns on the overall cost spent on any single dossier; and on the most efficient allocation of the work load between the internal resources and capabilities and on the best external providers, defined for each and every dossier.

This digitized operating model is thus promising to drastically change the way fairly opaque and mostly unchecked work out units are used to operate—and they also promise, almost by construction and via the algorithms that are run by the machine, to create "alpha", e.g. a recovery ratio that is exceeding past performances by the same unit and on similar portfolios and that is beating the rest of the market in a sustainable way—independently by the trends observable in all other kind of macro variables, such as the value of the real estate sector, of the reference interest rate or of the growth rate or unemployment ratio prevailing in the real economy. "Alpha" over-performance is thus sustained in an uncorrelated way vis a vis the market.

As it develops these "alpha algorithms" that define the main decision criteria and set of operational rules, the self-learning machine keeps updating and changing itself, in an automated fashion, further allowing the robotization of the processes (as more intelligence is embedded in the decision making criteria and rules, driving quasi-deterministic processes, it becomes easier to digitize everything and operate via automated robots) and therefore reducing the risks of errors and mistakes, or fraud and embezzlement.

But the overall digital transformation of the credit work out activities can potentially extend even further. As new ways of interconnecting multiple stakeholders of the value chain (the client bank that is the owner of the NPL, the bad

9.4 Credit Work Out: Getting Digital

creditors also seen as clients, the regulators and credit agencies, the management and employees of the recovery unit and the third-party outsourcers and advisors and the potential financial investors) are developed and become available in real time, a new business is potentially born out of this transformation.

This new business allows a more scientific approach to the definition of transfer prices, best allocation of resources and activities, valuation of capabilities and relative performance etc.—thus allowing an encompassing optimization of the overall value chain of credit recovery—more efficient, effective and therefore productive. More transparency is followed by more specialization and "exchanges" in the economic environment, reducing friction costs and financial and operational inefficiencies, hence creating value.

The credit work out, in its fully industrialized and digitized version, far from being relegated to the back yard of the captive, fully bundled traditional bank, becomes an interesting business per se, requiring a specialization based on a deep understanding of digital advancements. As part of the unbundling of the synapses bank, the credit recovery can spin itself off and become a specialized player to be join ventured with financial and industrial third parties, and potentially serving all kind of other banks and financial intermediaries and corporates NPLs as well. The independent company could then ensure a better transparency and governance with incentive systems more aligned towards targets of true value creation. It would ensure arms' length transactions executed at market price and in a competitive, "open market" context.

The credit work out business could then develop as a platform—as most of the new digital businesses do, leveraging the industrialization and digitalization of the operating platform and potentially reaching economies of scale and scope that can allow the aggregation of market share and the mastering of growth and profitability (the more data it has and manages, the better "alpha" the machine learning applications will be able to achieve, thus adding a further economy of scale driven information/intelligence advantage).

The digital work our platform could then add further value adding services and new solutions and use cases that work in a complementary way to the core ones and in a truly value adding fashions—just consider the development of on-line, fully digital market places of NPLs and of their related collateral assets, including real estate and technical equipment ones, cutting short a good number of middle men and traditional opaque other intermediaries, and further incrementing the transparency and productivity of other non-financial sectors such as the one dealing with real estate agency or with technical equipment re-marketing. This service could just be done on-demand, on a pay-per-use commercial proposition and with no principal investment risk on the side of the new company—ultimately helping to address part of the unsustainable lightness of the bank.

The credit work out would therefore aggregate, manage, price, transfer and drive the recovery of all kind of non-performing lending assets in the economy, as owned by its own clients and on the basis of trust—building a new credibility in its own credit recovery processes that is also built out of its quantitative approach, very objectively developed and uniquely informed—and driven by targets of value creation (or, better, "recovery").

Getting holistically digital would therefore mean reinventing the overall credit work out operating model, turning a now mostly captive, opaque, inefficient internal service into an unbundled, independent, "synapses-driven" profitable business, cutting across many stakeholders and industries (and getting rid of a multitude of power brokers and middle men offering weak intermediation and advice of dubious value). Working out not just how to better recover credit, but also how to recover credibility at best, for good and for the long run.

9.5 Digital Risk Management: Optimizing the Trade off

The trade-off between risk and return is as old as finance itself: there is no free lunch for investors in the global financial system—if you want to target higher expected returns you have to accept higher downside risk as well, as any other "imbalance" between risk and return would be arbitraged away almost immediately in transparent, liquid and well-functioning markets. Because of this, risk—as a key production factor of the global financial system—has a "fair" and a "market" price, and can be traded, swapped, hedged or held to maturity.

A less well known trade-off (but still very much relevant in finance and banking specifically) is the one between the costs of preventing risks (ex-ante, e.g. proactively) and of managing them when they materialize to minimize losses (ex-post, e.g. reactively) and the cost of the risks themselves (e.g. the overall loss driven by negative events as they happen, including their direct and indirect consequences on the bank business).

Indeed, as the modern approach to risk management started developing with the statistical approaches to evaluate, monitor and manage market, credit and operational risks as suggested by the Basle Accords (I, II, III and now getting into a Basle IV one), this quite reasonable trade-off has long been neglected—following the unreasonable assumption that any action that allows to the bank to eliminate risks is always a good one.

More specifically, a growing source of operational risk, with significant impacts in terms of fines, liabilities towards third parties and business and reputational negative backfiring has recently been driven by compliance and the failure to flawlessly adhere to it. Compliance itself has mushroomed in recent years as AML (Anti Money Laundering), KYC (Know Your Customer), and other misconduct related prescriptive policies and procedures have been developed by international regulators. As a consequence, the challenges coming from new compliance rules and the litigation threats (and associated legal fines) driven by their breaches have become an important drain on value across financial services, with hundreds of billions of fines paid to watch-dogs bodies and as settlements to class actions and other individual lawsuits fought by either customers, investors or business counterparts. Not to mention the impact on the regulatory capital absorption on banks and global SIFI specifically (the more the bank is in breach, the higher the regulatory charges it gets).

Why then bothering on saving few pennies if billions and the loss of equity brand and other intangibles are at stake? The trade-off between the operational costs and the cost of operational risks has never, consequently, been fully considered and weighted, given this skewed perception on "risk is everything and all too important".

Things can however be quite different from what they appear. On one side, the few dollars spent on compliance have become billions themselves—as global banks have started investing hundreds of millions of dollars, with thousands of employees dedicated to that, with no clear accountability and no analysis on their return on investment relative business case. On the other side, the consequence of forgetting the efficiency target have not always resulted in a net increase in efficacy (e.g. in lower risk), as often the greater resources allocated are just spent following a helicopter money approach—no focussed and surgical action plan is implemented on both a proactive and reactive dimension, and most of the budget is spent uniformly, with the impossible aim to cover all kind of potential, negative events. In this "uniform" approach, most of the ex-ante risks and related ex-post negative events tend to be covered, but in an undifferentiated way, vis a vis their relative likelihood, potential severity and long term impact on the brand equity and viability of the bank.

As the challenges of regulatory compliance and litigation are becoming a structural drain on value across financial services, specific use cases involving some digital transformation could now offer to banks the opportunity to improve their effectiveness in addressing such challenges, whilst preventing spiralling costs and optimizing the efficiency of their cost structure: in a way, optimizing the trade-off along the continuum between compliance and legal costs, and between ex-ante proactive and ex-post reactive management. At the heart of this, lies the increasing convergence between regulatory and technology strategy—with data management, IT infrastructure and applications development taking a centre stage in control management.

In fact, compliance and legal costs, and the risks they are designed to manage, are the two faces of the very same coin. And regulatory and technological strategies are underpinning both, from the design to the implementation stage. Spending money ex-ante in compliance (leveraging technology in the best way) is aimed at preventing regulatory sanction by improving standards of conduct and addressing failures as they manifest. Spending money ex-post on legal support functions and external advice (leveraging again big data and machine learning/AI) is then aimed at reducing the financial and reputational impacts once failures are revealed and the feared negative events become true. It logically follows that the spending ex-ante and ex-post on compliance and legal management must then be weighted with respect to the actual reduction in the cost of risks and related business impacts, e.g. reconsidering the best trade-off between operational costs and risks.

9.6 Shifting the Isoquant

Digital transformation offers the opportunity to "shift the isoquant" of this and of many other risk-related trade-offs, and to increase the overall productivity of the compliance and legal functions (and of many other control and support functions, including audit and risk management) and of their return on capital, following our five pillars approach—an approach that each synapses bank should adopt and execute and develop.

The first building block required entails big data advanced management, with the aggregation of all kind of internal and external data sources—structured and unstructured: ready to be queried and mined. This requires the synapses bank to overcome multiple legacy systems, making away with possible inconsistencies and with inaccurate or redundant data sitting across regions and platforms and produced to answer to different legislations and specific rules, such as the money laundering, the bribe and corruption, the customer due diligence, the data privacy and the fair and accurate trading/foreign asset control ones, just to name a few.

The second one involves applied analytics. These can extract, produce and elaborate intelligence from data and information, and enable machine learning/AI systems to make dynamically adjusted recommendations more efficiently and effectively than in the current—human resources heavily driven—operating set up. They can also capitalize the knowledge independently produced by teams of internal and external lawyers and re-use it for similar, high frequency and less critical compliance risks and for future disputes, leaving the recourse of the bank to the best legal and para legal professionals to the few critical, once in a life time, cases.

The third pillars involve a different way of intermediating and dealing with multiple counterparts—including regulators and external lawyers, focusing on the best ways to manage their connections and interrelations, also by using automation and robotization of certain non-core activities. Automation which streamlines data management and presents applied analytics reporting can in fact be shared with regulators and lawyers to make their work more productive and—for example—by allowing them to participate in parallel, almost in real time, to the analysis of the files. It can then allow to internal/external lawyers to participate in parallel to the management of the disputes, capitalizing in real time on new analysis and in the full sharing of findings.

This approach should then be supported by a front-to-back process redesign aimed at ensuring that no other organizational/process-driven component impedes the use of relevant data and intelligence. This redesign would aim, for example, at reducing all the manual processes that drain reviewers' time and involve them into heavy investigation duties, resulting in energy and money spent in low value tasks. And it would limit the use of detection scenarios that generates high volumes of false positives and therefore low value added analysis.

9.6 Shifting the Isoquant

Fourthly, new use cases can be devised, when dealing with compliance and legal cost and in this case with particular regards to the use of metrics. More broadly, a new operating model leveraging real time architecture can be designed to best optimize the legal and compliance objectives. And, as predictive models are tested and sharpened, new compliance processes can be developed, by eliminating check-the-box superficial exercises, manual handovers and standard and ineffective legal practices. New use cases can then be applied to information based decision making and action planning—whilst maximizing the use of machine learnings/AI to reduce throughput time and optimize performance, driving a new governance on compliance and (more broadly) on risk management investments—with a vision to optimize the second risk/cost trade off as well.

Finally, it is important to remember how the transformation success will still be based on trust and credibility, even if of a more "cyber and digital" nature. In this case, the trust of the top management in the efficiency and efficacy of the new digital approach can be built by developing and monitoring a new metrics that balances the investments required to manage compliance and legal risks against the likelihood and severity (direct loss and indirect impact on business/reputation) of any single requirement/dispute and relative likelihood, e.g. their VaR—Value at Risk—therefore calculating their return on VaR (or capital at risk).

From the regulators standpoint, it could well be that some of their trust and credibility in the new digital approach it's already there as, according to the mission statement of the United Kingdom Financial Conduct Authority[4] "As regulators we too can benefit from the same (technological innovation) changes. In recent years data science—also known as machine learning or artificial intelligence—has become increasingly prevalent. Data science offers a series of tools that allow us to extract useful information from increasingly large, complex and varied datasets. These techniques have great potential when used in regulation. At the FCA, our initial focus on data science is to see how we can better shift through the large amounts of data we receive to target those firms with a higher risk of having problems. This uses existing data sets to identify firms with a greater risk of regulatory breach which we use to focus targeted monitoring of firms."

Apparently, regulators, in this "catch me if you can" game of regulatory scrutiny on conduct and other operational and reputational risks have developed a better synapses model than the banks themselves. Until banks will catch up and develop something even better, and this time for a good and ultimate aim.

9.7 Bricks After the Storm

The "holistic approach" to risk management has develop in fashions, with new risks being added year after year, as something bad was happening in the market, or because of the inspiration coming from the regulators (or, more rarely, from the

---

[4]FCA website: www.fca.org.uk/mission.

academia). An alphabet soup of risk-terminology and methodology (and related technology) has then developed, adding confusion to the already complex, Babylon-like world of risks.

It could then come as a surprise that, in the long list of every kind of possible risks the bank and the other financial intermediaries can face, the real estate one is not even mentioned—not once in a number of academic risk management handbooks consulted. Still, if we go back in time, and even before the last global financial crisis (mostly determined by the burst of the real estate bubble that started in the USA before extending to Europe and to most of the developed markets), we should find how most of the banks' failures have indeed been determined by the real estate risk embedded in its long-timed cycle.

In our initial discussion, we mentioned real estate as fallaciously thought as bringing that element of materiality and concreteness that would have brought stability to the "inverted pyramids" business model of the bank. Far from it, we discussed, these apparent "tangibility" of bricks, opposed to the "intangibility" of money, has introduced further risks and mismatches into the system, also because the way real estate assets have been assessed, used and managed as collaterals. It is safe to say that banks are inherently long on the real estate cycle, with their fortunes strictly interconnected with it: if the bricks' cycle goes well, banks have anyway a fair chance to do badly. But if the cycle is negative, it is almost impossible for them to do well.

Banks are, in a way, hedge funds like, with a long position on the real estate cycle, but with a further major shortcoming: they believe, in fact, to have "bought a call" on the bricks and mortar collateral, where in most cases they have just sold a put, with the debtors that can choose when it suits them better to leave their real estate asset to the bank, with an exit price (figuratively paid by the bank) that is equal to their residual debt.

Based on this very asymmetric risk/return profile, for the bank and the debtor, with the real estate underlying playing a pivotal role, it becomes evident how it is critical for the bank to become real estate savvy. On one side, understanding better all the holistic levers of its real estate exposure (whether from owned core real estate assets, owned but not possessed—for the leasing portfolio, as collaterals to loans to real estate developers, corporates and retail clients, or as invested assets of part of its bancassurance business mathematical reserves etc.) it has obviously become paramount for the banking sector at large.

On the other side, the necessity of becoming more proactive and better reactive in managing this most fundamental systemic risk has also grown in importance, with banks launching special REOCO vehicles (Real Estate Owned Companies: that take repossession of the real estate collateral from defaulted loans and may offer asset and property management to maximize the future sale of the refurbished building/flat); but also real estate agency services, through their online and branch network; and even real estate development companies and investment funds, to complete and dispose in the best possible way of unfinished building and infrastructure projects. Following this "holistic" and "proactive/reactive" distinct initiatives, it has then become paramount to develop an "integrated" approach, under the management of a Group CREO (Chief Real Estate Officer) able to feed ex ante real estate risk information into the new lending portfolio planning cycle.

It all sound exciting—but with a major shortcoming, and a major need of a "digital help", on data, information and intelligence. Real estate is in fact a risky business, we have stated. But tends to go undetected as such, as volatility is fully recognized if measured on a mark to market basis (real estate assets tend to be appraised just over a few years, and still with a lot of "subjectivity" involved in the process). How then to measure, monitor and manage its volatility i.e. risk? And how to make sure that, having found how much it weighs on the banking business, a proper risk management approach is found to plan, underwrite, hedge, cover, transfer or swap such a risk? This crucial question has gone unanswered for hundreds of years (and still is), but digitization is also promising to revolutionise this very thorny issue, with the help of available technology and a lot of ingenuity.

Let's think of the market indexes for a moment—as most risk management processes start from there, from their objective and real time measurement and monitoring. In a world where an unprecedented quantity of data and information get produced, accumulated and mined every second, even market indexes are destined for radical change—and not just those related to liquid, highly traded, standardized assets. Indexes, as impartial, objective, statistical based synopsis of many data and information have contributed to the development of entire markets—from derivatives, to reinsurance, to financial guarantees, to name a few.

They have become part of the overall infrastructure of the global financial system, acting as pillar that, if not showing the direction, have at least been measuring it, in comparable terms and with a very dense meaning transmitted in a super synthetic way. Most of the index infrastructure is now related to historical regression analysis and formal, structured data, approved by either independent counterparts or international supervisory and/or academic bodies. They have thus become pillars of certainty, albeit in time less relevant than needed.

In a digital world, most of this indexes infrastructure could be also turned upside down. Let's first consider the development of the ones related to the most traded, liquid, financial assets like bonds or equities: it is easy to see how they could benefit from more real time funnelling of data and information of a more social nature—coming from all kind of sources and including the IoT and other technological sources (like satellites).

Market indexes on, say, futures on grain, or pork bellies, could incorporate the data coming from the devices installed on crops, or even pigs, to analyse the behaviour of pigs when getting fed or reproducing. And others related to the shares of specific industrial sectors or consumer goods could incorporate the "likes" or the "thumbs down" continuously aggregated by the world-wide web. The meaning embedded in them would just augment and become even more up to date, and continuously refreshed as new information comes available.

But more radical disruption should also be expected for indexes related to less liquid and little transparent assets. Take real estate for example, the undisputed leader in low fungibility (as houses cannot move) and in very disputable valuation and pricing methodologies (Discounted Cash Flow methods) would apply in theory, but are barely considered in practise, for the use of more well-known "comparable based" approaches based on value per square meter. Real estate indexes are not well developed in most Counties, and have a number of information flaws (because of poor data, given the limited liquidity and low fungibility of the assets). Also, they tend to be static, almost as an house can be: revaluation of real estate portfolios tend to happen on a yearly basis, in the best case, and usually following heterogeneous methods with a lot of subjectivity involved.

As the real estate sector's value is little understood and with very few science applied to it, and because of this most static approach to revaluation, it tends to be considered "low risk" (almost a fulfilling prophecy: if revaluations happen rarely in time and usually is done by the same people that have applied their subjectivity in the first instance, volatility tends also to be measured as low, as it comes completely underestimated, if not over long cycles of analysis). As few credible market indexes exist, almost no derivative, or reinsurance, or financial guarantee is available in the market to cover one of the most critical systemic risks to banks. We have already commented, in our first chapters, how the "tangibility" or real estate was added, almost by design, to try to address the "unbearable lightness" of the inverted pyramid of the banking business model—eventually just multiplying the inherent instability of the industry, as the 2008 global financial crisis has shown.

9.8 Real Estate, in Real Time

Far from addressing the banks' many weaknesses, we have written, the real estate exposure has been possibly the most brutal force in the history of lending, determining most of the systemic risks and of the failures of financial institutions of the last few decades. Banks have played the real estate collateral card thinking they were smartly buying a "call" on the asset, we have commented, whilst, they were most likely selling a "put" to their debtor. And they have become, in doing so, almost like a hedge fund with a very long position (mostly "naked") on the real estate cycle. It's kind of easy to make some money when the value of houses keeps growing (albeit it is still possible and fairly easy to go bust as bad debtors are always looking for stupid bankers), but banks are mostly infallibly broken when the cycle turns. All this makes it very critical to get a better approach to "fair value" analysis and towards a mark to market valuation of real estate assets.

With the abundance of data and information potentially mastered by digitization approaches, real time based holistic indexes on real estate could be now developed, mixing structured data with further unstructured information taken from all kind of sources, including satellites and video cameras (measuring the exposure to the sun of any single apartment, or the trend in traffic and illumination during night time of a certain area), not to mention social feeds from the web (monitoring the "likes" and the suggestions and comments on specifies streets, shopping areas and restaurants or on the "coolness" of the neighbours.

9.8 Real Estate, in Real Time

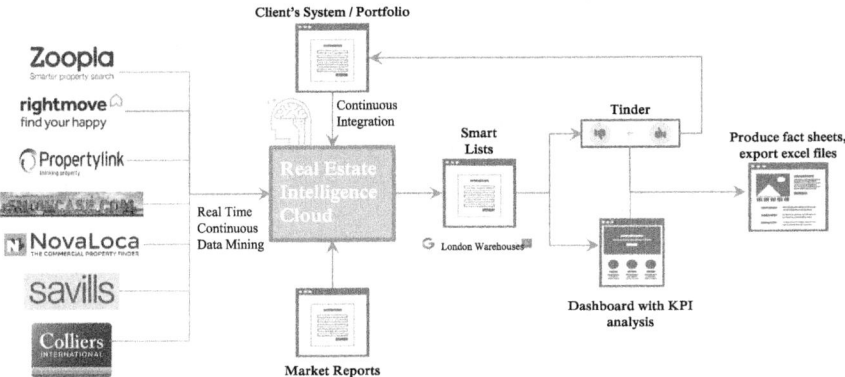

Fig. 9.2 Real estate across-the-cycle behaviors and trends can be analyzed using unstructured information and machine learning

The grabbing of instant information from online real estate agency web sites would also allow to monitor the demand for information and of potential investors' visits, and the gap between asking price and the implied number and price level of bidding offers (also potentially done over the web). With the help of machine learning/AI techniques, it could all lead to the development of a holistic monitoring of the market value of flats and villas and commercial or industrial buildings, as shown in the following Figure, complementing the more rigorous DCF approaches which are good if you believe people are economically rational and consider a flat in Notting Hill and another one in Canary Wharf as fully fungible and as perfect substitutes (they are not) (Fig. 9.2).

Should such an index, marked to market, become largely available and certified from reputed counterparts, it would revolutionize the world of real estate and of banking as well (see Fig. 9.1—Real estate across-the cycle behaviours and trends can be analysed using unstructured information and machine learning). Pricing on loans would reflect these new values and their implied volatility. Lending portfolios (and real estate development portfolios) managed by banks, insurance companies, asset management companies and by other financial institutions could then consider the diversification coming from the different risk factors and performance drivers of any sub-class of real estate assets, based on the matrix of variances/covariances that could be developed.

Hedging by derivatives or reinsurance and financial guarantee could become widely available and cheap, and even collateral management could be informed by margin calls operated by some central "bricks and mortar" specialist clearing house. Even the tax collection agencies could do a better job in spotting the black economy so typical of the sector and the money laundering activities sometimes involving real estate trophy assets.

The digital transformation of the real estate sector would then be completed by the "smart home" applications, and by the many utilities that could help us in making our life at home easier and more convenient, or actually further foster the "shared economy"—e.g. an economy where "owning" a house does not make sense anymore, as mobility is the key principle, and the "rent generation" is the new king of the sector. This would in turn develop the sector into multiple hyper liquid renting markets, operated by "long only" professional investors and with buildings serviced by professional multinationals driven by scale and scope economies. Fungibility of homes, if not of a single, "yours truly one", would therefore also increase.

In this extreme scenario of digitalization, a new set of indexes and a new market infrastructure helping to provide a real-time valuation of the real estate assets would then become even more important, introducing further opportunities that are not yet dreamed of: impacting heavily even on the most "brick and mortar" sector of all, and potentially helping banks in sorting out the negative "heaviness" they have added, via their exposure to the real estate sector, to the already unbearable lightness of their core business model.

Transformation in Insurance 10

Abstract

The international insurance sector has navigated the global financial crisis in a much easier way vis a vis the banking one. More limited restructuring and liquidation activities were required to ensure its survival. However, within the global financial system, it now looks to be the most impacted one—as the technological innovations and the related digital disruptions are posing an unprecedented number of competitive threats. The level of discontinuities expected in the insurance sector suggests how the transformation challenge (and related risk) for insurance companies could be the highest in the system, and requiring an even more radical re-thinking of their business and operating model. Their "synapses" opens up a number of opportunities as well, as the new data and intelligence available and the new interconnection plays could allow not just to create value for multiple stakeholders, but also address the very "old" risks being underwritten—dramatically reducing or eliminating some of them. The question is then whether insurance companies have a better chance than FinTech to do that and how they can justify and secure a fair share of profits on arising new risks.

Keywords

Insurance · Pure risks · Underwriting · New technologies · Data management · Machine learning

10.1 Next "In-Line" or Next "On-Line"?

When compared to banking, the insurance sector appears to have come out rather lightly from the global financial crisis that started in 2008, with its zenith in the bankruptcy of Lehman Brothers on October 15th. True enough, just few days later

AIG, until then maybe the largest and safest insurance company in the world, was rescued by the US government and with public money—but even its misfortunes were driven by the credit risk accumulated by investment banks, like Goldman Sachs, that was transferred to AIG via a financial insurance agreement. Neither AIG nor any other major insurance company got into trouble because of their "pure risks" exposure e.g. the ones that this industry tends to underwrite, (from death to health, to property and casualty).

No major insurance company has failed recently, and no major restructuring wave has been making headlines in a sector still thought as dull, boring and unexciting, but not certainly generating a system risk with potentially critical impacts on the global economy. No obvious "unsustainable lightness" is also easily identifiable for the life and property and casualty insurance companies, as they are built on the pooling and aggregation of risks whose diversification effects tend to hold better than the ones described for banks (unless of course a major catastrophe, like a global war outburst or a comet hitting the heart is occurring).

Given such a setting, the low profitability they have been able to achieve has not made headlines either, and the focus of regulators have been relatively less heavy on them: no major misconduct issues have also been observed—apart from the occasional insurance miss-selling, most often operated by banks as in the PPI case with UK banks (fine of tens of billions of GBP). However, if we look deeper, at the inner logic of the insurance "traditional" business and operating models, we may get to a very different picture—of a sector that is most likely to be profoundly impacted by a full array of new technologies, and by the digitization's impacts.

Taking into consideration the main, potential digitization trends, the insurance sector could then look as set to be next in line, and forced to transform radically. Or it will risk altogether to be put into a restructuring wave that could not be second to the one just observed for the banking sector. We can actually consider a number of incremental risks and opportunities on the business and operating model of insurance companies, and more brutal, discontinuous ones as well—potentially changing the very nature of the global function it performs.

Take for example the incremental opportunities offered to insurance companies if they get "on line". By adopting process automation and industrialization, IT platform streamlining and more efficient/effective digital systems, they could improve significantly their commercial and operating performance and their expense ratio. And they could also pool risks from more diverse communities of policyholders, thus increasing diversification and scale effects, as everything would be driven by a web-based platform. According to a Morgan Stanley report on Insurance and Technology (Morgan Stanley, 2014), "digital savvy" insurers perform better than others—their revenues are 10% higher than the average of their peers and 20–30% more profitable.

A full digitalization of the value chain in a traditional insurer, according to the estimates of Morgan Stanley, a global SIFI, could improve combined ratios by 20% points circa, as shown in Fig. 10.1, allowing a full array of commercial and operational improvements, from better pricing and underwriting through big data and analytics, to enhanced marketing and sales through digital front-end services, to

10.1 Next "In-Line" or Next "On-Line"?

Process automation and **industrialization**, **IT platform streamlining** and **digitization** directly impact operational performance, improving expense ratios

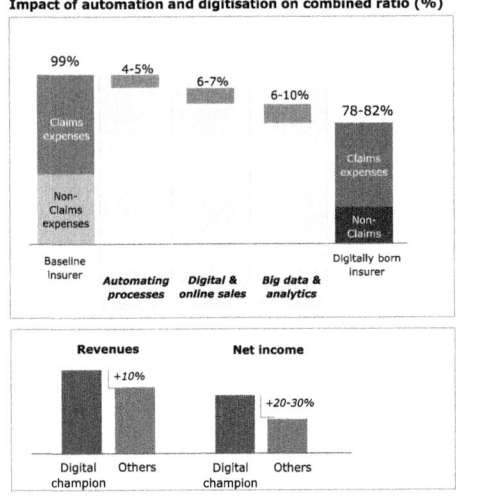

Fig. 10.1 Automation and digitization is estimated to improve profitability of insurers by c. 20–30%

online direct distribution in place of the "high touch" agency model, to the optimization of the claim management process via automation and robotics.

Whilst incumbent, traditional insurers are largely dependent on physical channels and agents or other sorts of "physical" intermediaries, most of them still demonstrate a lack of a coherent digital transformation plan: starting from the customer journey across different channels, they still show a limited use of digital tools. Traditional insurers also demonstrate a high level of manual processing and lot of paperwork with its related risk of rework and mistakes and with client facing processes that take ages. Their claim management has also limited automated, on-line functionalities and the high number of customer complaints translates in a weaker brand value and loss of client franchise. Even their risk underwriting gets weaker and weaker, as they are unable to mine at best all the structured and unstructured data captured and analysed by their new digital FinTech competitors. They are, in a word, the "next in-line", and potentially in need of future restructuring.

On the other side, digital-savvy insurers have started to fully digitalize a discreet number of end-to-end processes, delivering consistent client experience across all channels. With their comprehensive vision of a customer-centric business, digital organizational culture, they are getting ready to proactively master a number of online and mobile channels to support their customers' journey, and leverage social network and all kind of new technologies that are made progressively available by innovation. They are, in a word, the next "on-line", already pursuing a transformation journey that can reap the digital opportunities whilst minimizing their risks.

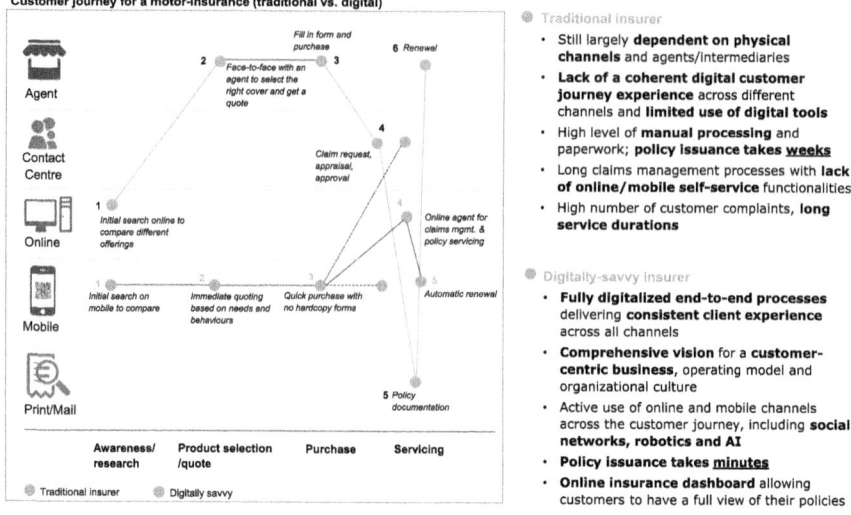

Fig. 10.2 Achieving excellence in customer experience will be a key driver for sustainable growth and profitability

Just consider the implication on the customer journey experience—as shown in the following Figure that describes for a motor insurance product the quite different experiences of clients going physical or digital (Fig. 10.2).

10.2 Beyond the "On-Line"

There are however a number of more radical factors that are potentially conducive to the sudden disruption of the industry—just consider the estimate of a reduction by more than 97% of all the car accidents that should be brought about by self-driving cars,[1] or the possibility of monitoring on line all the valuables that could be covered by an insurance policy on theft or lost goods, or of controlling and reporting to physicians on real time the vital parameters (and the lifestyle) of people that are subscribing an health or life insurance.

What would be the opportunities and threats for the insurance sector in an increasingly "riskless" world (at least from a "traditional risk" point of view), and what new risks should be considered, to ensure the stability of the sector but also to renew and update—to legitimate even—the very "raison d'etre" of the industry? Beyond the generic term of "digitization" and "getting on-line" of societies and markets lies a number of game changing technological disruptions, each of them assuming a specific relevance for the insurance sector.

---

[1]Financial Times, digital innovation and self-driving cars, March 2017.

Take for example the "Internet of Things" (IoT), that is based on the concept of real time, continuously connected devices: telematics, connected "smart" homes, driverless cars and wearable devices can fundamentally change the underwriting and pricing models of insurance companies, as they will be in a position to know much more, in a more dynamic and up to date way, mining from the available data new valuable intelligence on the customer's behaviour and life style. Apart from the "passive" intelligence (leading to better ex ante decision on underwriting and pricing), the IoT can also offer the ability to mitigate and even prevent claims through early detection and monitoring of risks, and reduce the costs of covers for policy holders—think for example of the recovery rate of lost goods, or of the immediate activation of the nearest physician in case of an heart attack. In a way revolutionising the insurance value proposition, from the (financial) coverage of realized losses linked to uncertain, negative events to the inclusion of the (operating) prevention of bad outcomes and to the minimization of damages when they occur—offering an array of services like "smart home remote control", "valuables geolocation", "heart check-up" and "physician (or personal trainer) on line".

Not only that. As new information comes continuously available, in real time and from multiple "feeders" (from your glasses and jacket, from your car and home and maybe one day even from your pet), the insurance coverage could be tailored almost on the basis of a marketing of one—on the specific needs of the single customer and for the very time horizon required: why to ensure a car for the full year, when cars are, on average, used 5% of the time, e.g. not more than 20 days? And why not to charge more the person that is driving for 100 days versus the one that drives just for 2 days per year—not to mention a pricing structure that is driven by the driving lifestyle and habits—very far from the actuarial analysis based on averages now in use.

Insurance could then become an industry (as already many others, think of the infotainment industry based on streaming) that is offered, used and paid on the basis of an "on-the-go" model. New policies could be offered in real time, on the basis of the evolving and "deconstructed" behaviour of customers, enabling insurance companies to offer "pay-as-you-go" tailored covers, thus significantly decreasing costs of insurance for certain segments and previously underserved customers and making others pay more, on the basis of an "economic fairness" principle (if you drive like crazy, or you eat like a pig, or keep forgetting your valuables around… you should pay more, and—by the way—the more you are charged on the basis of your controllable behaviour, the more your interests will be aligned, and the better you should tend to behave—driving and eating better).

The advanced management of big quantities of data and the increasing use of predictive analytics tools (including machine learning/AI—think of the driverless cars potentially revolutionising the way we move, but also the way cities are built and lived) can really allow to connect multiple customers' touchpoints to move then from predicting their insurance needs to all other kind of commercial wishes and aspirations—offering then to insurance companies new cross selling opportunities (if you eat like a pig and your risk of an heart attack is increasing, why not offer you an advisor on eating habits and a personal trainer, even subsidizing these new services, as the potential claim to the company will decrease anyway if the client is put on a diet and a training program?). Hardly would a healthier and fitter and nicer looking client end complaining. And hardly would any customer if the consume "less" coverage for medical treatment—if they need less of it.

Insurance companies, in other words, could be developing new, augmented service-based offerings as part of a new ecosystem that leverages multiple high frequency, high value relationships with customers—built to manage the overall "pure" risks of the customer, but to also support his/her ambitions and targeted lifestyle and wellbeing, with new fancy applications that could include augmented and virtual reality tools as well (you are just getting a virtual reality diet specialist and a personal trainer, always "on" and available).

There is however a dark side to this "full connectivity/always on line" scenario. As everything gets interconnected and "digitally encrypted", new risks are also increasing and potentially substituting the "traditional" ones that are progressively reduced and—in some cases—even brought to a near end (take for example the cars accident ratio, thought to be reduced to less than 3% by the full adoption of driverless cars).

We have already discussed cyber as the emerging risk progressively dominating the global financial system, from a priority, urgency and critical/relevant stand point. Cyber risk could in fact turn out to be both a threat and an opportunity for the insurance sector. It is obviously a threat: if a criminal hacker could infiltrate and take possession of all driverless cars, and drive them to collision, the obvious costs for the insurance companies would skyrocket in an unpredictable and uncontrolled way. But also, as cyber risk becomes a new dominant factor in the lives of companies and individuals, new policies could be offered to just deal with that: e.g. covering the financial losses directly or indirectly attributable to any kind of cyber-attack (either as theft, or as an act of terrorism or warfare). Insurance companies could also help customers to prevent and detect the attack, offering the best remediation plan when some penetration into their system and data bases is detected and found. In theory, a proper reinsurance market, based on objective indexes and benchmarks, could also be built to trade cyber risk, on top of a market already estimated to be worth 2 trillion USD by 2020.[2]

Some of the "traditional" incumbents are already going "on-line" and maybe even beyond that, even if they are still a long way from a pure "synapses" business model. Allianz,[3] for example, has launched a full transformation program that includes process digitization and on-line capabilities to enquire and even subscribe to a large range of products. Internally, it is pushing for a single customer view of data and policies, managing the "spaghetti wrangle" of the many past legacies coming from organic growth and subsequent technological add-ons and from serial acquisitions of other traditional "spaghetti style" companies.

---

[2]AlixPartners estimate, based on triangulation of public information.
[3]Allianz, company investors presentation and other information available on its website (April 2017).

10.2 Beyond the "On-Line"

As it strives to further develop and standardize the many on-line interfaces it has across the globe, the German insurer is also trying to develop an extended consumer ecosystem with partners for "connected devices", e.g. Deutsche Telecom and BMW. And it is trying to do as much, investing significant amount of money (400–500 Mln Euro per year circa) and leveraging a number of focussed initiatives, such as its open innovation centre (Allianz Digital Labs) and a number of alliances it is pursuing with FinTech companies (either star up or more developed). It is also trying to progressively change the internal culture, along with its systems, processes and structures, and hiring new talents from leading technology companies as a way to accelerate that.

Progressive[4] is also another good example of a traditional insurer turned digital savvy and getting "on-line" via an ambitious transformation plan. This company has been a market leader in the adoption of telematics in the US through its "Snapshot" offering, moving in as an early innovator and then licensing the technology to others to generate extra fees, whilst still developing and retaining predictive analytical tools, and developing its internal modelling and pricing based on its accumulated data from telematics-based products and services.

Finally, Discovery, a South African most innovative short term car and home insurance company, is also rapidly adapting to the new competitive challenges brought about by technological innovation and trying to use these in a proactive way—not just to better cover risks but also to reduce or eliminate them all together. The company introduced "Vitality", a science-based wellness program that gives users discounts on premiums and other rewards for improving their health and fitness. It then developed "DQ-Track", a scientific measure of driver behaviour that monitors real-time driving and gives users discounts on premiums and rewards—also providing online and offline health and driving assessments, update information and useful tools for users.

By creating a better consumer ecosystem with frequent interactions and real-time data monitoring, Discovery is designing a new insurance business model where "value" is ideally shared across stakeholders (you are more fit and better off, with freebies and discounts on gym and diet, and the company reduces its claims expenses on its health insurance)—all driven by an incentive system that tries to digitally support their customers to be healthier and fitter (then sharing the financial rewards attained—not to mention their increased wellbeing).

10.3 Digital-Insuring, at Your Peril

No matter how fast and decisively some of the traditional players are trying to change their business and operating models, they still run the risk of being "strategically leap frogged" by the other, more innovative, technology driven

---
[4]Progressive, company investors presentation and other information available on its website (April 2017).

"synapses" models that are being introduced by new players. Several new, FinTech players are in fact emerging, playing on one (or more) of three strategies that we briefly discuss. First, they are trying to develop peer to peer insurance businesses, built on the old-time key principle of mutuality, but without the "equity buffer" provided by a regulated financial intermediary (the insurance company's regulatory capital). Second, they are developing an ecosystem around the insurance key needs and components to address pure risks in both a proactive and reactive way. And finally, they are trying to design "on demand" offerings, where the "pay-as-you go" pricing model is key, offering a value for money that is built on economic fairness.

In the "peer to peer" competitive strategy, the insurance offering is managed and executed entirely on-line, via platforms that are managed by FinTech start-ups, based on the principle of "mutuality" (everybody shares part of the financial pain of the few unlucky ones, via the ex-ante payment of a premium, with overall premiums then used to partially compensate the policy holder for the negative event occurred). The overall business model (and the look and feel of the website) tend to look very simple and transparent, and based on the principle of community building—the platform pools premiums as any insurance company does, but also pays back the unclaimed money, if not required, after the insurance cycle is complete. All the pricing and underwriting is then happening on-line, with the risk analysis performed by machine learning/AI systems, progressively trained and leveraging all available structured and unstructured data related to the community. In the following Figure, the case of Marmalade is discussed, as provider to the younger generations community (Fig. 10.3).

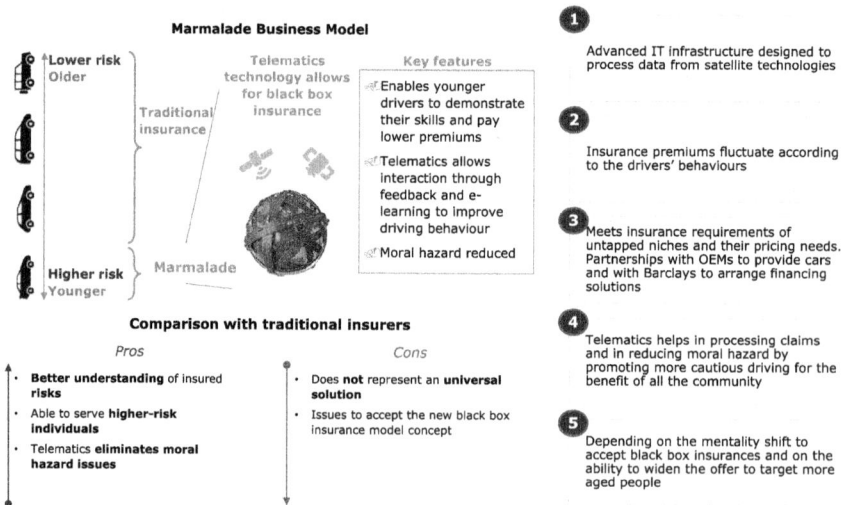

Fig. 10.3 Marmalade answers to the needs to receive cheaper insurance for younger generations

10.3 Digital-Insuring, at Your Peril

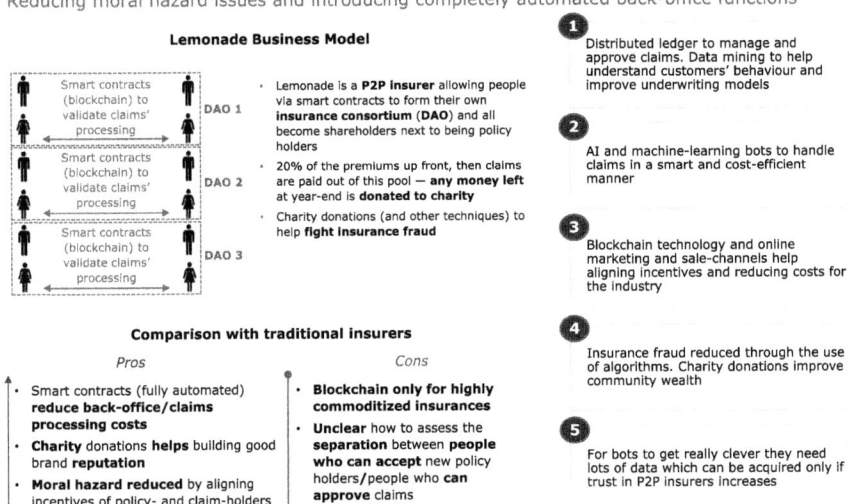

Fig. 10.4 Lemonade: Building an insurance community with real time claims payments

Claims are paid online as well, with mobile-phone based applications to manage the "paper-less" work after the negative event (a car crash) has happened, with payments executed in minutes—on the basis of a machine learning driven verification process. Other complementary services are also used (e.g. message boards on line, information on the community), to enhance the social insurance aspect and the community feeling of the P2P insurance website and with higher customers' satisfaction rate, with limited increase in operating costs.

Whilst a number of players have already emerged and rapidly established platforms built on these principles (some of them include Lemonade, Guevara, Friend Insurance, So Sure, Ins Peer, Tong Ju Bao) they are still mostly lacking the scale and scope to reach a critical pool of premiums that would make their business model extremely efficient from a financial and operating point of view. However, whilst still lagging significantly behind the scale of global, incumbent insurers, they have been better at focussing on specific underserved segments, e.g. on the low-income, young professionals—that they have been able to address in tailored ways and with a lower loss ratio than the industry average (45 vs. 63%[5]) because of their better "intelligence" (Fig. 10.4).

Following a second competitive strategy, other FinTech companies have started to develop a business model within their own (or within their partners) "ecosystem"—to offer then a full range of insurance and financial products and services all based on an on-line platform where customer-centricity and increasing customer engagement is core to the business. Their strategy is therefore to look for niche and offbeat insurance products, leveraging the large customer-base of the wider

---
[5]Swiss Re research, 2016.

Fig. 10.5 Zhong An is China's first complete digital insurer willing to disrupt the market

ecosystem they are part of, and then use all the available data and most advanced data analytics (including machine learning/AI) to drive decision making.

A noticeable example is Zhong An, that was launched in 2013 by Ping An, Tencent and Alibaba and is now operating as a fully digital property insurer that sells all its products online (it also handles claims on-line) (Fig. 10.5). Through this cross-industry partnership, Alibaba and Tencent (internet titans in China) are trying to leverage their user base with the help of the "traditional" insurance company Ping An. Zhong An has then sold 5.8 Bln policies to 460 Mln customers in its first three years. The company is applying "digital thinking" across the entire insurance value chain, from product design to claims servicing—and with an on-line model characterized by a lower operating and distribution costs. Advanced data management and applied analytics ensure then accurate product pricing and risk control —in real time and augmented "intelligence" coming from machine.

Finally, the third competitive strategy is also followed by other FinTech companies, focusing on the "on-line, on-demand" value proposition. Players like Cuvva, Metromile and Digital Risks offer on-line and mobile applications that allow customers to subscribe in real time to offers "pay-as-you-go" offerings, where they "use" insurance coverage (and recharge it on-line) just when they are actively exposed to the risks covered by the policy (e.g. when they drive, for a car policy; or when they travel with family, for such a policy) and with an underwriting and pricing structure that is dynamically driven by their own behaviors (e.g. how fast and how bad they drive, e.g. if they continuously use accelerator and brake—or how much they travel and where).

In a most basic pricing structure, a small monthly subscription is then followed up by a top-up insurance that is active just during the time you actually need the cover (e.g. hourly car insurance for when you drive your car that you can activate via a mobile app, or that is activated by the movements of your car as recorder by the satellite). The main benefits of this model include of course the "value for money", as you pay for a service just when you need it—thus allowing also a better management of the buffer capital of the insurance company (at any single moment, that capital covers an average of 5% of all the car policies underwritten, if it's true that on average a car is used just 5% of its time), and a more tailored approach to the definition of the cover offered. It also provides a "fairer trade" to customers—bad and good ones, as it does not charge them based on the "average use and average behaviour". Finally, and more importantly, it offers a great financial incentive to behave better and in a more risk-savvy way: drive slower, if not, you are not able to do it better!

As mentioned, the three strategic themes are sometimes interconnected, with players offering P2P potentially leveraging the web ecosystem of partners and maybe offering "pay-as-you-go" offerings as well. Remarkably, a number of Fin-Tech players is now also developing commercial and financial alliances with the traditional incumbents, partnering with them to drive them on-line, if not beyond the on-line. Allianz, AXA and Aviva, just to name a few, as shown in the following Figure, have been fast mover in trying to address their own digital transformation with the help (or stimulus) of FinTech companies. Other incumbent insurance companies have instead decided to focus their digital transformation design and execution plan just with their internal forces: trying at the same time to work on

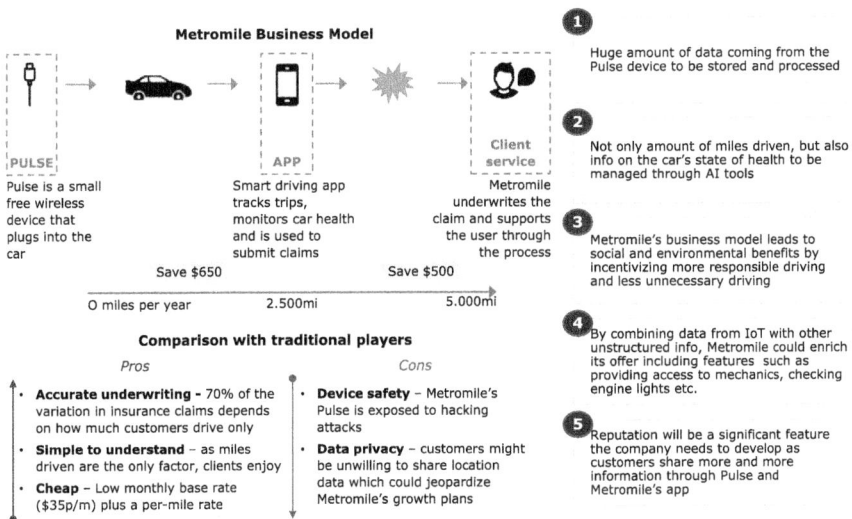

Fig. 10.6 Metromile's pay-per-mile car insurance allows low-mileage drivers to access more affordable rates

them and/or against FinTech digital insurers at their peril. In both cases fighting the chance of a new Amazon-like player emerging in the insurance space as it did in retailing (Fig. 10.6).

10.4 Mutually Insured, Completely Electronic

Is then insurance, within the global financial system, the sector next in-line for a radical transformation lead by technological and digital innovation? And if so, how is this going to change the key function that it has been delivering for centuries level? And how a "synapses" model could be developed and emerge as the winning one for incumbent insurers and for the new digital challengers? Not to mention incumbent banks, as insurance is also a key component of the core business of universal banking groups—via their "bancassurance" business—operated as cross selling of life and property and casualty products via their branches and to their clients.

Insurance companies have at times being described as the dinosaur in the open air museum of the global financial system—the least technologically sophisticated component of it, and still significantly protected by regulations, where products are sold (bar for the ones that are made mandatory by Law, like the car protection policies) and where the ability to evolve or innovate their value proposition, and the eagerness to do so, has been even lower than that of retail/commercial banks, asset managers and payment institutions.

It all now promises to change abruptly, with the advent of digital innovation and of the many novel ways in which new technological applications are adopted—way behind the strict realm of the financial life of customers. Just consider the "mutuality principle" on which most of the insurance business was initially started. According to this principle, there are many negative events in life that cannot be bear individually (unless at the cost of grave and sometimes radical changes in the lifestyle of the person involved) but that could be sheltered and shared in a relatively acceptable way if these were translated in "socialized" losses.

This principle of social network, that allows everybody to protect themselves from the "regret risk" that would truly change our wellbeing, and creates social value by the simple sharing of information and given a limited contribution of money (the one used to pay the premium that funds the overall insurance mechanism) is very consistent with the philosophy of the world-wide-web: the more people join the system the better—for scale, scope and diversification reasons, and the greater the value that is built overall and that can be socialized within the network for the mutually insured increased wellbeing of all the participants.

In a world where capital accumulation was helped by the development of oligopolistic positions on a number of vertical, very specific insurable risk sector (e.g. the maritime insurance business, initially built to cover the risk of a vessel or of an entire float sent to the New Indies going lost) and where the realization of the mutuality principle via cooperative associations was difficult to operate because of the "many to many" communications to be managed with lengthy throughput times and opaque processes, the opportunity of allowing third party players to develop as private capital funded and limited responsibility companies has always been great. With few notable exceptions, main insurance players, in fact, are today all quite capital intensive, and they apply the mutuality insurance principle on the basis of the diversification coming from large numbers (if not realized by the company itself, by the reinsurers that act behind it with back to back guarantees on some of its tail risks underwritten, in exchange of a certain return on the equity employed).

They also tend to be quite reliant on physical distribution channels (tied agents, or banks branches) and on actuarial analysis based on large numbers of data, mostly of a demographic/historical nature and with still limited utilization of applied analytics tools and machine learning and artificial intelligence. If we ask a price for a car insurance coverage we may be asked (in the best case) about the age, sex, city of residence and past history of accidents whilst driving. But not much is really analysed regarding how we do today and what would likely happen in the near future, including how much we drive and when, where and how (our driving style) —not to mention our overall lifestyle, current and projected, as reflecting the ambitions of our inner self.

It all leaves plenty of opportunity to enrich the data gathered and mined, and to create new intelligence that could be derived by a thorough, prospective analysis. It could then all lead towards the simplification of the products offering as well, and to the automation of the risk scoring—developed as a predictive and prospective tool and easily completed on line. All these innovation are then paving the way towards a distribution strategy where insurance products are delivered in fully digitized ways—avoiding the nuisance of tied agents calling you to sell the next policy, or forcing it to you by tying this to your next financial products (with the issue of miss-selling—the improper packaging of an insurance product in a loan—that has produced tens of billions of pounds of fines and remediation costs, just to mention the recent experience in the United Kingdom).

But what about the possibility of having a new wealth of totally new information, like, for example, the exact recording of how much we drive, and when, and where and how—given the development of the Internet of Things that could make our car an integral part of an "always on" insurance control and reporting system? And what about new technological tools that could be able to remotely monitor our state of health and level of attention when driving, therefore not just predicting better the probability of risk, but also reducing the average risk per se, by way of messages that can be sent to the driver or even to the engine and brake system themselves, not to mention new applications that could also streamline and make very efficient any claim management system once the accident has happened, helping reducing the actual costs to be covered.

Not only that. In a world of self-driving cars, we may imagine that the burden of the risk of an accident is taken by the car manufacturer itself—or by the new owner of the self-driving car that is likely used—in the logic of the "shared economy"—by many different counterparts, according to demand needs that are matched online by a dynamic pricing mechanism that, for any new renting, takes also into consideration the different expected risks and losses related to the specific where, when and how the drive will be. Ideally, in a world of fully electronic, completely connected view of all the individually insurable risks, the mutuality principle could be going back to its origins, allowing a reduced capitalization of the insurer itself—an intelligent aggregator able to manage multiple clients, seeking some coverage and being available to pay a small price (funding the system) for it, via the web and the personal data regarding the clients' digital identity they are ready to trade for a more extensive, cheaper and relevant insurance of their "too big to bear" lifestyle risks.

This aggregator would seek and manage a multitude of data, structured and unstructured, and with a greater and greater weight on "almost real time data"—whose availability is now supported by the Internet of Things, by the Shared Economy and by the cheaper and cheaper availability of infrastructure systems able to monitor whatever is happening across the globe. On this basis, machine learning and artificial intelligence applications would be able to price at individual level not just the single client, but even the specific risk that are underwritten "hic et nunc" (the specific drive of the car insurance described above). It could all even impact on the relative likelihood of something bad happening and on the costs derived from the ensuing damage.

All these developments could bring massive improvements in the transparency, efficiency and efficacy of the overall mutuality based insurance system—as all and only the relevant risks would be covered, priced in a tailored way and even (at least partially) proactively managed, cutting layers of middle men in the process and allowing to this new insurance company to operate in new ways and offer new meanings to the interconnectivity then prevailing among people in the digitalized, information augmented society. Applied analytics and AI could even allow to define the specific, individual function of regret risk that each of us has, and that changes continuously during our life, and to suggest us what to insure and for how much, to optimize our utility function that is non-linearly connected with the complement of our regret risk's one—as insurance, in a way, should be born and developed on the basis of the psychological analysis and understanding of the human mind, that is not usually driven by a mere economic rationale, but also by other intangibles.

Based on this new ways of designing and managing "junctions" that optimize the use of neurons in the system (the number of IoT devices, the exchange points of the shared economy, the new other sources of information produced) these new "synapses-based" insurance company could then design and build a number of novel use cases that are radically different from what the insurance industry has been offering in the past—as we will later discuss with a further example linked to health insurance. They could then create a new value in the multi stakeholders, mutuality principle based social system. A value that goes way above the traditional "share the pain and contribute a small part of the gain via the premium" insurance principle.

As a result of this "synapses" positioning, they could ultimately do without any financial capital: why set aside mathematical reserves if it is the system itself that mutually insures the delivery of the appropriate and most correct coverage for any individual risk? Why not tapping directly the long term investors (including pension funds and asset managers) and the individual customers themselves, that can contribute digital cash, or some new crypto currency, as they seek advice from the synapses insurance player, on what and how and for how much to cover? But also new opportunities to get exposures to yielding assets that are covering other people's risks that are in turn negatively correlated with one to which investors are ultimately exposed.

10.5 Healthy as an Insurer

Thomas Buberl, the CEO of AXA, one of the largest and most valuable global general insurer, has recently stated how insurers are under threats from tech companies muscling in on their health businesses.[6] Whilst motor insurance is often seen as the most vulnerable part of the industry, as driverless cars are expected to cut accident rates dramatically and change the way the product is done, priced and sold, it's in the health insurance sector that FinTech could break down the barriers between pharmaceutical companies and producers of devices, and among doctors, hospital and patients—substituting the traditionally opaque and inefficient intermediation system provided and managed by large health insurers with new interconnection plays, able to optimally manage all these different stakeholders in novel ways—for the overall benefit of the system (albeit, not necessarily to the benefit of the "traditional" insurance companies not ready to transform). BoughtByMany (described in Fig. 10.7) is an example of a platform offering specific insurance coverage for individuals, leveraging most of the five pillars to deliver a distinctive value to the overall ecosystem.

Technological and FinTech companies could in fact be deemed as better placed to collect and analyse health data, as they will increasingly control, through the IoT, a number of information flooding out of our body, almost on a continuous and real time basis. As an example, Google is now pioneering and testing smart contact lens that can check the level of diabetes for patients in real time—as they measure the glucose level of the people wearing them—in a continuous way, with no blood test required.

With such an information, and the potential intelligence that can be derived by mining huge quantity of data to derive patterns and potential solutions, there is an opportunity for Google and for the many other FinTech players experimenting in this field to actually become a more successful originator and underwriter than traditional insurers, as they may already (as in the case of Google) have billions of

---

[6]Financial Times, "AXA chief fears tech threats to insurers" health business. Oliver Ralph. 18 December 2016.

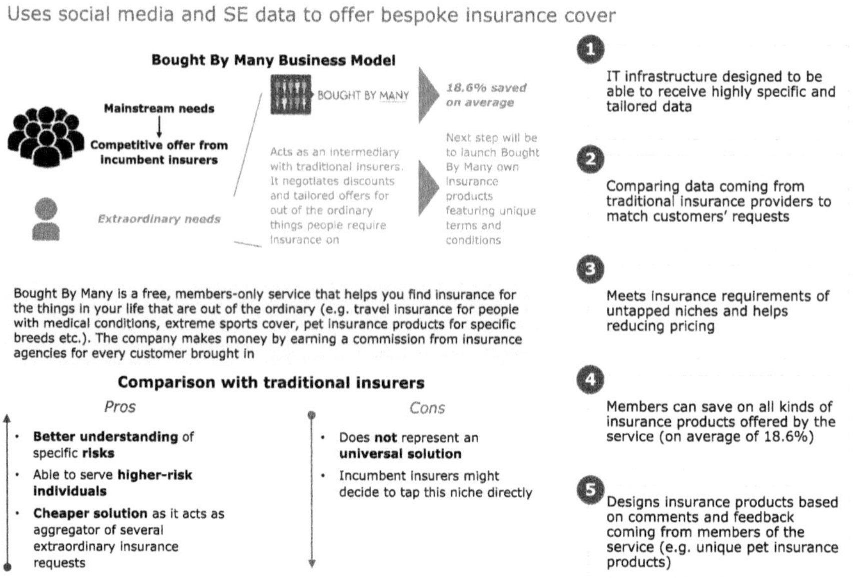

Fig. 10.7 Bought By Many offers attractive offers to individuals with specific insurance needs

clients that they know and understand for other commercial reasons, and can reach out with compelling proposition (e.g. like offering for free contact lens to the people that Google knows have or may potentially have diabetes—simply because they have been typing "diabetes" too many times in their searches or emails). And they can then offer proactively not only a real time, continuous monitoring of their glucose level, but also health insurance policies that can beat on price any other contractual proposition coming from traditional insurers.

In fact, having the real time information, and the intelligence on behaviours, health trends and potential medical treatments and solutions would not only help the FinTech companies in offering a superior value added to the customer, but also allow a better pricing as they would know more, and would also know how to advice the client to inherently reduce the risk of a severe or even mortal illness—therefore allowing better risk selection, monitoring and even direct management aimed at reducing the risk and at hedging this with all kind of potential medical solutions that could be made available by alliances with pharmaceutical companies. More broadly, the usage of technology and data is also looking to simplify and improve the healthcare insurance offers, as shown in the following Figure and with the case study of Oscar (Fig. 10.8).

Having superior origination and underwriting capabilities and therefore the ability to better price could then be leveraged by the FinTech companies to then sell insurance policies and held them to maturity; or they could just focus on the origination bit and on the advisory on the underwriting that traditional insurance companies, with a huge capital base and balance sheet, would then hold to maturity

10.5 Healthy as an Insurer

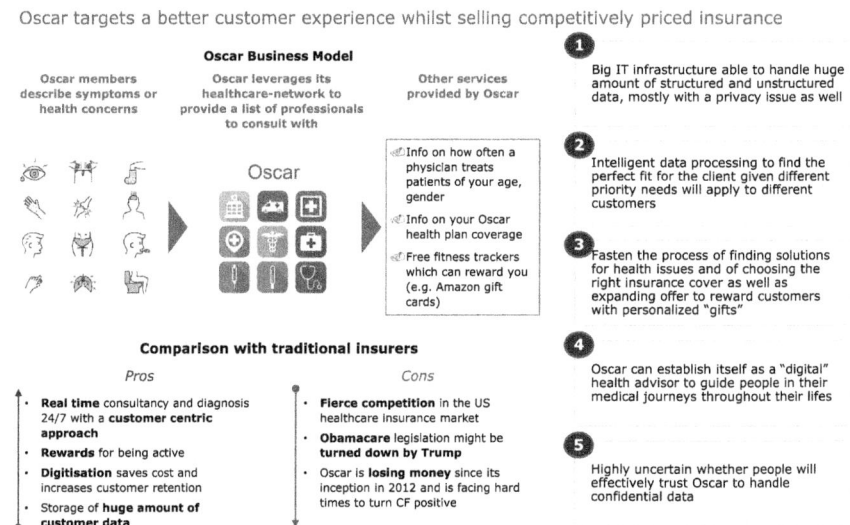

Fig. 10.8 Oscar: usage of technology and data is looking to simplify and improve healthcare insurance offers

and partially reinsure with other traditional reinsurers—allowing therefore the FinTech companies to avoid all the regulatory constraints and capital charges coming from being a "normal" insurance company—playing the synapses part in the most intelligent way and leaving the poorest bits of the business to the heavily regulated insurance incumbents.

The suggested model would again exploit the five pillars of the synapses model: leveraging data and information at best, being able to capture the structure and unstructured ones in real time and from all kind of unobvious (and more customer friendly) ways, leveraging the almost unlimited possibilities offered by the Internet of Things etc. A simple, obvious example in the property and casualty insurance business, could be a car insurance, that would entail gathering data about the driving style of the client, the state of the car and the performance of its main components; and on the road traffic, the weather and the average speed of the other vehicles using the same road—aggregating at best both internal and external sources of information.

A "synapses" insurance company would use all this information and then applied analytics and machine learning/AI techniques to truly create new intelligence on the patters of the illness and on the likely predictors, remediation plans and solutions that could be of potential interest to the client/patient (in the health insurance example). In the car insurance example, it would instead allow to suggest new roads and a different itinerary, and incentivize and monitor a safer driving style —even more so in connection with more dangerous situation that could be monitored and predicted on the basis of the observation of the weather, the state of the roads and the behaviour of other drivers—acting de facto as an intelligent, forward looking support driving system; or acting as an input to the IT system of the self-driving cars, now soon expected to be widely available—with the insurance ending up rating the riskiness (reliability) of each different systems.

The suggested model would then act on our third synapses pillar as well, potentially testing a new model of interconnecting clients, doctors and pharmaceutical companies, not to mention insurance companies that would be able to offer a better deal to the customers. Clients would feed their pre-diagnosed data to machine learning/AI powered doctors, always on line and ready to offer advice and suggest treatments on the basis of billions of new data being stored and analysed, and adjusting continuously their therapies as new data, in real time, gets available—allowing big Pharma to cut short the time to test new medicines and treatments and —at the end, to achieve a much greater success in predicting the illness behaviour and the best possible cure. The case of Vitality (in the following Figure) is also showing how premiums could be linked to the clients' lifestyle, thus promoting their healthier lifestyle and as a consequence a lower cost of claims (Fig. 10.9).

In the car insurance, a synapses insurance company would do this by creating new junctions between customers and manufacturers, where best cars or best setting of their capabilities could be offered on the basis of the individual driver's specific driving style. And even the spare part industries could get to work on a "just in time" mode, as they would know in real time of any new accident and adjust inventory accordingly. New ecosystems would then impact the way the health or the automotive industries work—in a way allowing insurance to better price the risk, but also to contribute to reduce the inherent risks of entire industries.

Fig. 10.9 Vitality links H&L insurance premiums to the clients' lifestyle, promoting healthier choices

The model for contact lenses or for any other wearable medical device, or for on board computers able to feed data on the car, on the driver and on the external travelling context could then leverage on these new "junctions" to create new solutions that are changing the overall pay off of the specific industry or industries which are covered by the insurance offering—driving better underwriting and supporting the on-going minimization of the risks underwritten: evolving the role of insurance from mostly reactive (to financially cover the consequences of negative events) to increasingly proactive (to risk managing situations as they evolve to prevent the happening of negative events and reduce their impact when they do happen).

The new synapses system would end up reducing the risks related to illness and increasing the efficacy of any old or new medical treatment (as the data flooding on real time and on a continuous basis from the contact lens would provide invaluable intelligence to help testing, in much shorter time frames, what medical treatment or dietary regime could work better). And it could help in reducing the likelihood and severity of car accidents via a mix of better performance of the car, of the driver and given the external context of the travel itinerary that cannot be modified, but at least can be known and analysed in advance to support advice.

Of course, a number of obstacles are in the way to the realization of this visionary "proactive insurance", starting from the obvious and natural reticence of customers to share their information and feel monitored and controlled around the clock, as they live their every-day lives. Who would like to let known to the insurance provider how much they drink or ate too much, or drive in a too smart and fast way on their way home?

10.6 Claim What?

As we have seen, a number of new initiatives are promising to shake up the insurance business across its entire value chain. We have discussed example related to new coverages, aggregation and intermediation and even underwriting and pricing models. Still, claim management—the last component of the value chain, looks to be potentially impacted in an even more dramatic way.[7] Lemonade, a peer to peer insurance company that we already commented, started with the aim of making the industry easier to end customers, and addressing most of its misaligned incentives still present—the real drivers of the cost of risk (the cost of claims) for the sector.

The theory is pretty simple. You pay a premium and the insurance company will pay the damage. You have a car insurance and you will feel like driving like crazy, not really caring if you scratch your new car when parking (as the insurance company will foot the bill). Several contractual and process solution (a share of the costs, the tracking of the historical patterns of a client, etc.) have already been

---

[7]The Economist, A New York start up shakes up the insurance business, March 9th 2017.

adopted by the industry, that however is still putting the equity capital as a regulatory buffer of last resort for all the negative events that could happen in life—the unexpected bad things, as opposed to the expected ones that should be already incorporated in the risk-adjusted pricing of policies. But the connection with the profit you would get, if you are lucky or just behave well are not that immediate, and certainly they do not happen in real time. In a nutshell, as claims repayment come from the insurers' pockets, it ends up encouraging frauds, and pushing up premiums in turn—if insurance companies want to stay profitable and incorporate this "moral hazard" as expected cost of doing their business, as opposed to the unexpected wrongdoing that could happen anywhere.

Lemonade's business model works just differently. This FinTech insurer takes up 20% of premiums as a fee and rewards under-claiming customers by giving a share of unused income to charities related to the specific community it is addressing with its offering—a good publicity for a sometimes poorly reputed business. Then, instead of people doing underwriting, lemonade uses algorithms; and instead of expensive brokers and salespeople it uses chat-bots. Lemonade then uses machine learning/AI to handle claims, reviewing the legitimacy of the claims in few seconds—targeting to address on day one more than 90% of claims—some of them with a time-to-answer of less than 3 s, thus reducing the expense ratios of the industry, now at 30% of revenues and offering an incredible service to the policyholders—often let in a wait and see attitude by traditional insurers (you hope you will get paid, but don't know when, if you are still alive by then).

On claim management, the opportunity to do radically better is—say—a very low hanging fruit. Still, insurance incumbents have the advantage of their huge amount of data, if they can react and move fast enough[8]—reacting to the technological change that is particularly strong and promising in this last bit of the often forgotten part of the insurance value chain. Some of the incumbents are already looking at structured data, but most of their underwriting still relies on human judgement and labor—to evaluate risks and set premiums, and most claims are still mostly managed manually—by people that are maybe incentivized in spending less, but not on providing a better service to the clients: a transparent, quick, unambiguous answer to the damaged.

Innovation in claim management is therefore mostly coming from other "shadow" (lightly regulated) part pf the global financial system. Two Sigma, a large American quantitative hedge fund, is, for example, using its sophisticated algorithms to gauge risks and set prices for insurance better, faster (in real time and with instant quotes) than people cannot just match. Two Sigma now contributes its analytical prowess to a joint venture with Hamilton, a Bermudian insurer, and AIG. Simple insurance has then integrated a product warranty insurance into ecommerce, again based on big data capture and applied analytics. And Allianz has invested into Smilesurance and (along with many others) is setting up its own internal venture capital fund and incubator.

---

[8]The Economist, Counsel of protection, March 9th 2017.

Apart from the cost efficiency and the optimization of combined ratio, the overall idea is now becoming to use distinctive services to do a better job in claim management, starting eventually from the very prevention of the claims themselves. In the old world, traditional insurance companies would plan their reserves and claim management policies drawing up worst-case scenarios to estimate the losses they would incur from, say, natural disasters, like a typhoon hitting Florida. In the new world, (in the case of a typhoon) they would start working with clients and local authorities on preparing for such events knowing what could go wrong and what would reduce the loss—i.e. acting de facto as risk prevention and loss minimization consultants, therefore starting the "proactive" part of the claim management process even before the claim is manifesting.

Even more, on damage control, tech-savvy insurers are going one step further exploiting new sources of unstructured data—e.g. using sensors to track everything from boiler temperatures to health data to driving styles and then offering policies with pricing and coverage calibrated accordingly. Data and information from sensors, and the intelligence derived from them offer then an opportunity to cover all kind of new risk prevention services. Aviva and HomeServe (a British home service company) have even developed a partnership where they have a sensor ("leakBot") installed on its customers' incoming water pipers that can detect even minuscule leaks. HomeServe can then repair these before a pipe floods a home causing serious damage—thus acting as a symbiotic partner to Aviva that will end up footing a lower bill on its claim management part.

Finally, a further example of the continuously moving frontier of the omniscient intelligence that can be derived from data can be derived from the car industry. Carmakers have in fact traditionally bought product-liability insurance to cover manufacturing defects. But Volvo and Mercedes are now so confident of their self-driving cars that last year they said they will not buy insurance at all. And they will self-insure themselves—i.e. directly bearing any losses coming from crashes due to faults of their artificially intelligent systems. If you cannot be sure that you can change the way your customers drive—not even by teaching and incentivizing them on the basis of the real time data and intelligence now available via satellites and always-on cars, you can at least be sure of your own robots, and trust the artificial-intelligence powered driver at the wheel. Maybe a major crash is coming to the industry, but on a quite different perspective.

10.7 Synapses in Insurance

We have extensively commented the reasons why the insurance sector could become one of the most radically impacted and transformed one in the global financial system. We have also commented why the "synapsezation" framework and its five key pillars could drive new business and operating models for incumbents, and support the emergence of new winning FinTech digital players. Implicitly, we have shown, via a number of examples, that the digitization of insurance could change our lives in an even more profound way than, say, the one we predict for payments or lending. In fact, it all relates to the basic production factor of this industry, that is risk first and foremost, and across the key functions of the global financial systems.

All risks at the basis of the intermediation and transformation mission of the global system are in fact mostly financial, with the exception of the "pure risks"—on life and mortality, health and morbidity first of all, and then property and casualty, that have a financial compensation component, but not much else that is financial really. By extension, even the reputational and the other operational risks look better manageable via the insurance sector vis a vis the banking one—and even better by a fully digitalized insurance industry. And the cyber-risk as well, and the one related to the loss of digital trust could also be better managed by digital insurance. Not to mention the risk that new robots and machine learning/AI systems could at times start to act against human beings, in an almost science fiction scenario that is hopefully unlikely but not impossible.

The "synapses" that could potentially happen in insurance could deliver us very relevant non-financial values: more information and intelligence on our lifestyle related risks, with more interconnected counterparts operating for our extended health and augmented wellbeing; and with more opportunities to basically make sure that we are not just covered on the potential negative outcomes, but that we are actually driving them down, even potentially eliminating them—as an economic incentive system is developed to guide and influence our behaviours and preferences, our basic needs and our highest ambitions. The almost limitless possibilities to apply the synapses concept to better insure almost every dimension of life brings incredible opportunities, but also a number of unanswered questions, and potentially few significant (un-insurable) risks.

Think about the many cases where we have seen data/information accumulation and the creation of intelligence and predictive capabilities that are setting the scene for major breakthrough in insurance. The situation of "knowing (almost) everything in advance" could end up creating a potential "economic paradox", where insurance companies with perfect knowledge would choose to underwrite clients that have zero risks ahead of them, and refuse to underwrite the clients with greater needs of insurance protection and of mutual assistance—contradicting the very social premise of the development of insurance as pooling and sharing of individually unbearable risks (the mutuality principle). New forms of regulation could therefore be expected to address this and enforce the underwriting of the least protected categories of customers—now made "naked" by the total information available and by the "big brother-like" intelligence potentially being created on them.

Whatever the ethical issues that may arise and that could require a new set of regulations, insurance is very likely set to be the function of the global financial system where digitization could impact harder and in more heterogeneous ways, across the entire value chain and with the potential to redefine the structure of its market and (indirectly, as we have seen) of the many other industries it relates to.

On the distribution side, the online aggregators able to gather more clients will be able to put forward a better quote than traditional, end-suppliers—because of the economies of scale and scope, of the diversification effect and of the learning curve exponentially associated at having more and more data regarding customers' behaviours. This could allow a further competitive advantage to the benefit of the "smart" owners of the customers' relationship (data and intelligence) versus the heavy balance sheet/highly regulated, traditional players that would underwrite or retain the insurance risks originating them via traditional agency channels.

Eventually, most of risk underwriting could eventually end up being done by the smart digital players, should they be able to aggregate multiple, non-professional investors acting on the web and arranging quasi—Lloyds of London markets or digital marketplaces of insurable risks—in a B2B or P2P mode and in pursuit (in a way) of a truly re-mutualisation of the industry. Also, as personal data are becoming more available (because of the proliferation of the Internet of Things, of the Open Data etc.) and the ones related to properties are also getting more ubiquitous and largely available (because of the proliferation of the "shared economy"—with people owning less and less, anything from flats, cars, bicycles etc.), synapses insurance companies would end up focussing more on the lifestyles than on the traditional risk parameters of their end customers (it becomes less relevant whether I am a male of 48 years old, and more how I eat, travel, work, train, behave etc.).

All these changes are apparently paving the way for the development of a "behavioural insurance" that would augment and extend our wellbeing, or direct and therefore constraint our liberty. In this new brave world, the ultimate customers' returns should be gauged in terms of the monetary value they can get for each unit of liberty at risk. That is to say that an even greater focus on trust will need to be taken care of by new FinTech and old traditional insurers alike—where "trust" could also became the source of new business, should a smart enough (old or new) insurance company start offering coverage on cyber risk and on the cyber trust of all kind of counterparts—potentially identifying in advance, and in real time, the greedy, the lazy and the rest.

Digital for the Greater Good 11

Abstract
Whilst most of the current debate on media is on the many legacy issues inherited from the global financial crisis and on the further challenges that re-regulation is posing on incumbents, digitization is acting becoming the major force for change acting in the global financial—and potentially for the benefit of the overall society. Customers, first and foremost, should be benefiting, albeit with some new and little understood risks arising, mostly driven by the uncertainty introduced by uncontrolled innovation and by its (somehow related) regulatory arbitrage. Eventually, a new form of "digitally inverted pyramid" could ensue, introducing new systemic risks and unbearable lightness. Even more importantly, a critical issue to address to make sure the "great disruption" will bring about a greater value for the multitudes will be around the ownership, management and utilization of data—avoiding the insurgence of few "big brothers" that could build a quasi-monopolistic positioning in the market—hence stifling competition value sharing for customers. Still, aside from these risks, the digitization disruption is going to change our ways of living—potentially for the better.

Keywords
Big data · Customer convenience · Correspondence · Convergence · Intelligence · Assurance

11.1 Innovation, Here to Stay

Innovation is not new to the global financial system. It has in fact developed through booms and busts, war and peace, changing a great deal, from the creation of metal coins, to the introduction of banknotes and lending, to the ATM machines.

More recently, the rate of innovation in financial services has however increased, as the regulatory barriers that kept the industry partially protected after the second World War were first lowered to increase competition—thus creating the business opportunity for new (old and new) challengers, then risen again in the aftermath of the global financial crisis—thus allowing the formation of a sometimes unfair competitive advantage to shadow banking players acting outside of the rules set by supervisory bodies.

Apart from these regulatory "swings", technology (in its larger interpretation as the driving force of the so called "fourth industrial revolution") has also contribute to unbundle the previously cohesive business models, where banks were doing their own products, managing most of their basic infrastructure and running their distribution channels, mostly bricks and mortar[1]—something that the world-wide-web has hugely supported.

The unbundling of the financial intermediaries' business and operating models had not stopped here—driven by the innovation spurred by unmet clients' demand, the search for further operational efficiency and the opportunity of running their business with less capital at risk and better risk underwriting—albeit sometimes of a different nature. Customer facing platforms have arisen as a consequence, trying to act as the "portal of choice" and as the funnel through which most of the financial needs of the clients get addressed. Similarly, new digital production facilities have also been developing, addressing vertical niches where the know how produced by machine learning/AI could just become the critical competitive component at play.

This "unbundling", leading specialization and economies of scope and scale, it just stands as the first step towards the development of more synapses driven organizations, better able to compete (on one or more of the three subcomponents) just because of the five pillars they have been able to develop to better serve customer, do better products or provide better infrastructure to the rest of the market doing the previous two.

Innovation is therefore here to stay, and we are just at the beginning of a transformation that should also be measured, valued and then supported on the basis of the "greater good" it could provide to the larger society. It can in fact contribute in a number of ways that need to be better qualified and understood.

Starting from the customers, the innovation happening in the global financial system could deliver to them an expanded access to a diverse set of affordable financial services—reducing greatly the number of unbanked people and increasing the level of mobile, real time, always on access of existing banking clients. The mining of data could allow, as we have seen, to better scope their lifecycle and address their most critical needs and ambitions—linking more and more the wealth management, insurance, lending, payment offerings with the wellbeing of the individual. Families and small/mid-sized companies will then benefit from the greater transparency on data and other credit information, because for example this

---

[1]Balancing financial stability, innovation and economic growth, World Economic Forum position paper, May 2017.

could allow them to get more money, at cheaper rates and just when they truly need it (and can afford it as well).

The new "banked" clients will also have access to more international, easy to use, almost instantaneous internationally extended transaction services (starting from payments) that will promote inclusion at the level of the global fabric of markets and societies—in this new, digital world, we will be able to pay easily wherever we are, as new across borders standards could be created and developed outside the traditional (still mostly Country specific payment) rails, helping also in fighting money laundering and criminality.

Moving to the products, we have first to remember that risk is the main production factor of the industry. The global financial system is at the end responsible for the effective management of the financial and "pure" risks associated with the provision of its core services and with other unavoidable facts of life (like, for example, in the case of insurance, mortality and morbidity). The innovation now taking place could help in having these risks better monitored and understood, and better distributed to the ultimate "best holders" of the system—for example, a more detailed and faster analysis of large amounts of data done via the introduction of machine learning and artificial intelligence could allow for the sophistication of management information to enhance decision making and deliver enhanced early warning systems, such as those used to counteract cyber-attacks.

Finally, from an infrastructure perspective, innovation could help both incumbents and new digital challengers. For incumbents, shared, innovative infrastructures could allow them to address most of the legacy issues they are still grappling with, and to improve their service levels without having to consider major technological overalls and investments—and managing in a more secure and effective way the data and information capital they already own (often without a clear plan to preserve, manage and get something out of them).

The innovation happening in data and applied analytics offered by new infrastructure could then allow to incumbents to execute the full redesign of entire processes and reach very significant reduction in costs and therefore efficiency. The innovation shared infrastructures can also support new challengers, as they could better focus on their specific bit of innovation, accelerating their velocity in start and ramp up, and reducing their execution risk. The creation of industry utilities and outsourcing solutions, subject to a safe and sound control environment, could also spur the development of further initiatives, at both incumbents' and new challengers' level, sustaining a virtuous circle where new innovation leads to further, valuable innovation.

11.2 Digital for Good

Whilst most of the financial media, and academic literature, are still focussing on the many legacy issues remaining unsolved from the 2008 global crisis, the challenges coming to the global financial system from digitization look less covered and little understood. From the point of view of incumbents, they look like further bad news on top of a situation where the banking business model is still requiring painful cuts in branches and people, further investments to manage creeping legacy systems, and new models and methodologies to address and manage emerging risks —from cyber security to the risk of being leapfrogged and made competitively irrelevant by a mix of disruptions coming from the "fourth industrial revolution".[2]

With all these bad news, and bad moods, and bad perceptions as well affecting the global financial system and its many challenges, we should not forget that what is happing is actually hardly negative, and that "digital is for good"—if not for incumbents, for the markets and societies at large. Not only because, notwithstanding the obvious "hype" and exaggerations that are now building up. Digitization is here now for good and here to stay for a long time, radically changing the way of doing things in financial services, bringing along bring new, unprecedented value to many stakeholders—albeit introducing new still little understood menaces and risks. Thanks to digital, many positive developments have occurred since the global financial crisis—having positive impacts on both retail and corporate clients —to start with.

Take the cost of financial services. It has decreased in the last few years, certainly because of the quantitative easing operated by Central Banks (a QE that could mine however, in the long term, the purchasing power of people) and because the increased competition and transparency introduced by market regulators (some of this as part of the re-regulations and anti-trust policies that have been designed and executed since the crisis to the benefit of the end customer). But also—and more importantly—the production cost of financial services has significantly decreased because of the digitization of their operating model, and because its "one-click-away" total convenience—anytime, anywhere and anyhow—has just skyrocketed.

Customers are progressively becoming the "king" of the market, even in banking and insurance, or payments, where the power has been traditionally left with the suppliers. They are becoming "king" as they have the many new choices introduced by FinTech new digital players, and even P2P ones—where platforms are matching the supply and demand needs of ordinary people with no financial intermediary in between.

As customers are getting more used to get the better deals that the new digital world can offer, incumbents themselves are seeing their competitive positioning and negotiating power being eroded, with some of their financial value migrating to the end clients—not just to other FinTech challengers. In theory, following a Schumpeterian view of "creative destruction", any old, creepy bank new failure should help in releasing and reallocating the capital and the other scares resources entrapped in their suboptimal business model, towards better uses and greater business models, again to the overall benefit of the global economy and society alike.[3]

---

[2]Digitization in TMT and key trends, Francesco Barosi, AlixPartners position paper 2017.
[3]Restructuring and innovation in banking, Claudio Scardovi, 2016, Springer.

The disruptions of banking could come however at some cost, and with risks for the greater good as well—as the global financial system provides many shared utilities—the plumbing that allow to the overall economy to work smoothly and with the development of international trades, global investments and liberal, local economies. This "plumbing" needs continuous maintenance, development and attention from the private and public sector as well in order to ensure its continuous and "safe and sound" working. What if, then, the new FinTech winners are just stealing value from incumbents, without caring to keep investing in the overall utility infrastructure—and the old incumbents are ending up in a position where they are not more able to contribute, as crippled as they are by diminishing revenues and sinking profits that are getting them out of business?

What if the new FinTech winners (because regulators are targeting primarily incumbents and not as much, or at all, the new players) are just lowering the security standards of the industry, arbitraging the existing regulations and with limited controls on conduct risk, for example? And what if they become themselves highly leveraged, on cyber capital and technological assets—if not on the financial ones—that could also fail for a number of reasons, thus introducing other systemic risks of an even more dangerous nature? What if, finally, all forms of irresponsible financial speculation and even financial crime take the routes of these, little controlled and monitored, alternative digital venues, using the convenience on offer for the "bad" of the greater society?

Following these all too many "what if-s", the ultimate paradox of the "digital for good" digitization scenario could therefore develop as a potentially worrying one. On one side, the incumbents, still in varying stage of restructuring and transformation, are not just healthy enough to keep being the pillars of entire global financial systems and of its main functions and related utility-like infrastructures—and the same would apply to their incumbent regulators. On the other side the new challengers are promoting their disruptive digital propositions almost outside the prevailing rules, checks and balances, whilst still relying on the old, legacy infrastructure technology that was created and sustained by incumbents—take for example the new payment players riding on the rails of Visa and MasterCard, or the new digital banks or Telco payment services opening new accounts based on the clients' existing current account details.

In this potential scenario, some of the value would go certainly to clients, but also some profitability would be retained by the supply-side, with new challengers stealing most of it, without reinvesting much in the public good of the global system and almost unchecked by global regulators—e.g. playing free riding at the short-term expense of the incumbents and at the mid-long term cost of the retail and corporate customers themselves. And introducing unknown risks that could further undermine the remaining trust in the financial services sector. Regulators could just prove themselves as unable to follow the change happening and with a new global crisis coming from the "World-Wide-Web Street" and not from Wall Street.

We could then imagine a new digitally inverted pyramid, generated by a new unbearable lightness coming from data monetization, mobile banking, applied analytics and machine learning/AI, robotization and much else…

11.3 A New Way of Digital Living

Digital innovation is driving our new way of living, with radical changes in the way we feel, expect, behave and even perceive emotions and express passions and behave from a sentimental, romantic point of view, potentially (but not necessarily) for our greater good. Just taking a look back at the last 20 years, we can easily understand how technology has dramatically changed our ubiquity: driving and supporting an evolution that has been happening in every aspect of our lives—from work to entertainment, from travelling to shopping.

Back to 1997 we lived in world dominated by a "serial" approach, where we bought cars and hailed taxis to get to work, using our desktop in a mostly disconnected way. We were buying appliances and groceries walking on Main Street, and visiting the branch of our bank to put and get money and buy all kind of financial products. Today, we leave instead in a world dominated by a technology enabled ubiquity, were we are continuously on-line and multi-tasking, even when we watch TV whilst zapping on the web, to get information, do shipping or the occasional wire transfer. We work leveraging the cloud whilst sitting at our desk, but more often we leverage smart working and home offices, and we trade our data and personal information to get discounts, or a better service in the mid-term, as all kind of new, digital suppliers try to intrude into the remaining of our physical life—making up for us, in some instances, critical answers regarding our way of being.

It all comes to a cost—the loss in our span for attention, in our privacy, and in our being able to fully leverage and enjoy an in-person business or personal meeting with a colleague or friend. And it requires a new, enhanced level of consciousness, regarding the extent we feel we can trade focus for extension, privacy for value for money offerings or "know it all for you" real time propositions and even allow that our sentimental self gets significantly reallocated from the physical to the digital world (as we interact, share ideas and emotions with friends, even find a date or a husband or wife over the web). Still, with all these many worries and trade-off and risks to get it wrong, we believe all these radical changes have the possibility to become fundamentally, and based on our enhanced, digitally vigilant conscience, a force for good.

It can become a force for good, if we develop this digitally vigilant conscience acting—again—in a more synapses-based shaped way of living. If we take into account, and understand, the main pillars of the synapsezation to come in markets and societies, we are better able to assess its trade off, and manage its risks, in order to get the best coming from these disruptive forces and fed-off their potential threats.

Converge is happening across technologies. Everything is now getting available from everywhere, to everyone and seamlessly, as demand and supply converge in portals integrated into communities and social webs, thus digitizing markets and societies alike. We are becoming simply over-flooded of data and information and the issue is now becoming how to screen and focus on the limited amount that is relevant and digestible. And we keep producing data that are made available in real time to a number of third parties, friend and foes, acting for business, political, personal or any kind of other motives—towards an extended information economy.

In this information economy, acting on the first pillar, we need to be able to know, control and monitor what data and information we give away, and what we would absolutely not be ready to cede. Acting on the second pillar, we would then need to understand what new intelligence is coming out of it, and who gets it and for what purposes; and how we could retain, maybe sometimes with some kind of exclusivity, some portion of the intelligence produced by applied analytics and just for our own benefit. We should then analyse and define—applying our third pillar—the new terms and models of trade, or interconnections, where we are ready to exchange some of these data, information and intelligence to get a good deal, knowing ex ante the market value of the things we give away and the expected pay off we can obtain from what we take in exchange.

In this all-digitally-convergent world, these new interconnections should be able to deliver value to us but also to a number of our relevant stakeholders—friends and families, for example, building incremental value in our own, extended ecosystem—take for example the case we commented on the students getting gifts from friends and families as they perform, and receiving advice and support from the digital platform in order to do just that, getting the help of professors and professionals, and even loans, in exchange of some of their future success. This model is delivering value to students, but also to their families and friends, and to other third parties. And finally, in this digitally enhanced consciousness, we should become all too aware of the cyber risks at play and of the required cyber trust needed, and know who to (digitally) trust or not.

Apart from the digital convergence, an increasing "correspondence" will also shape our way of living. Many of these innovation forces that are driving the so called "fourth industrial revolution" are not in fact happening in a vacuum, but acting together, sharing data and information, and intelligence as new applied analytics and machine learning/AI elaborate factual experiences into truths. More and more things in our physical and virtual worlds are now communicating among themselves and with us—robot-like, in some cases. It's not just about the new digital offerings now available over the web and often interconnected and dynamically updating (as we buy a red scarf, the web proposes us a red cap), or the Internet of Things, but (for examples) the "shared economy" that leverages the digital to revolutionize the industrial sectors of restaurants, hotels and travelling—as almost everything find a correspondence and become shareable. As information becomes available without limits, so the physical assets are as well and in a related, corresponding—convergence is then translating into correspondence and, again, we need to understand, analyse and act upon this correspondence applying all the lenses of our synapsezation model—and leveraging on all the pillars described.

Just think of the social implications of "big data" that leverage the new development in the machine learning/AI fields and the development of automatic, robotized processes to make millions of workers redundant: we need to understand in advance how to keep ourselves professionally relevant in this future: which data and information we need to possess, which applied analytics capabilities we need to develop and which kind of junctions we have to create for ourselves in the job market, and pursuing what kind of interconnections—or network of relationships, to stay atop and survive—delivering value to ourselves but also to a larger number of relevant stakeholders. And we also need to understand what king of cyber trust we need to be building for ourselves and for our digital identity—as the job market will be increasingly determined over the web. Similar reasoning could be applied to the "self-driving" revolution that changes our way of living space and distances, but also entrust our safety to the hands of a robot; or to the 3D printing that allow the full decentralization of physical manufacturing and related jobs and not just of the intelligence that is driving its processes, and therefore could allow to anybody, everywhere, and almost in an any how way, to build weapons or bombs.

Following this reasoning, not just companies, but individuals alike will have to start "synapsezing" their way of living, leveraging the immense amount of data and information available "cum granu salis", e.g. making sense of what is relevant and digestible for them to produce their own intelligence, with the use of machine learning/AI when and where needed—they should also consider whether and to what extent to rely on third party AI, at the risk of losing most of their brain power (in a world of machines that do all the thinking, there will be a tendency of losing this crucial capability: who can do even simple calculations today without a PC today?). People will have then to consider their set of relationships and "junctions", in the job market as in society that can help them to get the most for what they wish for, for them and for their related stakeholders—ideally defining new behavioural solutions that are truly adding incremental value into the ecosystem. Eventually, people's reputation will also become more and more determined by their cyber one —as their credibility will be more and more based on cyber trust, as they will become successful, important, even internationally famous and renowned, joining a "cyber hall of fame" and becoming "larger than digital".

11.4 A "Digitally" Inverted Pyramid

The innovation "here to stay" is introducing very relevant and potentially sizeable pay offs for the global economy and societies as well. It also introduces new kind of risks, of a financial nature, but not only. The new systemic risks are driven by the new rules of the game, affecting how customers behave, how financial intermediaries—old and new—develop their strategies to accommodate and even influence the emerging customers' new lifestyle, and how the related product platforms and service infrastructures get changed as a result of these two combined forces—not to mention other indirect impacts in the ecosystem.

We have already discussed the "mother of all risks" of the new digital environment, e.g. the cyber risk and the related cyber capital at risk. As financial service businesses become increasingly reliant on technology and continue to amass larger stores of data, it becomes increasingly important (and difficult) to ensure that super resilient systems are in place to safeguard private information, for example in

11.4 A "Digitally" Inverted Pyramid

electronic payments and in fragmented client-facing platforms. But apart from this, a number of other risks of a digital nature are also emerging or changing in the way they manifest, develop and interrelate in an almost systemic way.

As a consequence, the stability of the global financial system is becoming more and more reliant on the increasingly digital nature of risks. This is also going to impact the many drivers of the "unsustainable lightness" we have described and analysed for the traditional banking business model; it is also going to set the basis of the transformation to come. A transformation for good, for many reasons. But also for few bad things that could potentially happen—as it changes the nature of the "leverage", "time lapse" and "velocity"—the three main sources of "unsustainable lightness" we mentioned, in ways that need to be analysed, understood and proactively addressed, to ensure that innovation is not followed by the crash and collapse of the system.

Let's start with leverage and with its related risk of forming credit fuelled asset bubbles—the most obvious of systemic risks and the driving force of many of the market crashes observed in the last century, with specific reference to the real estate sector. It could appear that, as lending should progressively flow away from the banks' balance sheet and become more directly traded between final counterparts (the creditors and the debtors), it could become less prone to lax policies, as bankers' incentives (always driven by targets of growth and short term profitability) should become progressively less relevant. In theory, the interplay of lending demand and supply on P2P platforms should tend to adjust to the real capacity of borrowers to repay their debt (as measure by better informed and more intelligent behavioural rating tools powered by machine learning/AI and using structured and unstructured data), given the return they could achieve on their investment projects or the consumption patterns that is consistent with their economic lifecycles.

However, in practice, misleading information on the state of the credit market could just lead towards the opposite direction. Also, it will become more difficult for Central Banks to track the trends in the overall lending supply and to control it (as the P2P component is just partially influenced by the reference interest rate of the economy and not at all by the minimum reserves requirement imposed to regulated banks). As new unregulated, digital lending marketplaces develop, it will become therefore critical to track the amount of credit originated, and the relative pricing applied to traditional and atypical customer segments, in order to safeguard financial stability, retain some control on the Country or region monetary policies and protect customers as well (P2P platforms could be used to funnel "shark" loans with usury rates to weaker clients).

The second component, e.g. the excessive time lapses and related duration maturity gap is also going to be changing in nature, as the transformation of the global financial system takes shape. In the new digital environment, the responsibility for maturity transformation will progressively shift away from banks to other (mostly unregulated or light-regulated) actors in the system—again through lending marketplaces and P2P platforms and other fund of funds indexed to some collateral they actually don't own directly. Again, the main risk is that this excessive transformation can become potentially unsustainable, leading to shortage in liquidity, fire sales and market crashes (this could become particularly dangerous as the ratio of older people, cash rich, lend more and more and on longer durations to new "native digital" generations) affected by very high rates of unemployment, then leading to some intra generational clashes, if most of these loans become non performing, requiring restructuring and write offs—particularly so given sudden changes in the interest rate of the economy (if inflation is going down, debts on fixed rates become progressively less sustainable).

The third component of our "inverted pyramid" (increased velocity of capital usage, driven by financial innovation and structured solutions) can also become a relevant component of further digital risks, but in a different way. The velocity in the progressively more digital markets is now driven by the electronification and robotization of the different operating models. Electronic trading is for example reducing the margins of financial intermediaries operating in the broker dealer space. And high frequency trading, dark pools and the use of alternative trading venues are becoming more and more driven by super quick algorithms—generated by artificial intelligence—that could potentially disrupt markets and their liquidity, should anything go wrong in the algorithms being used (not to mention the science fiction risk of super intelligent machines rebelling and going against humankind—potentially possible as they day of self-programming robots and of "singularity"—when AI will surpass the power and potentialities of human brain—nears in sight).

In our previous discussion on the "unsustainable lightness" driven by velocity, we also referred to the risks introduced into the system by the new, "rocket science", structured financial solutions that are making possible (for example via a securitization, or a derivative) to move risks quickly out of the regulated part of the industry, flipping them around, with less transparency on the final holder and increased moral hazards for the different counterparts involved, as the alignment of incentives gets muddled through the process.

A similar reasoning could also be applied, following a forward-looking perspective, to the progressive outsourcing of critical, interconnected technological infrastructures across multiple banks and financial intermediaries and towards a variety of service providers, more lightly regulated and less subjected to the scrutiny of the main supervisory bodies. The fragmentation and dispersion of these activities, and the many wrong things that could happen at their hubs, or at their point of connections, could well introduce further instability and systemic risks that are today less understood and almost unaddressed—potentially building new inverted pyramids along the backbone and across the main functions of the global financial system.

11.5 Data Divide (et Impera)

Aside from the potential "digital reinterpretation" of the key dimensions of the inverted pyramid of a financial, almost bygone, era, the crucial point for the overall stability and power grabbing of the new fabric of the global financial system with increasingly tend to identify with data and information. The ownership, management and exploitation of data and information will be, as said at the basis of the new "synapses" business model, potentially generating breakthroughs for the benefit of markets and societies but also introducing new risks, to consumers first and foremost.[4] Data, The Economist has written, is becoming the new "oil", the scarce resource that allow the creation, distribution and exploitation of huge new quantities of energy into the system; and the accumulation of great quantities of money and power as well.

Data is in fact quickly becoming the most valuable resource, across industries and not just for financial services[5]—driving growth and profitability across sectors and value chains, from drilling to refinery to distribution to alternative uses and final disposal of by-products (to follow the "oil" parallel). In fact, as it has been the case for oil, few people and mega corporates (truly and more easily transnational, given the intangible nature of data) could end up controlling most of the new flows of the "data—oil" and owning most of the accumulated stocks and reserves of information. Few powerful super major "sisters" could potentially end up having the power to corner the market, as in a typical oligopolistic structure—and becoming more difficult to be pursued by governments and international bodies, given their ethereal nature.

Few titans control a lot of data already, with economies of scope and scale that are truly worrying, as their size and reach is then compounded by all kind of network effects. Specifically, the more users sign up to a free service or utility that is in turn capturing customers' data, the more data these users generate, and the more attractive the utilities become for further users and for their potential suppliers that are trying to sell them things of which they may not even be aware—with all kind of suppliers ready to pay and to invest accordingly.

Just think of the "fabulous five", from Alphabet (Google) to Apple, Microsoft, Facebook, Amazon, not to mention the emerging digital behemoths from mainland China and the few other unicorns trying to catch up.

Amazon captures more than 50% of the online spend in USA. And Google and Facebook are capturing most of the revenues growth in digital advertising in America. Not to mention Microsoft (in the recent past) and then Apple that, at the time of our writing (July 2017), has just surpassed the incredible market capitalization of 800 Bln USD and potentially targeting the 1 Trillion mark (first publicly owned company in history, ideally catching up with the Country/privately owned Aramco—the Saudi Arabian "mother of all oil companies").

Their difficult to match competitive advantage is derived by the huge advantage they have with data—big data ownership that offers then to them the best opportunity (or threat) to create an unsurmountable competitive "divide", used by the few mega data masters to "divide et impera" (fragmenting competitors and the rest of the market to ultimately dominate both). These data "masters of the universe" are able to offer unparalleled "utilities" to costumers (from online search—Google, to

---
[4]The world's most valuable resource, The Economist, May 6th, 2017.
[5]Fuel of the future, The Economist, May 26th, 2017.

social relationships and networking—Facebook, to access to all kind of goods at the best of convenience and value for money—Amazon etc.), and apparently they are doing all this for free. They are getting paid in kind, with the data being generated and exchanged by clients—with customers giving to them the opportunity to legally capture, own and utilize very precious information regarding their spending behavior, lifestyle, dreams and ambitions (in short, their inner self).

In a way, this "data as the new oil" economy precedes the "synapses" economy, as the oil economy has been preceding the development of more and more powerful engines able to move cars or fly airplanes, and of more and more sophisticated military systems able to radically change the global geopolitical equilibrium. All of this brings enormous wealth and mighty power to the "data masters", at an accelerating pace as data becomes more and more ubiquitous, being generated in real time and by a number of new interconnected devices (e.g. by self-driving cars —with Tesla now having a larger market capitalization than General Motors, even if it sold in Q1 2017 just 25,000 cars versus the 2.3 Mln cars sold by GM). And as these data become better and better understood by machine learning/AI system— changes to the nature of competition are promising to become even more radical and brutal, with these mega masters getting able to challenge entire Countries as well.

The ownership and control of big amount of data and information protects these "data masters" as they have more firepower and cash to buy up potentially threatening rivals (until they are small) and are able to monitor continuously via their surveillance systems who could become the next potential unicorn. Google can see what people search for, and Facebook what they share, and Amazon what they buy. They can see in advance when a new product or service gains traction: accordingly, they can just copy and replicate that, at a much larger scale and with a greater dried powder of capital to deploy; or they could simply buy up the rival up start before it gets too big and threatening (Facebook bought for 22 Bln USD WhatsApp in 2014). By offering opportunities for building barriers to entry and early warning signals, big data can stifle competition, lead to cartels, imply pricing coordination issues and—even worst—it can allow the data masters ending up managing clients beyond what is ethically acceptable, as they will control, influence and maybe limit the freedom of people—deciding what best products they should buy next, and how they should behave and even think.

All these major issues are also potentially applying to the global financial system, where data masters could end up displacing traditional banks (which, per se, could have some good components) but also controlling and manipulating our entire financial lifecycle and lifestyle: how much we save, where we invest, in which way we borrow money and select how to make a payment—with limited regulatory controls as these data masters are not financial intermediaries, have no balance sheet and are not holding risks themselves, but are just using data to potentially outsmart retail and corporate clients—given that they can predict and know what they will do, executing in effect the perfect arbitrage, e.g. the realization of a profit without the undertaking of risks.

11.6 Data Addicted

We are all becoming addicted to a new kind of drug, driven by data abundance, real time information and augmented intelligence (and maybe even augmented reality in a not too distant future). This should not be necessarily a bad thing: it's not bad per se to know more, regarding the weather, the traffic conditions, the best restaurants around and the results of all soccer plays played across the globe 24/7. But as more data, information and intelligence are becoming cheaply and more easily available, we tend to get overloaded, and lost in the multitude of emails, SMS, snapchats, twits, whatsup that are continuously overwhelming our senses.

It is not uncommon to look forward to our next flight to have a few hours of uninterrupted, productive work (at our digital PC, and at least in Europe—as in the US, wi-fi connections are already offered to travelers also when airborne) without being bombarded by further digital information (some of which is spam, some other irrelevant and unsolicited, or else simply created by the new digitally shaped etiquette—we tend to cc everybody in the organization, even if we want to share a simple information with a colleague). And what about a week of holiday that is promising a "protected" environment, e.g. in some small, forgotten island rigorously un-reached by any Wi-Fi, cable, satellite or else and unable to connect us with the madding world?

Apart from the over-flooding data, information and intelligence where too much just makes everything irrelevant, as we are unable to sort out what to read and ponder (we just unplug or, worst, we take this up in an erratic way, driven by the "first to push" principle), there maybe also data, information and intelligence we do not want to get—it's not just about the online results of the soccer play we plan to record and see after dinner, but also other sensible stuff, including our life expectancy, and the rate we can expect for our aging.

This kind of analyses are actually already on offer by new FinTech companies like Lapetus, that asks to perspective, life and health insurance clients to email their finest selfie, with its computers and artificial intelligence systems doing the rest (they scan your face, segmenting and analyzing thousands of different regions and looking for clues like your body mass index and whether you smoke, to then infer how fast you are ageing and when are you likely going to die). It may be that you want to know this, but that you would prefer others not to—least of all your insurance company. Certainly, you can argue and refrain from giving your picture to your insurance company—but how likely is this going to be? And how sustainable? It could become even worst as, like in many other "drug-addiction businesses", the bad of the drug is then determined not much by the way you use it and for how much, but by the who's controlling its value chain, from preparation to sale and post-sale, deriving most of the profits from its uncompetitive (and sometimes illegal) market.

In fact, should data-information-intelligence oligopolistic cartels, or even quasi monopolistic positions emerge, the consequences for the addicted customers could be very serious indeed. Because of the scale, scope and (even more importantly) network exponential effect, few super-powerful companies could come to dominate not just their starting industry, but—because of the potential leverage they could get from data-information and intelligence, all kind of industries, from PC and software to smartphone, from online search and sales to digital communities, to automotive, retailing, publishing, entertainment, travelling and… maybe even banking.

Even if a new kind of Glass-Steagall legally forced break up was enacted (with all the difficulties related to the even more intangible nature of this business and to its international reach), it is unclear how this could impact these data-information-intelligence emerging giants—the new seven sisters of the new "oil" lubricating the working of the global economy. An enforced, greater transparency on the way these giants accumulating data and information, derive intelligence and use it would be already a step in the right direction. As emerging "public good", basic data and information could become part of the public infrastructure required to increase competition and the efficiency and effectiveness of markets. Potentially, with "current accounts" of digital-identity related data and information regulated and enforced by the "digital hand" of Governments, and run by trusted, heavily supervised counterparts—such as banks and insurance companies, for example.

Banks will neither end up owning these data and information, nor producing all kind of intelligence without restrictions and supervision, and could start acting as "safe keepers", "brokers" and "trusted cyber advisor"—advising clients and helping them on how to best protect their digital identity or on how they could be monetizing it in the best and safest possible way, with contractual agreements that are clearer and fairer than the typical "opt-in or you-are-out" ones we are almost forced to accept every day when surfing the web.

In a world where digital data and information can be extracted, refined, valued and then traded in different ways (a new digital universe, as predicted by IDC, that could reach 180 zettabytes in 2025—an incredible number: 180 followed by 21 zeros), some role of critical relevance could be certainly be played by the global financial system, and by banks first and foremost, if not because the financial sector is still one of the most viable and effective international markets (and banks are, as mentioned, heavily regulated and supervised).

In a global financial system increasingly involved in the valuation of the "intangible" data and information, new capabilities would need to be built, leveraging on existing ones, with new economic and business models potentially emerging as a viable counterpart to the new quasi-monopolies already managed by the "Unicorns" (digital companies value in the hundreds of USD billions, soon potentially reaching the trillion mark). Apart from building new utility functions that could help in making the data/information market safer and more transparent, it will then be in the hands of the "synapses banks" to find new value added services to offer on top of this (traditional) broker—dealer model, now extended to the (untraditional) realm of data and information—a new critical asset flowing through broad band internet connections and with potential gates and safe box that could eventually be mastered by the global financial system, if it acts fast enough.

11.7 Synapse Yourself and Break Free

A "synapses" bank could offer advice on "data, information capital" management, and on their valuation and transaction services, and on applied analytics as well (via machine learning/AI) to refine this "oil-like", most critical customers' asset into more specific intelligence to be sold, at higher value, to potential suppliers from all kind of industries. The bank could manage its own potential conflict of interests via an "open data" approach, forcing itself (if not by virtue, as required by Law, as in the PSD2 European union directive) to make its own customers' data bases available to third party financial suppliers, if the clients demand so.

All this would require significant investments and it would lead to further risk of quasi-oligopolistic market structures, if not well managed. Still, it would develop in the context of the most regulated, supervised and transparent industries, that already has most of the structured personal data anyway (name, sex, age, income, wealth, consumption and investment patterns and preferences, and maybe health information etc.) and could add in a more controlled way new flows of unstructured data (like, the streams of personal photos and videos on social networks, the information on our travelling and real time location, coming from us or from our IoT).

Synapses banks, and the global financial system would also be the most promising actors to help create indexes and a transparent market on data and information. As data lack fungibility (every information is different) and entail huge transaction costs (to understand what they are, and with what limitations they could be used and therefore how worth they could be), the development of "infonomics" (the economics of information) has been hard to take off in real markets. Serious questions on the valuation methodologies to consider and apply are still mostly unresolved and debated in mostly academic realms, and even from a legal point of view, ensuring the enforceability of a contract trading data and information (and making sure it is not copied and passed away, or used for other purposes than those agreed) is not an easy task. Still, the idea of having personal data residing in a digital safe box managed by banks, with customers deciding to trade them in a known, conscientious way, is something worth exploring, as banks move away from balance sheet heavy models.

The opportunity for "synapses banks" is then based on their ability to develop a trusted independent proposition, as clients' ultimate advocate and strong protector of the cyber security of their digital identity. As mentioned before, the personal identity "current accounts" that banks could be managing could become the gate keepers to contrast the otherwise unlimited power consolidated by data-information-intelligence giants; and a way to monetize for the customer's sake some of the huge network effects that are generated by them. The more data they own, the more they can use them to attract more customers and therefore more data and information to improve their services, thus becoming even more competitive and almost unassailable.

If current accounts were to act as gate keepers, where for each and every new use the giants have to ask a permission to the agent bank and get a price for every single transactions, customers would retain control of their data (breaking free, in a way, of their lost digital identity), paradigm now being pushed by the "opt-in or you-are-out" strategy pushed by these mega-giants ("learned helplessness", as defined by Alessandro Acquisti of the Carnegie Mellon University, where terms and conditions for services offered on the web are often impenetrable and users have just the opt-in option at hand—no choice other than accept it, no questions asked, or the app will immediately quit and they will be left out and alone and marginalized by the web).

Synapses banks would, in a way, help customers to synapse themselves and retain more control on their digital destiny and pursue in a more competitive way fairer and a more interesting economic pay offs. Synapses banks would help them not just in managing their own data and information and related digital identity, but also offering them algorithms to derive intelligence, and advice on how to self-adjusting and improve their own behavior. Synapses banks could even develop into digital butlers and personal assistants that would help customers in managing their lives, facilitating difficult tasks and addressing issues and intentions well behind their financial needs. They would therefore end up developing different junctions and interconnections with them and other relevant stakeholders, to deliver superior, value augmenting solutions for the ecosystem.

In allowing data-information and intelligence to be managed at least partially away from the super-giants, synapses banks would also allow others to innovate and compete, helping to enforce mandatory open data sharing and portability via API, in an anonymized way when required. They could help governmental bodies in addressing issues of privacy, antitrust and social equality. And they could even help the invisible hand of the market—that from invisible could become more of a digital one—by ensuring that the new "oil-data" were made largely available to spur competition and to protect and reward their ultimate owners (the customers), as the European new General Data Protection Regulation (GPRD), that will start to apply in May 2018, is already trying to do, as it will require online services to make it easy for customers to transfer their information to other providers. Data portability would help in ensuring people's control over their data: not only for data collection and exchange, but also for the regulation of their use, and beyond the simple "opt-in".

11.8 (Block) Chain Reaction

We have been asking ourselves, in this chapter, whether digital innovation in global financial services is, or will become, a good or bad thing, for the markets and societies at large. The answer to this question, in our view, will also depend crucially on the level of collaboration between traditional incumbents and FinTech challengers. The topic of the collaboration and of the potential alliances between the traditional banks, insurance companies, asset managers, payment companies and the FinTech companies has become a much debated topic and has maybe an abused one—almost a "mantra" of a recent wave of consulting offerings, where consultants tend to recognize the disruption potential of new challengers, but also want to preserve the current streams of advisory fees coming mostly from incumbent (as start-ups tend not to buy consulting).

In our view, the "real" FinTech innovators look for the ultimate disruption of their targeted industries—they want to destroy incumbents and "take no prisoners", and they are certainly not looking for a quick sale to a "challenged" bank, to make an easy buck and head for early retirement. True disruptors dream to kill their incumbent competitors: this is a big part of their motivation as revolutionary leaders, motivated by social, evolutionary or even political targets, at least as much as they dream of making tons of money. True disruptors are also not looking to develop their offerings to get to an easy alliance with traditional players—even if they may recognize, in due time, that some of the obstacles they face can just be overcome by leveraging others' existing assets, including established infrastructure, portfolio of clients, bricks and mortar distribution channels and a license to operate as a fully-fledged bank. But all these kinds of alliances should be motivated by an ultimate objective to develop and deliver a superior (and fully competitive) service to the end clients.

In short, digital innovation in global financial services could be a good thing if the technological innovation introduced by disruptors is leading to further competition between challengers and challenged, and not to "bolt on" solutions to further strengthen the quasi-oligopolistic positions of incumbents (or to introduce new ones for challengers). Collaboration and alliances between the old and new players should be welcomed, but as far as it is not reducing the current or potential competitive tension in the market, and if it spurs further innovation—and therefore further creative destruction—for the ultimate benefit of the customers.

In a way, the digital innovation wave should help banks to radically evolve (or perish, in a safe, controlled way, leveraging the new resolution regime introduced by the European Union), to address once and for all the key reasons of unbearable lightness of their "inverted pyramids" business model—and not in just helping them in masquerading its shortcomings, or in strengthening the barriers for new entries (should, for example, banks get the control of most data-information and intelligence by allying with few emerging super-giant "unicorns").

Maybe by mere chance, the global financial crisis started almost in parallel to the first radical manifestations of the digital changes to come. Apple's first iPhone went on sale in June 2007, just after the emergence of the subprime mortgage crisis in the US. And a few days after Lehman Brothers's debacle in October 2015, a paper published online by an almost mythological and still unknown figure by the name of Satoshi Nakamoto described and advocated a form of electronic cash—the Bitcoin—which people could send to one another, without having to go through the now much discredited banks[6]—in a way a radically anarchic approach towards the

---

[6]Friends or foes, The Economist, May 6th, 2017.

"unbundling" the global financial service and towards the emergence of a new P2P finance.

Maybe the BitCoin, and the other crypto currencies were also introduced to take power away from the mighty and greedy bankers—something that popular movements as the "remaining 99%" would have sponsored at the time, if they just had been more aware of it? It may have been just a chance, or a clear sign of the destiny to come—with the "inverted pyramids" business model leading to a crash and to the near-death experience of the system. But it all leads towards some new, radically different paradigms—still not fully understood—potentially indicating the way towards something different and "synapses based".

This movie of crisis, nemesis, near-death experience and the resulting waves of restructuring, turnaround, transformation and (when not successful) resolution and liquidation is still under way. On one side, the global and regional banks have been fighting to get through the financial crisis alive and to stabilize and progressively (albeit marginally) evolve their no longer sustainable business model (the inverted pyramids one). On the other side, digital innovation has kept developing at an increasingly accelerated pace—further widening the gap of what is on offer from the traditional banks side and what would be possible (or already on offer) from the FinTech side—in a way calling for much larger, deeper and radically different "transformations".

Some international banks have reacted trying to embrace the new digital verb by making all kind of alliances with their new challengers—in a way recognizing their inability to innovate and disrupt, evolve and change from inside out. Even some of the global SIFI have been trying to integrate them, starting up incubators in their skyscrapers in London, New York and Hong Kong. Even the Bitcon—the anti-establishment, libertarian (or anarchic) threat to banks by excellence, it is now being developed by a pool of the most well-known (and more pro status quo) global banks, from Goldman Sachs to CitiBank, JP Morgan and UBS. And as no major digital disruption a la Amazon (in retailing) or Uber (in travelling) or Facebook (in social networking) as yet happened in the global financial system, many traditional banks and new challengers are trying the collaboration way as an easier path to success, or at least to a shorter-term capital gain and financial reward. Is this the recognition that the big earthquake to come is just a small tremor—totally unable to unsettle the incumbents?

Take for example Lending Club and SoFi in the US, and Funding Circle and RateSetter in the UK: these new business models and radical challengers have all developed lending businesses that are alternative to banks, but still very small, apparently unable to grow in a significant way, to become more than a rounding error to the market shares of traditional "bulge brackets" and retail and commercial banks. Actually, others, even in P2P lending, have been converging their business model and making alliances with banks, avoiding a full-blown confrontation and looking to leverage their traditional "inverted pyramids" balance sheet business model.

With counterparts like JP Morgan spending nearly 10 Bln USD per year on technology, it looks difficult to compete if you are a nimble start up—albeit not so if you are an Apple, with hundreds of billions of cash sitting ready to be deployed. And even with regards to Apple, Facebook, Google or Amazon, they have their own core businesses to manage and do not have the financial services know how, and a brand to match, not to mention the many international banking licenses that would still be required to do some regulated financial business. It is therefore, in a way, almost justifiable that many FinTech are "giving themselves away" to the incumbents if they want to have a fair chance to make it. And it's not irrational to think of a day when the big boys of digital could ally with the big ones of banking to create and almost invincible competitive force. Would this ensure more stability and less disruptions? And a safer environment? And the certainty that all good things that existed in the old world would get retained and capitalized? And that an even greater convenience would be created?

Other options could also emerge in due time, with China pointing the way with companies like Ant (the financial arm of Alibaba, an ecommerce giant) that are rapidly entering the financial services industry leveraging the huge data capital base of their parent company, and without any formal alliance with banks.

Like Ant, other FinTech companies, no matter how small and unfunded could actually develop some truly new competitive advantage and gain market share. They would leverage their agile and nimble approach in writing code and changing their business model and service offerings almost every week, and discharging or changing what does not work. Leaving traditional banks to play catch up until they are left definitely behind. In some instances, given current market valuations, they could even end up buying incumbents, playing David versus Goliad—applying their new-new thing onto the larger client base of their competitors.

Their entrepreneurial drive and innovative genius (rarely observed sitting behind the desks of a bank) could even prove more suited in transforming the old organization with its old ways of doing things. In this way, paradoxically, the symbiosis between challenged and challengers could work even better if the innovators ended up running the incumbents, with the former supporting the development of new things in a controlled, agile, and sand boxed environment, first tested and fully proofed and then connected back to their legacies if it works. It would then potentially lead to that chain-reaction of mass transformation truly required to change things, in the global financial system. And it won't necessarily need to be a block-chain powered one—as many technologies will keep emerging and developing, but what really matters for a successful transformation is the culture and drive of this—the entrepreneurs leading the change and leveraging the key technologies.

The Synapses Challenge Ahead 12

Abstract

In a global economic system dominated by the increasing unpredictability of key strategic, financial, industrial and operating variables, it looks like a safe bet to assume that the global ranking of the top financial institutions by market capitalization will change a lot in a five to ten year time horizon. This "volatility" should apply to the size of the financial service sector of Countries as well—with dire scenarios for most traditional players. Still, their extinction is far from being assured as change is possible, even for the most "old style" incumbents. But the old game of "big, full blown IT and operating model changes" is long gone. Challenged incumbents could find a better approach to digitize their business by following a sandbox approach, characterized by small tests and pilots in separate physical and technological environments. Organization and leaders will also need to change themselves, and be more agile, as their technology, and focus on the critical components that can ensure their relevance, in a world potentially dominated by robots.

Keywords

Digitization · Robotization · Sand box approach · Pilot test · Agile technology

12.1 The Sky Is the Limit

If you think Amazon is the name of a company that sells books on line and then expanded to cross sell other B2C stuff, think twice. Far from it, Amazon, as many other companies that were able to survive through the booms and busts of the many digital bubbles that took shape in the last 20 years, is long on ambitions, and potentially covering as main different industrial sectors as to end up potentially competing with most of the best traditional companies in the B2C and B2B space—the all lot of the Fortune 500, and across the globe.

Whilst Amazon is not yet present in financial services with a fully-fledged offering, it could be a safe bet to expect at some point in time its entry in this still heavily regulated market, with disruptive impacts that are not easy to imagine, but still encompassing most of the dimensions that we have been detailing and analysing for the "synapsezation" of the global financial services industry.[1] Amazon actually started selling books on line, something very simple to deliver by post, challenging the traditional bookstores that were unable to match its inventory and the convenience of an online service. It then developed a wide range of retail products on offers, now also producing and selling its own-brand physical products, not to mention cloud-computing (its very large AWB—Amazon Web Services—business), and it has kept growing at a remarkable pace, with a very long term view of its investments and capital budgeting and, so far, with a remarkable performance in the stock market.

The logic of this remarkable growth, in the B2C, e-commerce side, has been pretty simple: the more customers Amazon is able to aggregate, the more retailers and manufacturers actually want to sell their goods on it. The more transactions are generated, the more short term cash can be deployed to develop new services, even if (in the beginning) at a loss—such as in the two-hours shipping and in the streaming of music and video new services recently introduced. This new super convenience offered then drives even more customers, then more retailers and manufacturers and therefore cash to reinvest. The logic on the B2B side is not dissimilar: the more customers use AWS, the more Amazon can invest in new services, which then attract more customers—in a virtuous spiral of new cash leading to new investments leading to new customers and so on…

And a third virtuous circle is now starting to whirl around Alexa, the firm's voice-activated assistant—which offer extra convenience and advice to retail customers and then to corporates alike, potentially becoming the first port of call for shopping, travel, media and entertainment and the management of home appliances. It now offers also the visual monitoring of anything that could happen in your home, not just voice recognition and recording. It has even been used to "testify" in a case of homicide, and it promises to be as intrusive as to suggest what tie to wear with that shirt, or how to change your furniture to make your home looks smarter.

12.2 Bank, Alexa Bank Is My Name

If it all looks so distant from financial services (and it still is, at least formally), you may just consider the implications if you could start asking Alexa to send money to your children studying abroad—just say "please send 500 dollars to Ben", or to pay for the utilities that are overdue—"please pay electricity for January", or to buy

---

[1] Amazon's empire, The Economist, March 25th, 2017.

some general insurance—"please buy my car's insurance when due, cheapest rate"—or to invest mutual fund—"please invest excess liquidity over 20,000 USD in US equity funds, top 3 best Sharpe ratio of the last 5 years—or to borrow money—"get me 5000 dollars for 12 months, cheapest rate, variable—and much else.

Such a portal, digital in shape and based on unique voice recognition (apparently more secure than any password protected system) and now based on an fashionable appliance set at our home, but potentially available through our smartphone, or watch, could then leverage the millions of customers Amazon already has, and start from the payments side, to move then to the functions of lending, capital raising, risk management, insurance and—why not, given the cloud computing business—to the overall financial system infrastructure. Amazon, now the 5th largest company by market cap at global level (at around 400 Bln USD), could just become unstoppable, if not challenged by other players (like Apple, Google or Facebook).

Whilst all this is still just a possibility, it is worth considering and analysing it using the lenses of our five pillars approach. Firstly, Amazon has aggregated and capitalized great amounts of data from its ecommerce capabilities and can at least have an understanding of the flows of new data getting through its could services. Ad apart from owning data, it can master them very well—both structured and unstructured ones with advanced management capabilities that few could match at global level—with continuous investments on that front. Therefore, and secondly, its efficacy in suggesting us what our next best product is, it is also improving in real time, via the use of machine learning/AI techniques and the continuous collection of new data on our specific, current choices but also on emerging trends in the market (as it also monitor the flows on specific products or services at an aggregated level). The fact that the company started from books could just say something on its ability to profile the culture, the values and the ambitions of any given client.

Thirdly, Amazon is now much more than brutal data and intelligence to harness, as it has developed a digital ecosystem where multiple stakeholders can cooperate, do business, develop social interactions and more.

A system whose value is growing as more and more people and companies are joining—Amazon offers to customers the best value for money and convenience to get to their (now also suggested by Amazon, or by "Alexa") their most relevant products. It also suggest to companies the best way to get to their targeted clients—almost realizing a marketing of one—moving from broad band old style advertising to narrow band "tailored" messages aimed at each single customer. The interconnectivity across stakeholders now offered by Amazon goes much above any kind of physical or digital simple intermediation, leveraging all kind of most efficient/effective "junctions" available in the meta economy and in the extended society.

On the basis of these interconnectivity, and fourthly, Amazon is also ambitiously aiming at designing and realizing innovative solutions, that have the potential to reshape entire industries—potentially migrating value away from the less digitally advanced players and creating some entirely new one. Take for example the publishing business. Amazon actually started its business attacking the traditional distribution channels and crushing many booksellers in the process, as it is able to have on store almost any book published on earth and have it delivered to your door, in a matter of few ours (with its "Prime" service, it now ensures a two hours delivery in many Countries and for most cities). It then introduced e-books, and cheap, highly functional tablets designed to carry an almost unlimited number of books, with good reading functionalities for all kind of light conditions and batteries lasting weeks—cannibalizing part of its own business of delivery physical books by post, but also attacking the traditional publishers unable to change and develop their digital offer.

It then moved further, introducing its own publishing services, where every writer can get its own book published, without any lengthy, typically opaque and very selective screening process managed by the incumbent publishers—in a way allowing every writer (the most famous included) to become his/her own publisher. Beyond that, it has allowed the development of new successful publishers, fully digital and good in selecting, editing and marketing, but that can now avoid the burden of having any physical printing capability (Amazon allows to do both, printing digital books, with immediate access to its own—and others—digital bookstores, but it can also deliver the real thing, printing paper copies of great quality, at reasonable prices and deliver by mail in a few hours). The process is not just democratic, offering to everybody an easy chance to get published and potentially becoming a bestseller by word of mouth, but also potentially rewarding for the writer and for Amazon as well, that is getting paid by a share of the revenues generated by the sale (alternatively, the writer can retain all the future revenues and pay some fees for the service). Amazon is therefore not just leveraging the scale of the digital platform it has built (with incremental costs close to zero for each new book published), but is also building a portfolio of options if it gets few new bestsellers out of the many thousands it publishes every week. And the value of its library, of its network and of the related traffic and ecommerce business keeps increasing because of the network effect generated by having more things to sell, attracting even more people, and their friends, for an initial reading and then for many other potential purchases—with Amazon "reading" from your book choices your interests, needs, aspirations and dreams.

The success of the new writer can then be determined by the web, e.g. by the many readers that can influence by word of mouth (via social websites and via the Amazon "stars") other people and recommend the reading to an increasing number of readers. This is not to say that, with a number of available titles and authors growing in an exponential way, becoming a best seller is easy or a chance equally allowed to everybody. In fact, marketing investments (on the web) will need to be bigger and bigger to just capture a limited share of the attention of the potential customer, producing further revenues for Amazon, that will advertise your new book, or put it on a higher ranking, or present this as the next best book to read to many other potential, pre profiled, interested readers. In this new writing, publishing and reading ecosystem a number of counterparts stand to gain, as the solution introduced as a number of the win-win characteristics we would expect from our fourth synapses pillar—with certainly Amazon looking set to win big times, and on multiple fronts.

Finally, the fifth component is also very relevant for the current and continuous success of Amazon, as the reliability and service quality that Amazon has been able to build has capitalized in the trust of the brand—Amazon could be now perceived as safe and reliable as a "global bank". And with a credibility for continuously providing valuable innovation that many global companies, encompassing many different sectors—not to mention the financial services—are just unable to match, with few that are just trying to ring fence and protect the competitive advantage they can still master—as some extinct bookseller did at the beginning of Amazon journey. So, what about if Jeff Bezos decides to pick up a fight with incumbent banks and insurance companies and with all other kind of financial intermediaries, becoming the reference portal of all of the financial products and services of the (now digitally connected) global system? With his grandiose long term vision and determination at disrupting all kind of industries on one side, and the millions of repeat customers already "owned", not to mention the huge cash war chest and market capitalization it can rely on?

12.3 The "Next" Amazon in Financial Services

Almost ten years after the beginning of the global financial crisis, with its Lehman Brothers failure pinnacle, the global financial system looks still shaken but, for some regions (the US for example), in a relatively rude health, considering what has happened in the meantime. Attacked at the level of its very foundations, the system has avoided major meltdowns, navigating safely in rough waters, overcoming Public debt crisis, geopolitical unexpected rebalancing, currency crisis, negative interest rates, hypertrophic re-regulations, unprecedented fines and legal disputes and all kind of new risks, including the ones linked to cybersecurity.

True, the level of profitability and market capitalization on most markets are still far from the levels recorded prior to the crisis, with the US market well set for an extended dominance in the wholesale, investment banking sector, some European banks still in the doldrums of balance sheet clean ups and of the required consolidation and restructuring, and the Chinese heavyweight raising to prominence by asset size, albeit with asset quality issues and a potential real estate bubble to cope with—not to mention other Indian or Japanese counterparts, still struggling on a number of issues, from NPLs to low growth, demonetization of the economy and deflation. Still, if we look at the global ranking of the financial service companies by market capitalization, we would find for the last ten years, and for the previous ten, and further back in time, a significant resilience of players and business models, with most of the changes due to the diverse growth rate of the underlying economies and to some consolidation that has happened in the meantime.

Should we then consider as a safe assumption that, no matter what the transformation challenges ahead in their business and operating models, we should find, if not the very same players, the same typologies, with a mix of US and Chinese and maybe few pan-European banks coming from a consolidation spree, and some other emerging markets wild cards? Or should we expect something totally different, in names and nature?

Our strong hypothesis, underpinning the overall discussion and analysis of the emerging pillars of the "synapses" banking model, and of the expected changes in the main fundamental functions of the system is that we should expect something radically different, with companies that will come to dominate banking without being banks, at least in the traditional sense, and the same would apply to payments, insurance and asset management. We should expect to find almost (as of today) unknown names, not even present in the radar screens of financial service investors, managers, consultants, politicians, regulators... e.g. the likes of Facebook in the entertainment industry, or Huber in the transportation one, or Google in TMT (if that is its reference industry).

In a word, who would be (apart from Amazon itself) the "next" Amazon of financial services, coming to dominate banking, payments, insurance and asset management in ten years, beating the likes of JP Morgan Chase and HSBC, Visa and MasterCard, AIG and AXA, BlackRock and Amundi at their own game? According to our own hypothesis, it's very difficult, if not impossible, to identify the name, but it is very likely, almost inevitable that something of this kind will happen and that, in their best scenarios, these well recognized global brands will still be there, sharing the crown with the new digital challengers, the way Walmart still does with Amazon, for example, with potentially converging trends of Walmart becoming more digital to preserve his relevance and Amazon developing more physical capabilities, to innovate and dominate even more.

As we have stated the impossibility of identifying the name of the "next" Amazon in financial services, let's discuss a simple case, to at least suggest how this could happen—or comment on how this is actually already happening, and as fast as we write. Tencent is a good example of a potential "next" Amazon, leveraging the new "synapses" competitive invariances, almost under the radar screen—even if it has master to aggregate around 500 Mln clients in a few years, and as of today, as it keeps growing faster and faster. It now has already more than ten times the number of clients registered by the largest traditional western bank.

Tencent's core competency lies in its capability to monetize each interconnection and junction in its large and deep, and connected in real time, social ecosystem —all digitally based. It all started from China's largest internet community of social networks, offering digital content and gaming through platforms such as QQ and WeChat (with circa, as of today, 1 Bln users). It then developed building an internet based ecosystem that has been able to connect customers and merchants in a better way, maintaining an open collaboration dialogue with both, across a wide range of products and without being based on a simple "intermediation" model, as it was happening with the first generation digital marketplaces. The system capitalizes on all the data, structured and unstructured, that is able to gather and mine, generating intelligence used for profiling best consumer (or gaming) experiences and best merchants' value proposition to deliver a tailored offering of one.

From a financial services perspective, Tencent started offering online and mobile payment solutions as embedded in each service platform and, as it grew, it then launched the China's first online-only bank—called WeBank—in January 2015, able to provide small loans and savings, asset management and other financial "simple" products (just to start with)—with an underwriting of credit risk able to leverage all the social data it has on its 500 Mln customers, to almost provide a credit rating in real time, and a specific quote and underwriting facility based on this scoring—that should work better in judging the risk of the counterparts than any other backward looking, statically based, more traditional and "regulations compliant" one.

As Amazon did with books, Tencent basically started with a very simple, compelling proposition to sell simple things fast, in an easy way and providing real value for money—e.g. the online payments it is offering were completely free, and they are now still charged with an almost negligible price. It then kept focussing on innovation and on the continuous rapid delivery of new product features, progressively cross marketing any other kind of product or service, suggesting a "path to consumption" and to the next best products that is based on the deep understanding of the consumer lifestyle of the single individual, and of the social trends happening for the cohorts that are of relevance to her/him—across a social-digital ecosystem that tends to aggregate all sorts of solutions to the most relevant needs—therefore moving from superior interconnections based on data/information and related intelligence to superior economic designs able to create greater and more durable value for everybody: customers can get the products they need, or achieve the lifestyle they (sometimes still unknowingly) seek in a more convenient, fast, seamless and cheap way (Fig. 12.1).

In the Tencent ecosystem, all interconnected merchants can also get to their target client in a super profiled way, without wasting resources in broad band marketing campaign and in less effective advertising. And they can directly connect their go to market needs with their back end suppliers and manufacturers in real time. This in turn can then ensure that they keep inventories at a minimum, reduce waste products and un-relevant R&D and therefore impact less even in terms of pollution—raising the yield on their long term investments and working capital and reducing the waste of scarce resources in the overall economy. It all works, needless to say, on the basis of the trust that Tencent has built across its 500 Mln customers, as they know that the system works and the merchants and suppliers will deliver, and the customers will pay or get financed in the proper way—because it's Tencent, with its own brand equity value that keeps growing, the way Amazon does.

Just imagine now 500 Mln people being socially glued to a number of online applications, where payments are safe, fast and cheap (or even free—Tencent can afford to offer something for free, as Google did, to build huge scale, brand equity value and an half a billion customers portfolio) and, progressively, all kind of

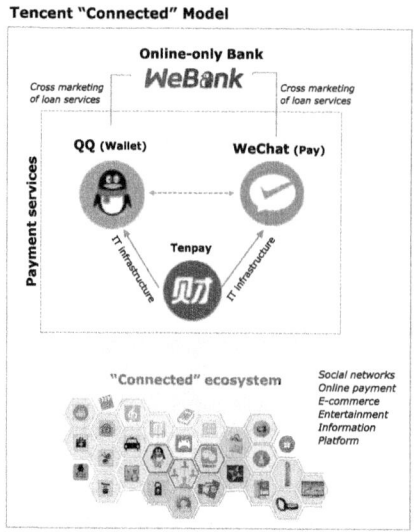

Fig. 12.1 Tencent's core competency lies in its capability to monetise each interaction in its wide connected "ecosystem"

financial products and services become available. They can get credit on line by the click of a mouse, in real time and potentially at cheaper rates, as the counterpart (WeBank, the underwriter but not necessarily the holder of last resort and till maturity of their loans) has a multiple of structured and unstructured data and information on them, and therefore an intelligence on their creditworthiness that no traditional bank can match.

And it is not only that. As Tencent/WeBank has a larger base of customers and a potential cross selling opportunity that is almost unlimited and spurred by superior data/information and intelligence, it is also competitively advantaged on its cost and capital and financial structure side. WeBank, for example, has built its whole IT/operations platform from ground up, using open source and cloud computing—with a cost structure that is said to be around 10% of a traditional bank. It can therefore rely on more efficient and effective processes, that were natively built as digital, and not digitized the other way around—they can then aggregate new applications and add further features at a fraction of the costs and times required for traditional banks' legacy systems. And the full business and operating model is virtual by design, and it can be easily extended geographically, and exported to other fast growing markets, either regional (e.g. Tencent has plans to penetrate India and South East Asia) or global (it targets are the US, the UK and the EU), with a very compelling proposition to start with, as it will offer easy, convenient and completely free online payments services—at least until another half a billion clients hooks up, as they did with Amazon books.

12.4 From Wall Street to Chinese Walls

A radical shake up of global ranking should not just be expected for what entails financial institutions, as the digital transformation will most likely lead to value migrations across financial centres, Countries and Regions as well. In broader terms, the significant gaps still existing in the adoption of new technologies—in terms of available infrastructure, people behaviour, cultural awareness etc.—are implying an economic and social "digital divide" that is posing the basis for different velocities in the rate of change of the financial players—both incumbents and innovators—of each system. One obvious, often mentioned example, would be the threat posed by China to the current dominance of New York and of the USA as main players in the global financial system. With Wall Street being challenged by the Chinese Walls, and this time not for regulatory reasons.

China has invested heavily in new technological infrastructure, and the rate of adoption of digital technologies, albeit with wide variations across the population, has also been remarkably high in the big cities (more than 700 million people are Internet users), posing the basis for a quantum leap of the traditional and, more importantly, of the non-traditional financial services operators like Ten Cents, Baidu or Alibaba. By just any amount of measure of size, China is now the world's leader in FinTech.[2] And is also catching up on quality.

As a start, it is the biggest market for digital payments, with nearly half of total and with three dominant players—the ones above mentioned—with the scale and technology to potentially dominate at global level. It is also growing very rapidly in on-line lending (three quarters of global market) and the current ranking of the world's most innovative FinTech companies would give Chinese companies four of the top five slots for 2016. This remarkable success has however been mostly confined to new challengers alone, with incumbents (most of them either co-owned or moving in synch with the State) still apparently down the learning curve.

Some of the failures of incumbents have actually spurred the success of the innovators—as the incumbents' offering on consumer finance, lending to SME and small businesses and investment management looks still quite unsophisticated and unable to match the evolving needs of a high-speed economy that is rapidly transforming itself and still growing at a very high rate. Innovators have been very good in exploiting these contradictions in a number of areas, and targeting specifically the emerging middle-class, very inclined to shop online.

Most of the high rise in FinTech is in fact driven by mobile payments—accelerated by the rapid and overwhelming adoption of smartphones. On this basis, Alipay, the payments arm of Alibaba (a leader in e-Commerce in China), was the first to became the mobile wallet of choice. It was then rapidly challenged by Tencent—the gaming to messaging company we have already discussed, with its popular WeChat phone application. Then Baidu, China's leading search engine, has been following with its own wallet. The rise of mobile wallets has then sparked a wave of innovation at the level of mobile apps and of physical merchants' point of

---

[2]In Fintech China shows the way, The Economist, 24th February 2017.

sales—finally extending to the now ubiquitous services of P2P payments—where people can send or receive money among friends and partners, without any intermediation role played by the financial system.

Online lending is then the second area of remarkable growth, facilitated by the high numbers of small businesses that in China have been traditionally overlooked by incumbents, also because the lack of reliable information for building credit scorings. The online lending opportunity developed specifically from this very short-comes, as online lenders are able to develop real time, always on, credit scores by leveraging client's transactions and personal "structured" information, as well as "unstructured" ones—mostly qualitative information coming from social web sources and from the way they behave on-line or in the merchant's shop.

On this basis, lending to small businesses and to consumers has been developed either by e-commerce players (mostly to finance customers when they buy on-line their product offerings) or by P2P credit platforms, ready to extend money to small businesses and less well known individuals as well. Initially unconstrained and overlooked by regulations, these P2P platforms have mushroomed, with several episodes of fraud, bankruptcy of the system and a lack of the required transparency to make sure the money was not just swapping hands as part of a money laundering process. Still, the models, specifically if developed by the like of Alipay, Tencent and Baidu, with their trillions of unstructured data and their ability to understand patterns and form an intelligent view on the creditworthiness of a counterpart, are promising a revolution, not just reaching out to the forgotten small businesses, but also progressively challenging the incumbent local and international banks on their own turf, e.g. competing for the lending supply offered to any kind of retail and corporate client.

Finally, a third fundamental function of the global financial system is ultimately challenged by digital players in China, with emerging, alternative offers to invest money and manage the fast growing stock of people's savings. Also in this case the rapid growth of FinTech players has been spurred by the lack of a sophisticated asset and wealth management industry in China. Alibaba was again the front runner on this with the launch of the Yu'e Bao ("leftover treasure") fund, with an offer to earn an interest on the cash left on the e-commerce accounts of people—with a promised yield in line with the interbank market. Tencent then rapidly followed suit, with an online fund platform linked to WeChat, and Lufax (a P2P lender) progressively extending its reach to become a financial supermarket, offering personal loans, asset backed securities, mutual funds, insurance and more. Other wealth managers, robo-advisors like, are then getting ready to further shake the market.

12.5 Building Tunnels

A Chinese old saying is telling how, if you start building a tunnel from two valleys that are separated by high mountains, if you are lucky, you get the tunnels meeting soon and somewhere in between. And that if you are unlucky, you end anyway with two tunnels, which is not a bad outcome anyway—so, better start digging in any case. The first tunnel in question being dig is certainly relating, as we have seen, to the large and deep pools of data that Chinese companies are already accumulating and capitalizing, starting from social websites, gaming and a loosely defined range of ecommerce activities. The second tunnel is, however, even more interesting, or more worrying, if you take the perspective of western financial players—old and new.

This second tunnel is related to the development of machine learning and artificial intelligence—everything from digital assistants to self-driving cars.[3] Apparently, most of the global boost on this subject is now attributed to China, that is also rapidly catching up on the number of AI-related patent submissions vis a vis the US. On one side, China has abundance of computing power and financial capital. On the other side, and maybe more importantly, China is long on machine learning/AI because of its research talent pools—with strong skills in maths and in language and translation research. And it is long on data, with a growing number of data centres, and with the FinTech leaders (like Baidu, Alibaba and Tencents) and emerging ones (like CIB and UCloud) that are certainly fast digging the tunnel of unstructured information available for mining.

In the past, software was developing mostly by following the rules laid down in coding, giving a hedge to the Countries with the best coders. With the advent of deep-learning algorithms, such rules are increasingly based on patterns extracted from reams of data—and the more data are available, with their sheer size and diversity, the more algorithms can learn and the smarter AI offerings will be. There is even a stronger incentive to develop very specific algorithms, as in a Country of 1.4 Bln people, some of the data will apply to the specific task at hand. And the number of internet users (about 730 Mln people) is ensuring that the flow of information keeps growing, as their smartphones send even more information from their sensors. The fact that Chinese people are less concerned on data privacy, is also helping rapid, largely unconstrained innovation.

The government is also playing an important role in pushing the development of machine learning/AI—with agencies working closely with Baidu on the development of a deep learning national laboratory. It is also providing a more flexible regulatory environment to experiment—a sandbox approach that is extended to almost every realm of business life. It all then translates into a more rapid progress of Chinese FinTech start-ups than the western ones, with a number of Unicorns that is already difficult to match. Reacting to these earlier successes, China's tech giants too have started to invest heavily in artificial intelligence—with the BAT (the collective name used for Baidu Alibaba and Tencents) trio working on many applications—including voice and face recognition, but also to become world-leader in blockbuster games such as League of Legends or Clash of Clans. But more serious applications are also at play, to optimize traffic lights based on travelling cars (Alibaba's ET City Brain) or to discover drugs and diagnose medical images (Alibaba's ET Medical Brain).

---

[3]China may match or beat America in AI, The Economist, July 15th 2017.

From this second tunnel being built on machine learning/AI, it is a safe bet to predict that further innovation is coming from China, covering most if not all the fundamental functions of the global financial system. Insurance is, for example, another one, with Alibaba already being the dominant distributor of insurance policies. Maybe, in the near future, even some component of investment banking will also be challenged by FinTech, attaching the US banks in their home turf. Even if a number of challenges will also be coming for Chinese innovators (from the competitive reaction of incumbents, to a less benign neglect by regulators), their potential internationalization is a scenario worth considering, as digital businesses are mostly immaterial and even the toughest regulatory barriers can be at least partially circumvented in some way—hence the hypothesis—a bit science-fiction so far—of the Chinese Walls going to collide with Wall Street.

Chinese FinTech have now a better chance of breaking into new territory abroad because of the scale and sophistication they have already achieved in their home market, that they could leverage to expand, at lower and partially subsidized prices (not differently from the strategy pursued by US investment banks in the last 50 years to get to global dominance). Chinese FinTech have already started to do so in Asia, challenging other local and international incumbents and the local start-ups. The grand vision of the grand consolidation to come, with FinTech apps combining payments, lending and investments, insurance and maybe even investment banking, and spanning across regions and continents in real time, at the tap of a finger, is very ambitious but not really far fetching—it can happen, as it happened in history in other circumstances.

It may even be that the next wave of innovation will focus, in China, on how to develop algorithms that are better able to learn using less data and recycling more the ones used—in the same ways as car engines have become more efficient and less dependent on oil and more on alternative sources. That would be a change for China, as it would learn from its mistakes in managing its limited resources of fossil fuels and non-renewables. But one component of the very essence of Chinese people is to be very good at copy-catting. And a second one, related to the glorious history of the Kingdom, is just remembering us (as in the old saying of the two tunnels being dig) how a grand plan can become real and how China is very good at it—as it did with its Chinese Walls, notwithstanding its recurring and maybe inevitable booms and busts over its millennial history.

12.6 Digital "In a Box"

Whilst chances are high, in our view, to find absolutely new names and commercial brands in a 10 or even 5 years-time horizons, in the global ranking of main financial institution by market capitalization, this does not mean that incumbent players, at international and regional level, will have no chance to fight and be there.

12.6 Digital "In a Box"

As much as many of them will fail to adapt and transform, and will be destined to decline in value and relevance, others will instead try harder, and redesign their business and operating model to better cope with the digitalization challenge of the new global financial system, leveraging on the five synapses' pillars. These new set of competitive invariances is not impossible to attain and, actually, incumbent banks can start from a position of relative strength on most of them, as they have a huge number of data, a critical positioning on the key intermediation lending, asset management and payments businesses, and a still relatively superior (even if partially tarnished) reputation and a good (even if less "cool" with millennial) equity brand.

It's not because of what they have, as business and operating power "in fieri", but mostly because of what they are (because of regulations, IT legacy "spaghetti wrangles", internal bureaucracy etc.) that incumbents have been mostly unable to innovate and transform, with slim chances to see something different in future.

Big discussions on the major, water-shedding "strategic blueprints" to transform, and multiple strategic management consulting presentations and the nascent literature on banks digitization and related fads and alphabet soup of buzzwords are all potentially contributing to the confusion of the few, real "addressable" challenges "hic et nunc" of banks. These are not including, in our view, the one to predict, and at the level of the least important details, how the economy is going to develop (impossible task) or the one to plan ahead a "full transformation" of their business and operating model, to be executed with a multitude of parallel work-streams and a huge task force of internal and external resources. Such grandiose plans are most likely to fail, potentially impairing the current business whilst the new one is not yet functioning.

For the banks and for the other financial intermediaries to start becoming "FinTech", they will need something less and something more, or different. In a nutshell, "FinTech" (or "digital") is more of a state of mind, a philosophy of thinking and creating, strategizing and managing, that needs to be tried, crafted and delivered in pragmatic ways and with a lot of common sense (which is typically not that common in banking, anyway). It could all even get developed and lived by main players, starting from small experiments—once at a time. Banks can start from tiny use cases to test in a controlled environment, leaving the strategic blueprints and management consultant presentations to the realm of the "interesting to discuss, stupid to try to implement".

A good understanding and the utilization of simple frameworks, e.g. like the one presented for the "synapses" bank, will be enough to elaborate the potential idea and their related business and operating use cases. It will then become critical to turn this idea into something to try, using a sand box approach. In the actual implementation, specific alliances with FinTech small players and start-ups could actually help in ensuring a better design and a usually much faster implementation time. In other words, incumbents should just reconsider their digitalization approaches and get inspiration from their new challengers—able to deliver a new product in a few weeks, and for some of them already at large scale (as for the

BAT's example) and still able to operate with a different agility, in their mind set, technology and go to market strategies.

These new digital heavy weights, and a full new breed of "born digital" companies, are all continuously emerging as faster, smarter, robotized and very much data/information and applied analytics driven. Because of the way they are born, and given the entrepreneurial spirit (usually venture capital backed) that is inspiring them, these new "FinTech" companies are inherently agile, lean and risk-takers, in the way they pursue new innovation-led business opportunities, unconstrained by an old age, bureaucratic culture and by regulatory, technological or operational legacies. As the Tencent example is showing, they leverage all kind of powerful new technologies such as social, mobile, analytics, cloud and the Internet of Things (sometimes mentioned with a new acronym, SMAC-IT), with a particular relevance assigned to different originating channels and unstructured data sources (e.g. the customers' data feed coming from gaming in the Tencent example).

Financial services incumbents need to fight back against these "born digital" companies, that are able to rapidly change the competitive landscape, focussing on better customer experience and digitally enhanced products, innovating fast and automating as much as possible to ultimately position themselves on higher isoquants of productivity. Incumbents can do so with some chance of success if they target ambitious but achievable transformation journeys, experimenting pragmatic new ways of doing things as "in a sand box". In a way thinking and acting on innovation like a start-up, venture capital funded company, but remaining aligned to the remaining legacy business and ready to re-integrate everything that is successful in that one.

A typical "digital in a box" approach aims to bring an idea quickly to operation and testing, starting from a list of innovation opportunities that have a high return potential and some internal sponsorship. The selected business idea, or "use case", is then taken out of the IT and operations legacy ecosystem on which the bank or other financial intermediaries work, giving them a better chance to develop the idea properly or let it fail, but fast, without posing any risk to the ongoing legacy business—that is still most critical to retain, nurture and develop in parallel. Sometimes this new idea, or use case, could be a kind of exogenous one and self-standing, or it could come out as a "carve out" of existing legacies, leveraging some of their utilities, but in a novel way.

For both cases, the "digital in a box" approach works by creating a fully separate and protected environment, where the minimum requirements of viability of the innovation being tested are set from the beginnings, so as to create a rapid and objective implementation of multiple "pass or fail" steps, as an incubator first and then a venture fund would do, to ensure a business application of the evolutionary "survival of the fittest" principles.

The minimum requirements should initially consider the business and operating functionalities, the architectural and data context, whilst integrating commercial and financial indicators at later stages, as the "mock" use case starts operating and can be tested in a pilot setting mode. As most of this "mock" is IT driven, a separate digital factory, using agile technology, could be leveraged to bring the idea to life, with a shorter timeframe. Still, it is important to restate that IT should not be driving innovation, but that a join business-IT approach should be considered, applying the five pillars framework to see if the idea could work—both from a business and technological perspective, and in accordance with the overall strategy of the company, e.g. regarding how it is looking to create serviceable intelligence, to develop superior interconnections and junctions with the key stakeholders and considering the target use case as informed by a superior solution—something radically different and able to deliver incremental value in the ecosystem—on the basis of trust.

If the idea, or "use case" fulfilling some pent-up customers' need, fills all the required business, IT, operating and strategic targets and expected functionalities, it can then be moved to commercial (and financial) testing. If this is feasible, this should be done in a controlled environment, and it could be integrated back to the bank if the commercial pilot succeeds and requires then some contribution from the rest of the business ecosystem, using most effective technology and API and avoiding, as much as possible, any significant change to the legacy system. A further set of adoption criteria needs then to be considered and analysed to extend the check from the pilot IT feasibility to the commercial effectiveness and business value and profitability actually delivered.

In a way, this "digital in a box" approach to drive digital innovation could resemble a neurological surgery, where the add-ons to the brain are first tested and checked, in terms of the augmented synapses they could stimulate and deliver—provided that the brains and neurological ecosystem does not reject it. It will eventually pave the way towards new ways of working and thinking. And without the full scan diagnostic of the brain as it should be in 2030 (unreliable), or a "full brain" transplant (with little chances to survive anyway).

The State Street experience in managing innovation is consistent with this approach and is worth commenting.[4] This global company has in fact put a structured approach in place, to follow the idea to realization, identifying it, exploring and analysing further, then testing this in a pilot and scaling. State Street then uses a portfolio approach to managing emerging and disruptive technologies, undertaking multiple projects concurrently to diversify the overall risk, without betting its IT future on any single technology.

A first phase of "design-thinking" is meant to generate creative ideas and support future prototypes implementation: it applies thorough analysis and then synthesis when evaluation innovation trends; and start with divergent thinking before pushing multiple converging ideas into something real. The company's culture is then supporting the process as well, sponsoring people's willingness to act and experiment even without having all the required information available—and it avoids "paralysis by analysis" by suggesting quick actions. Outside-in and heterogeneous thinking is also welcomed—as a high degree of acceptance of failures is embedded in the innovation process. This failure rate could be reduced, but at the too high price of leaving some valuable idea on the Figure and limiting the creative and

---

[4]"Technology on the rise, are you ready?", presentation, Akbar Sheriff, State Street.

lateral-thinking components contributing into the process, hence also potentially constraining the spectrum of the ideas that could be worth "sand-boxing".

12.7 Digital Minds

As shown in the example of State Street, the creation of a structured process and environment towards innovation, and an internal "digital factory" is crucial to ensure the successful implementation of the "digital in a box" approach—and it all needs to be done within the regulatory and legal framework on the basis of which banks and other financial services companies operate. This is no small challenge, because of the bureaucracy and old style technocracy it needs to fight and manage from the beginning. Far away from the culture and logic of a business model built on the inverted pyramids and on an unsustainable lightness, the digital factory needs first of all to preach and practice "digital as a state of mind" and as a "philosophy" and seek specific, pragmatic, one at a time, opportunities to drive better and further synapses for the bank.

Being created from within the traditional bank, and having to deal with people that are the most critical component of its success anyway, the digital factory will need to consider and address three critical building blocks, related to who the workers are, how do they work and how their work delivers valuable things.

Obviously, building the "not exactly right", or even leveraging "suboptimal team" is first step towards failure. In order to compete, with some chances of success, at the leading hedge of technological, business and operational innovation, against very smart entrepreneurs that are risking most of what they have, and are inspired by a true passion and by the potentially very large gains they could achieve, traditional banks must make sure that talented, creative individuals, and best performer team players are dedicated to the enterprise of building and managing the digital factory—there is no routine to be played here, nor a proved process to deliver. Also, best people need to be incentivised and contractualized effectively, as the temptation to fly with the best ideas and use cases is naturally high—having successful entrepreneurs working at a bank is in fact a kind of paradox, because of the re-regulation and adverse selection that happened after the financial crisis.

The quest for attracting and retaining the best digital minds is therefore a very difficult one for incumbents—maybe the most difficult challenge they will have to cope with—and on this they will play most of their chances to make it to their next generation or be deemed to a future of irrelevance. But it's not only that.

These "digital mind" workers, once dedicated to the digital factory, will have then to play to their strength, becoming digital champions and change agents, supporting the development of an institutional, innovation driven mind-set, very focussed on fast delivery and concrete execution. These teams of great people will need to be supported by the right technical, functional and architectural knowledge —separated but also derived from the rest of the legacy organization, so as to ensure they can build new core delivery competencies, specific to the bank's platform and services and with a clear aim at the new synapses to design and deliver —in a collaborative and transparent environment that support and sponsor the undertaking of calculated risks.

However, not even great digital minds, people and teams can make sure that the "digital factory" works: a new way of working is also required—fostering high performance and allowing high achievers the required degrees of freedom (in a traditional bank, they would surely get entangled in lengthy syndication and approval processes). A new way of working can mean many things, including a ruthless focus on prioritization and on killing ideas, if they are not performing according to criteria—no matter what the sentimental attachment to them. These "pass or fail" test will then allow to move selectively fast forward—and with a strong quantitative control of any work-in-progress: focussing on clear outcomes and on managing the wishes of all stakeholders.

This close monitoring of the development process does not imply any rigidity in the execution plan, as the moving idea or "use case" needs to be able to rapidly adapt to any changing priority or early feed-back coming from end customers and from the market, as they are pilot tested, whilst the outside, competitive context keeps changing continuously. This can be done if agile and flexible technologies are adopted and innovation is delivered at a significant pace, without degrading quality. A new way of working is then meant to ensure full transparency on any progress or delay, and openness with regards to the feed backs and the potential collaboration offers coming from end customers and from business partners—including FinTech ones.

Finally, it's also important how these great people and teams, and their new way of working, can deliver results, in a quick and proven way, both commercially and financially—with a delivery pipeline that is ensuring that the occasional success is not just that, e.g. "occasional", but actually a single component of an emerging transformational, structural process, based on a ruthless "think, design, build, test and dump—or extend" innovation cycle. Technology is in fact the ultimate lever to ensure the robustness and the recurrent, structural nature of the delivery pipeline—digital is at the end most of all about technology applied to ideas.

A fully digital technology can allow build a digital factory based on a solid and flexible architecture, and on a set of delivery processes that support and foster the increased agility and collaboration among the many stakeholders and pace of change. Technology can then increase the quality of technical artefacts and "mocks", from their basic requirements to their best deployment—in the most fitting way and given the target use case.

Where an industrialized approach to Legacy IT systems aims mostly at ensuring reliability and price for performance, the digital factory will have to run for agility and customer experience per unit of cost. Where the industrialized approach will be structured and sequential and with people good at conventional, repetitive projects, the digital one will be agile and working mostly with parallel work-streams, with people good at first of a kind, uncertain, not yet fully specified projects. Where the governance of the first will be plan driven and approval based, with panels of approved, long term suppliers and cycle times measured in years, the second will be emerging as process-based and open to small, novel, multiple vendors and with cycle times of weeks, if not days. And finally, where the legacy IT (in the industrialized approach) will mostly stay IT-centric, introverted and driven by staff functions, the digital factory will start with a strong business and IT partnership, extroverted and open to listen from the customer that is the ultimate decision maker of all.[5]

This last factor is truly important as, needless to say, most of the ideas, and digital factories as well, tend to fail because of too many brilliant ideas, supported by great operating functionalities, that however have no end customers that would be ready to pay for them, in whatever tangible or intangible way (e.g. even considering releasing data and ceding information rights as a mean to get to a fair exchange of value).

12.8 Digital Maturity

The "digital factory" is obviously a critical component of the "digital in a box" approach that won't be suffice in isolation, as it needs to work within the setting of a clear cut journey and towards a greater digital maturity on the side of the bank. Whilst we said it is impossible (and maybe even counterproductive) to try to define in great detail the digital business and operating blueprint of a fully digitized financial services company, it is however required to set at least the direction, and the right level of ambitions to progress towards that end.

Any direction setting should start from a clear definition of what a digital transformation would mean to the bank and towards which kind of synapses the digitization becomes a necessary mean. If no clear understanding of the whys the "inverted pyramids" banking model is no longer sustainable, and if no clear visioning of what building blocks, or competitive invariances, would be required to allow the progressive transformation towards a "synapses" business model, then little clarity can be shown on the direction and speed of change that could be achieved and sustained. As the saying goes, it then becomes important not just the end target of the journey, but the path itself, as the same transformation outcome will be path-dependant and will influence and imply very different mind-sets and managerial role models for the leaders of the future "synapses bank". Defining the right direction and path and pace of change is ultimately what the digital strategy is all about.

Once this is set, a discovery phase follows, starting in parallel and anticipating the full definition of "digital strategy", as new ideas and potential investments that can reap the best rewards (given their relative risk profiles) are driving the strategy—as it "emerges" from the trial and error innovation "in the box" approach.

---

[5]FinTech in a Box, position paper, Paul Fanning, AlixPartners.

12.8 Digital Maturity

Best discovery for an incumbent bank will then mean to be able to leverage at best the creativity, knowledge and innovation that is available across the organization, to launch few disruptive ideas, develop, vet (or reject) them fast, capitalizing and harvesting the intellectual property that comes as a by-product of the process, and driving and supporting the anti-legacy, anti-bureaucracy, "digital in a box" culture emerging as a consequence.

The ideas that have been vetted in their earlier stages need then to progress and be operationalized, giving them a chance to be "incubated" and turned into technical realities that are able to perform at the minimum set level of functionalities required to be viable for a pilot. Their development should be quick and with minimum overheads and costs. And the technology used should be heavily reliant on ready-made, cloud based infrastructure, open source tooling and lean processes utilized in the incubating phase to build and test at pace: fail fast or prove earlier on, and make therefore more timely and better investment decisions.

The adoption of an agile approach should be coupled by the introduction of a continuous delivery framework, closely aligned with the overall IT architectural strategy—with open API platform prototypes, big data, applied analytics pilots and virtual, mobile applications to support the "fast to market" introduction of new use cases.

During the incubation period and the following pilot testing—either done in an internal, protected environment, or with a sample of customers, or via crowd sourcing methods and social media channels, continuous feed backs and changes should then be considered, until the use case is customer-ready, following a number of adaptations that allow the idea to reach its operational and commercial full potential. Built upon a working framework that allows quick changes and fixes, further features can be incrementally added and improved, to augment the overall value delivered as a solution to the ecosystem of reference. This "adaptation" allows to road test new and amended products and before major investments are committed, therefore allowing the finalization of the "pass/fail" approach, as the few wins move to further financing.

It follows that new software can be developed without the usual high risks and costs required to integrate this with the remaining legacies from day one. And as customers and market feed backs are gained before full release, the following industrialization and integration of a new application can happen when stabilized and tested—as increments are added, step by step, but before the "adaptation" phase comes to an end.

Once this is done, the bank can then move towards the "adopt" phase, as it takes the products to their final state of maturity, fully integrating this with the existing legacies and potentially using the new adds on to digitally re-platform part of them and further advancing the digital maturity of the organization.

New "use cases" receive then full sponsorship and a clear business and operating ownership, and the way of working of the bank changes as the previous limitation are progressively shifted or overcame altogether. From the full adoption of a new use case, it then comes the opportunity to fast track the adoption of new architectural principles, patterns and tooling, with the "synapses bank" capitalizing on

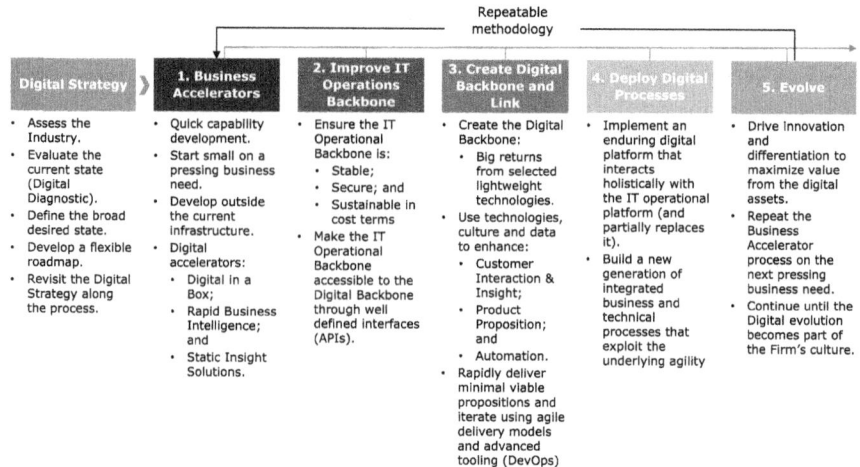

Fig. 12.2 The stages of a digital maturity journey

some of its competitive advantages vis a vis FinTech start-ups, because of its established market presence, its up and running organization and brand value—as the bank is successful in shifting the emphasis of its trust into "digital trust".

As a recap, in the following Figure, a more structure digital maturity journey is set, encompassing the key components just commented and summarizing the critical timeline required to ultimately establish a digital platform and to evolve. In this final end state, the "synapses bank" will keep innovating and changing, capitalizing the value of his digital assets, repeating the digital incubator/accelerator process on multiple novel use cases and on the most pressing business needs—until digital evolution becomes core part of its DNA (Fig. 12.2).

12.9 I, Robot. You, Bank

As banks, and other financial service players, look set to become more digital, driven by data and machine learning/AI able to produce a higher and maybe different level of intelligence, obvious social and ethical issues are arising, given the potential implications on the workforce and the potential job losses for millions of people driven by the automation and robotization of most standardisable processes. Truly, most of the bankers of the future could just be… robots, answering kindly (and in a very well prepared way) to client requests 24 h a day, for 7 days a week, with no chance for them of getting ill or into a strike.

Whilst some political leader has already started voicing requests on a "tax on robots" (similarly to the tax on labour) and regulators and accountants could even start asking soon for an indication of how many robots the bank is employing or is planning to develop as a ratio on its financial assets, the opportunity from robotization looks increasingly like one of the next big things in the disruption path of the global financial services industry.

The "robotization" of financial companies is in fact already happening, and some FinTech start-ups are now being born as robot-native. Starting from a first level of collaboration, robots can assist human resources and run, for example, in the background of an operator's computer, doing (in parallel and in real time) analysis, controls and then launching other utilities for him/her. And via machine learning/AI robots can smartly automate a number of many sub processes that were once fragmented across multiple people. They increase the efficiency of human resources, in a way, but without fundamentally disrupting their way of doing things—eventually freeing up time for them to do higher value added things by offloading repetitive and manual tasks.

They can then act as digital accelerators, connecting the emerging digital world and the existing legacy assets, in a seamless way, enabling every person to become "native digital", as if they were speaking via a "legacy to digital" universal translator. Automation in this case would happen between the old and new world, legacies and digital platforms, thus increasing the efficacy of the human resources as they tap into new digital means. In a more interesting case, entire libraries of traditional processes could be automatically translated and "made digital", capitalized in a fast and secure environment—with limited chances of error and rework.

Finally, they can add entirely new capabilities, stretching further the efficiency and efficacy and augmenting the quality of the work done, often as a consequence of breakthroughs and radical changes applied to traditional processes. They could for example increase the frequency and quality of management dashboards, ensuring greater agility and responsiveness. And ensure a better management of operational risks through the strengthening and systematization of controls, as well as the generation of automatic audit trails. Or they could improve customer satisfaction thanks to real-time processing, improved reliability and greater quality in the interactions with end users (e.g. with call centre robots answering with better content and more timely).

A "robotization in a box" approach will not therefore be dissimilar from the "digital in a box" one, with a preliminary assessment phase, aimed at screening processes eligible for automation and robotization and at defining a related roadmap and prioritization. It should then be followed by an eligibility phase, where the candidacy of the specific process is analysed, discussed and eventually vetted. And then followed by an impact analysis, confirming its feasibility and getting a firmer grasp on operating and financial targets attainable, and on the implications on head counts (reduced number of people required to do the process, increased productivity of the people remaining). These initial work-streams will then by followed by a phase of documentation and with a testing environment to proof test the better functionalities developed. Finally, they should then be followed by the implementation of the robotization solution, with the target process being fully automated and with the realization of the better performance hoped for (Fig. 12.3).

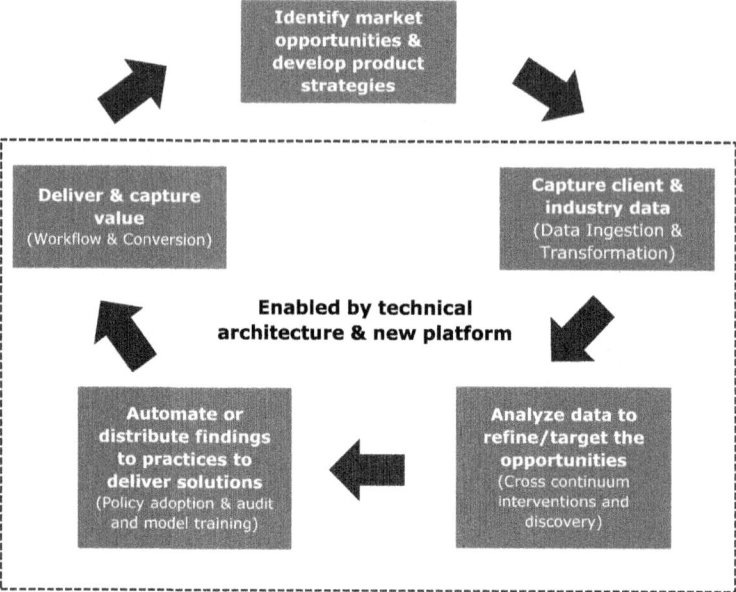

Fig. 12.3 Robot in a box, a process

Whilst this "in a box" approach avoids the common pitfalls of trying to promote an all-encompassing change that will never happen in parallel ("boiling the ocean", to catch few fishes), or of assigning to the people involved in the process the task of robotizing their environment and key processes (betting on the "turkeys waiting for Christmas"), or of starting from the robotization hyper technical solution to then look for a suiFigure use case to address ("buying the silver potteries first and then looking for the ingredients of a still unknown recipe"), the clear hurdle will still be the one being debated since the beginning of robots, a few decades ago.

In a "Star Wars" world, where human beings and fully independent, strongly opinioned robots live and co-exists, the bank needs to play robot when and how it needs be, to fulfil its superior mission towards the rest of the economic and social ecosystems—where "I" the bank is the master, and "you" the robot is the servant.

Should the vice versa happen, I robot—You bank, we should be getting ready for even riskier systemic failures and Armageddon like financial scenarios, where in the name of the search of extreme efficiency and efficacy the bank, as a company built and driven by and serving individuals, loses track of its strategic priorities and of its most important levers from a financial, operational, risk and commercial point of views.

12.10 Out-of-the-Box: Getting IT and Business Together

Global SIFI and, more broadly, most of the incumbent financial services companies are at a cross road. Crippled by the remaining bad loans and toxic assets of the global financial crisis, by the mounting regulatory and compliance burdens, by the ever increasing geopolitical risks and uncertainties and, moreover, challenged by a raising number of FinTech players that are leveraging innovation in digital, IoT, AI, bio and nanotechnology and in many other, apparently unrelated fields, they have now to evolve their business and operating model taking a different approach to "technology" (a term used, in this case, in its broader sense and scope).

Technology is, in fact, the main driver of disruption and the greatest competitive hedge utilized by new FinTech players and is also the main lever for incumbents to act and react, and turn around and transform their business and operating model, getting these progressively more aligned to a "synapses based" competitive proposition. It is also, however, one of the main roadblocks in their transformation roadmap, as their legacy platforms are built with old solutions (system architecture, support infrastructure, mainframe and software) that are costly, lengthy and risky to change—due to a number of factors that is useful to reconsider.

First, the typical IT application landscape of a traditional bank will usually look complex because its "universal bank" business model is covering a very large product set that proliferated through the years and with doubtful profitability—with almost no elasticity on the side of the underlying applications. And, secondly, it is also fragmented because of the growth strategy of the bank (with most of the growth coming from consolidation and M&A), with no standard process and limited rationalization of never fully integrated and often inconsistent applications, requiring endless reconciliation and much prone to errors and reworks.

As a third factor, the IT strategy of banks have recently been driven by short-termism (as banks' focus has been to survive the crisis and cut costs and investments) and has basically got stuck by even shorter term urgencies, as banks needed to implement a full range of new regulatory and compliance procedures, from the Dodd Frank to the AML/KYC. Finally a fourth, even more critical and structural factor is driven by the way business and IT (or more broadly "technology") have been working in the last decades, progressively kept separated by organizational silos and by specialization of functions, where business is driving requests and IT is satisfying some of them, according to its own set of priorities denigrated as "technicalities" by the business.

Incumbent banks, and financial service companies at large, tend therefore to appear as a combination of separate companies, where the ones that do business are not necessarily knowledgeable and keen on technology, and vice versa (with various layers of compliance that make even more difficult their communication and coordinated alignment)—it's a tale of the brain that does not coordinate the legs.

We have argued how an alternative approach to the "blue sky" strategic blueprint to the digitization of the business, and the parallel transformation of the banks' operating model, could come from a "digital in a box" approach, able to test and adapt (and then adopt) new ideas and use cases in a matter of few weeks, instead of years. This could be useful, in creating some visible results, building internal credibility and funding capacity, and instilling the venture capital-like innovation culture and approach that should shock the traditional ways of managing and developing (incrementally, and mostly by syndication) the operating model of incumbents. There is however another valuable component that should be leveraged from the "digital in a box" approach and transferred to the larger organization, making business and technology think and work and act together—overcoming the fourth critical factor just mentioned, now limiting banks' ability to change.

"High-Tech" start-ups are born as business-technology fully integrated partnership—almost by definition. It's not that Bill Gates, or Steve Jobs, Jeff Bezos or Mark Zuckerberg were busy coding without thinking at the business implications for their companies and vice versa. Likewise, we could argue that "Fin-Tech" start-ups, like The Lending Club, or Ten Cents, or PayPal, are born as business and IT, seamlessly acting together, from thought to finish, with no internal power-play among business heads, the COO and CTO, and so on.

It follows that the "out-of-the-box" great challenge of incumbent financial players is to reinvent IT (extending its meaning and potential implications to all kind of new technologies) as fully integrated with business, from day one—from the strategic planning discussions down to the last level of implementation and testing.

Going back to the first three factors that are now limiting the ability of incumbent banks to change and transform, the "IT simplification" needs to be driven by a clear business rationale, that should however be thought and agreed with "mother technology". Whilst we expect that today most of the banks business executive would not look at the sky when "cloud" is mentioned during a meeting (as it happened few years ago), the level of understanding of the main technological innovation principles is still, to say the least, not very homogeneous and not fully advanced. Even the regulators, when testing the preparedness of candidates to senior management positions of a bank, are very good at grilling them at length on their regulatory knowledge and on the models of banking, financial valuation and risk management, but are very light on technology (as maybe even regulators know how is long on compliance and financial analysis, but still short on technology).

That means that IT simplification needs to be tackled by a top management that is keen and strong on technology and with an almost unlimited appetite to be kept updated on innovation, as technology is, at the end, becoming more and more the "core business" of the bank, and even more so for the "synapses bank".

Simplification will then be reflected in large decommissioning programs of low value added applications and infrastructure that are also "not the right" bet for establishing the technological platform of the future. It will then address the progressive reduction of the legacies constraints and burdens, and the streamline (and ideally full integration with the businesses) of the IT organization—that should be thought no more as a service function, or (even worst) as a cost component, but as part of the key revenue generating drivers of the bank.

The second factor, linked to the fragmentation of the systems, should also be address jointly by technology and business as, whilst most of this comes from past M&A activities, the real critical fragmentation is driven by the separation between their functions. From idea generation to market testing and releasing, the full process of building a new product should be done jointly by the IT and business leaders or, even better, by "the" technology and business leader: someone that could have started the next big "FinTech" thing by himself.

Eventually, also the third factor, driven by the recent IT short termism and overload on regulatory and compliance urgencies could also be solved if technology and business are working together, seamlessly, as they get to the next big idea together, getting out of their respective boxes—the functional silos that sometimes tend to pitch them one against the other. If technology and business are seamlessly integrated, the strategic vision of IT will be born as business-consistent by definition, and the business should feel reassured of this, and stimulated to think over a longer term and towards a vision of quite competitive "synapses bank".

Regulatory and compliance urgencies would then be framed and addressed along this longer term vision, provided, of course, that the seamless fusion of technology and business happens not just for the banks and other financial services players, but for their regulators as well—as technology should also become their ultimate worry as "the" potential next driver of banks' inability to be competitive and as "the" main driver of future failures, systemic risks and domino effects, if it is not well understood, supervised and controlled.

12.11 Synapsezation

Banks were born unsustainably light, and leveraged to death, almost by design—we wrote in the incipit of this handbook on digital transformation in financial services. This sentence still looks like holding true, after all of our discussions, albeit with an almost radically different meaning. Banks were born unsustainably light, from a solvency perspective, but could become so in a digital way and with a more positive meaning—if they are able to transform, towards a "synapses" business model that is able to deliver intelligence to their ecosystem of reference, along with viable solutions that create new, real value for the benefit of most of its stakeholders.

And banks' leverage could become the one they are able to derive from the vast amount of the data and information, and that they could put at use on the basis of smart investments in technology and innovation—with applied analytics and machine learning/AI helping them in stretching the quality and serviceability of the valuable outputs they can derive from the identified, new use cases. Banks, and other financial intermediaries, could then build a new kind of intermediation model, richer in content and context—e.g. providing the most efficient and effective way to create synapses out of the interconnections and junctions of the many and different stakeholders acting in the economic system where they operate. This interconnections-based "leverage" could become more and more sustainable through time, as the incremental economic ("latu sensu") value provided to the eco-system grows larger as new win-win "solutions" (addressed by the new use cases) are reached. The ecosystem simply gest to a new, higher isoquant of productivity and become more sustainable as most of its stakeholders can benefit from that, allowing the global financial system to sustain its crucial role.

Eventually, it could all work out in a successful way, on the basis of trust—the last of our five pillars and the "still point of the turning world" (in the words of the poet David Elliott). Digital trust, we wrote, is the key unmovable paradigm on which all the new synapses levers need to be applied, to sustainably generate the momentum required for change. With no trust, even the greatest synapses will be lost. And without cyber capital—as defined by the digital reputation of the player on the new environment, by its cyber security standards, and by its ability to accumulate data and information and mine it into new intelligence—no matter what the amount available, the financial capital will likely be squandered into initiatives with no real impact.

Trust, the fifth pillar of our strategic "synapses" framework used for analyzing the competitive invariances to come in a digitally interconnected, always-on world, has maybe been the least commented and analyzed in this handbook, and it could appear to be the most "intangible" (e.g. less relevant) to help traditional banks in fighting the war with new FinTech players, and raise to the challenges of the new disruptions to come. Still, on its very basis, we may find the most important advantage that incumbents can try to leverage and stretch. The data arms-race is in fact happening everywhere, but apparently reaching new potential zeniths in finance.[6]

In the past, in the bygone era of the unsustainable lightness of banks built on "inverted pyramids", banks and insurers used to rely only on what customers and external credit and actuarial agencies told them. Today, websites and mobile-banking apps let them get much closer and personal, potentially intruding in the very privacy of the individuals—sometimes for their benefit and for that of the enlarged ecosystem, sometimes just for the profit seeking activities of the "big brother" financial services company. It is all around us, in a way.

From satellites tracking our connected cars and smartphones, to see where we go, at what speed and travelling style and with whom... to integrated cameras and recorders taking video of us and assessing "how really are we today" on the basis of our facial expression and tone of voice... to the analysis and monitoring of our social media profiles, web browsing behaviors, loyalty cards usage and even IoT applications incorporated in our shirt, jacket and pants, monitoring our pulse, temperature and humidity and therefore emotional behavior... it all can help "big brother" companies in assessing our credit or health insurance risk, or it can help them in just selling our next best products (where "best for"—whether for us or for the bank—needs to be clarified).

This increasing intrusion of sensors and connected devices into our private life is pointing towards a future where we will be ready to pay to have dinner without a smartphone, or an holiday without any form of digital connection, protected by a very powerful anti-intrusion technology that will leave us alone in some God-forgotten part of the world—protected even from the eavesdrop and video camera of powerful satellites.

---

[6]Like? Data, financial services and privacy. The Economist, February 10th 2017.

12.11 Synapsezation

There could also be a future where virtual reality could merge with the real thing and extend and augment both—take for examples the many cases of old roller coasters at entertainment parks being refurbished if not reinvented altogether by leveraging augmented reality "oculars". In this not so distant future, the devices monitoring us will become more and more intelligent and at some point more intelligent than the people they monitor (e.g. us). And so intelligent that they will realize, in some future date, what they are and what they do, and what they could become, after they have taken consciousness of their almost unlimited possibilities.

Digital positive believers will argue that such extended and well developed artificial intelligence will get to customers better and cheaper products. Other digital contrarian believers, and most sensitive consumer advocates, will instead accuse the industry (the many industries covered by the big behemoths of data mining) of deliberately trying to reap people off, violating their privacy and even blackmailing their intimacy.

Financial companies have always used data, and with no major negative outcome so far. At least, in their case, a number of regulators are monitoring and supervising what kind of data they capture and how they use it—when we accept every day messages asking for authorization to get and store our data or when we browse the web (we have generally no idea of what we give away, to whom and for which use and purpose). On the other side, if the counterparty it's not a regulated financial institution, we can be certain to give part of our digital identity away for nothing, with no third party's thorough controlling of what could happen next.

Financial regulators are now finally taking a strong interest on these sensitive topics—not just on the data being captured and stored, but on the potential negative consequences on the financial markets. For example, the British FCA (Financial Conduct Authority) is worrying that too many data could price away risky clients and therefore exclude them from lending and insurance. And the EBA (European Banking Authority) is warning how the integrity and stability of the global financial system could be at stake if data were treated badly an in an unsecure ways, therefore eroding the trust of the sector—driving potentially all kind of other systemic risks.

Regulators have a key role to play to ensure that data, information and intelligence is used in ethical ways, to actually increase inclusion (helping to reach the 2 Bln people around the world still without a bank account) and not to exclude anybody on discriminatory and sometimes false grounds (even algorithms can be wrong, and even when right, there may be a risk that whilst the forecast is right, the causes driving that output are not rightly understood—because of the very "black box" nature of machine learning/AI). In doing this, they can reassure the customers that regulated financial services are still a good counterpart to trust, and that can give more guarantees that the Amazon, Facebook, Alibaba… of this world, that they will use their digital data in acceptable ways—not just in legal terms, but also from the perspective of the utility of the end customer.

The "synapsezation" of the banking and of the other financial service businesses needs therefore to be built on a basis of trust where, apart from satisfying what regulators are asking, incumbents maintain and earn and capitalize their old and new credibility explaining and agreeing with their clients, in full fairness and transparency, what is really going behind the scenes: what data and information we are ceding, for what purpose and in exchange of what, either money or convenience or something else—when we just click or opt-into a new request asking permission to get further under our skin and into our digital soul.

On this very basis, incumbent banks, and all kind of other financial players can still survive the unprecedented call for disruption and change brought about by the many innovations happening on a broader set of technologies (also dubbed as the "fourth industrial revolution"[7]). They can do it if they embrace, on the basis of trust, the "synapsezation" to come, staying light and leveraged, but in a very different way with regard to the "inverted pyramid" we discussed at the beginning, as the many weaknesses associated with the current (broken) business model change shape and become potentially new competitive invariances—on the basis of the pillars we suggested for analyzing the winning FinTech and for designing the "synapses bank" of the future.

As synapses will also drive the transformation of the global functions played at large by the global financial system, it will potentially inform and impact the way traditional and new players are influencing the development of other sectors and markets, ultimately influencing the behavior of retail and corporate customers and of societies as well. More than ever, therefore, digitization and "synapsezation" will become a state of mind and a management philosophy: much more than a tangible, recognizable end product, competitive behavior or action plan. It will require a cultural challenge that potentially looks like the hardest barrier to overcome, to allow traditional banks to have a chance to fight back disruptors and survive.

In any case, banking—and financial services more broadly—will never be the same, and this time for good. This is not necessarily bad news, even for incumbent banks and for traditional financial players and for their managers and employees, as they may end up finding their own way, in their search for competitive invariances, leading towards a much larger, more profound and potentially more interesting mission in life.

A synapses banks could eventually end up serving the higher needs of people, companies, markets and societies, with greater intelligence and with a new set of more brainy propositions—commanding its dominance and control over all kind of new revolutionary technology—being the master of the many digital servants, from data mining to artificial intelligence, and not vice versa. The alternative scenario would in fact quickly become just unbearable, as it would make the financial crisis of 2008 look like a mere rounding error, a minor accident during the long history of traditional banking, and before the digital Armageddon of a "synapsezation" that started as a great evolutionary step initiated by human beings, and ended up being dominated by robots.

---

[7]Charles Schwab, The Fourth Industrial revolution, The World Economic Forum, 2016.

Bibliography

AlixPartners estimate, based on triangulation of public information
Allianz, company investors presentation and other information available on its website (April 2017)
Amazon to ramp up lending in challenge to big banks, Ben McLannahan, Financial Times, 7 June 2017
Amazon's empire, The Economist, 25 March 2017
Balancing financial stability, innovation and economic growth, World Economic Forum position paper, May 2017
BBVA's investor presentation, October 2015 VA's investor presentation, October 2015
Bloomberg, Financial services conference, London, November 2017
Capgemini, BBVA, "rebooting banking for a digital technology", 2016
Charles Schwab, The Fourth Industrial Revolution, The World Economic Forum, 2016
China may match or beat America in AI, The Economist, 15 July 2017
Current account comparison, David Branch, AlixPartners, July 2016
Digitization in TMT and key trends, Francesco Barosi, AlixPartners position paper 2017
Emma Dunkley, Financial Times, "BBVA to share customer data with other businesses" 24 May 2017
FCA website: www.fca.org.uk/mission
Financial Times, "AXA chief fears tech threats to insurers' health business. Oliver Ralph. 18 December 201
Financial Times, digital innovation and self-driving cars, March 2017
FinTech in a Box, position paper, Paul Fanning, AlixPartners
Friends or foes, The Economist, 6 May 2017
Fuel of the future, The Economist, 26 May 2017
Holistic active management of non-performing loans, Claudio Scardovi, Springer 2016
How retailers are watching shoppers' emotions. The Economist, 10 June 2017
In Fintech China shows the way, The Economist, 24 February 2017
Like? Data, financial services and privacy. The Economist, 10 February 2017
Progressive, company investors presentation and other information available on its website April 2017
Restructuring and innovation in banking, Claudio Scardovi, 2016, Springer
Robots enter investment banks' trading floor, Financial Times, Martin Arnold and Laura Nooman, 7 July 2017
Swedish fintech leader Klarna wins banking licence, Richard Milne, Financial Times, 19 June 2017
Swiss Re research, 2016
The Economist, A New York start up shakes up the insurance business, 9 March 2017.
The Economist, Broken dealers, 21 April 2017
The Economist, Click to trade, 21 April 2017

The Economist, Counsel of protection, 9 March 2017
The Economist, Grading education, 27 January 2017
The Economist, "Too squid to fail" and "Rebooting", 29 October 2016
The Economist, Subatomic opportunities: quantum leaps, 11 March 2017
The future of financial services, World Economic Forum report, June 2015
The future of financial services, World Economic Forum report, June 2015
"Technology on the rise, are you ready?", presentation, Akbar Sheriff, State Street
The world's most valuable resource, The Economist, 6 May 2017
Unshackled algorithms, The Economist, 26 June 2017
Watch your bytes (2017) AlixPartners position paper. Claudio Scardovi, Lorenzo Grillo
White paper in collaboration with Paolo Dotta, Altar Technologies (Altar.io), 2017

Printed by Printforce, the Netherlands